The
South
Atlantic
Quarterly
Spring/Summer 2000
Volume 99
Number 2/3

The *South Atlantic Quarterly* is published, at $112 for insti-
tutions and $32 for individuals, by Duke University Press,
905 West Main Street, Suite 18-B, Durham, NC 27701.
Periodicals postage paid at Durham, NC. POSTMASTER:
Send address changes to *South Atlantic Quarterly*, Box
90660, Duke University Press, Durham, NC 27708-0660.

Subscriptions. The annual subscription rate is $112 for institu-
tions and $32 for individuals. Subscribers outside the United
States should add $16 per year for postage. Single copies are
$28 for institutions and $12 for individuals; back volumes,
$112. Direct all orders and subscription queries to Duke
University Press, Journals Fulfillment, Box 90660, Durham,
NC 27708-0660; 888-387-5687 (toll-free in the U.S. and
Canada) or at 919-687-3602. An electronic subscription
to the journal may be purchased from Project Muse at
muse.jhu.edu.

Photocopying. Photocopies for course or research use that
are supplied to the end-user at no cost may be made without need for explicit permission or fee. Photocopies that
are provided to the end-user for a photocopying fee may
not be made without payment of permissions fees to Duke
University Press, at $2 per copy for each article copied.

Permissions. Requests for permission to republish copy-
righted material from the journal should be addressed to
Permissions Editor, Duke University Press, Box 90660,
Durham, NC 27708-0660.

Library exchanges should be sent to Duke University Library,
Gift and Exchange Department, Durham, NC 27708.

The *South Atlantic Quarterly* is indexed in *Abstracts of
English Studies, Academic Abstracts, Academic Index, America:
History and Life, American Bibliography of Slavic and East
European Studies, American Humanities Index, Arts and
Humanities Citation Index, Book Review Index, CERDIC,
Children's Book Review Index (1965–), Current Contents, His-
torical Abstracts, Humanities Index, Index to Book Reviews in
the Humanities, LCR, Middle East: Abstract and Index, MLA
Bibliography, PAIS,* and *Social Science Source.*

ISSN 0038-2876

ISBN for this issue: 0-8223-6502-2

Mysterious Actions: New American Drama

SPECIAL ISSUE EDITOR: JODY MCAULIFFE

The
South
Atlantic
Quarterly
Spring/Summer 2000
Volume 99
Number 2/3

To my mother, Joy McAuliffe,
and the memory of my father,
William J. McAuliffe
—J. M.

Jody McAuliffe

Mysterious Actions

It is strange that two of the titles of the plays in this collection contain the word *mystery*: *The Mystery of Attraction* and *The Mystery at the Middle of Ordinary Life.* That which is mysterious excites wonder, curiosity, or surprise while baffling our efforts to comprehend or identify it. That which is mysterious is beyond our powers to discover, understand, or explain.

It is passing strange that critic José Muñoz uses the word *mysterious* to describe the appearance of Maria Irene Fornes's plays in his discussion of Nilo Cruz's play *Two Sisters and a Piano*— a work that he regards as saturated with mysteriousness. Both Cruz and Marlane Meyer cite Fornes as a pivotal influence in their formation. Muñoz goes on to describe this mysterious quality as "strategic, measured, and interventionist."

That which is strange deviates from what is ordinary, usual, or to be expected. So the greed for the strange is also the poet's search for originality in style, the desire for "the pleasure of the original, a pleasure sought in reaction to a culture of numbing sameness" (Frank Lentricchia). The middle class, as Wallace Stevens so

The *South Atlantic Quarterly* 99:2/3, Spring/Summer 2000.

effectively noticed, has a "common preference for *realistic* satisfactions." Desdemona, on the other hand, inclined seriously and greedily to devour strangeness, so much so that she in part wished she had not heard it, "yet she wished / That heaven had made her such a man."

Some friend of Othello must have taught these playwrights how to tell their tales, for they have most certainly wooed me. All five of these plays shatter gradually through the icy surface of our "culture of commodity." All of these writers risk work that goes beyond realism, beyond the palliative of the middle class, beyond the capitalistic demands of the culture of commodity with tales that would win any daughter (or son).

When we speak of the action of these plays, what Francis Fergusson described as movement of spirit, we must dive deep into mystery through poetry, the supreme engine of their dramatic action, toward a radical deviancy of experience. The Monster of Neal Bell's *Monster* is really Victor Frankenstein himself. How Desdemona loved the stories of Cannibals and Anthropophagi! Follow the trail of Erin Cressida Wilson's *The Trail of Her Inner Thigh* into the secret of the womb—mystery itself. Is it witchcraft or craft? Let you witness it.

We should walk out of the theater after seeing any of these plays with the same amazement Nick Adams experienced after encountering *The Battler*: "He *found* he had a ham sandwich in his hand and put it in his pocket." Oh, to be so knocked out by a play, to get the craziness that's coming to us without knowing quite what happened—or how. When was the last time you "found" you had a ham sandwich in your hand? Looking back we see the firelight in the clearing of our mind's eye: We see these playwrights' visages in their minds.

Neal Bell. Photo: Peter Cunningham.

Neal Bell

Monster

A reading of *Monster* was presented at La Jolla Playhouse, which commissioned the work. It will receive its premiere in New York in January 2002, at the Classic Stage Company.

A play from the novel Frankenstein *by Mary Shelley.*

Characters

FORSTER, *second-in-command of the* Aurora
WALTON, *young captain of the* Aurora
TWO DOGS
VICTOR, *a young doctor*
FATHER, *of Victor*
MOTHER, *of Victor*
ELIZABETH, *Victor's cousin*
CAT
CLERVAL, *Victor's friend*
JUSTINE, *a servant in Victor's household*
WILLIAM, *Victor's little brother*
CREATURE, *Victor's creation*

Monster can be performed with a cast of five men and two women, with VICTOR, ELIZA-BETH, and the CREATURE being the three non-

The *South Atlantic Quarterly* 99:2/3, Spring/Summer 2000.
Copyright © 2001 by Neal Bell.

doubled parts, and the following doubling or tripling of these characters: FORSTER/FATHER/DOG, WALTON/CLERVAL, CAT/WILLIAM, and JUSTINE/MOTHER/DOG.

The Artic and England in the early nineteenth century. (Prop note: The Leyden jar, which appears in the thunderstorm-scene in act I, is a metal-lined glass jar, with a metal rod sticking out of the lid.)

Act I

Scene 1

On board the ship Aurora. *Somewhere in the Arctic Ocean.*
The young captain ROBERT WALTON *stands on the deck, looking out at the polar twilight.*
Lieutenant FORSTER, *an older man, approaches. He watches his captain anxiously, then finally speaks.*

FORSTER   If we turn back now . . . (*He gets no response*)
Captain?

WALTON   (*pointing out*) What do you see?

FORSTER   The jaws of a trap.
And we're sailing into it.

WALTON   (*not disagreeing*) For a moment, I thought I could just make out
the tracery of a rose window.
Through that wall of ice, the sun—
what little sun there is, blood-red,
and fading—almost gone.

FORSTER *regards his captain with concern.*

A cathedral.
With an empty pulpit gleaming in the final light,
a rat in search of a crumb—
Our Savior, "this is His body, take, eat"—
skitters across the altar—*there,*
do you hear it?

FORSTER   Sir, that's drifting snow—

WALTON Tiny claws,
a tiny beating heart—
a blood-red eye, glazing over,
dimmer, and what is it thinking, Lieutenant?
What are the thoughts of a dying rat?

FORSTER It's thinking, "We've come to the end of the world, and my captain's insane, and we're all of us bloody well fucked." Would be my guess.

Captain WALTON *is jarred.* FORSTER *renews his appeal.*

If we turn back now—

WALTON (*interrupting, in mock amazement*) You're on fire.
I can see the smoke of your breath—

FORSTER (*trying to be patient*) No, sir: if you could recover your wits,
you'd feel the cold—

WALTON (*ignoring*)—ambition burning: "All my life, I have wanted, in
some spectacular way, to fail."

He waits for FORSTER's *reaction, which doesn't come.*

"Let us *almost* find a way, to the
Top of the World, let us come *this* close—
and then turn back.
We're only human."
Like that smell.

FORSTER What smell?

WALTON The drizzly shit running down your leg.

Pause.

FORSTER (*having had enough*) Look at the walls of ice.
On every side of us, closing in—

WALTON Then we're already trapped.
We can't turn back.

FORSTER One channel is clear. Right behind us.

WALTON We don't have room to come around.

FORSTER (*correcting*) We won't, sir. After nightfall.

Pause.

WALTON The sun sets—

FORSTER In less than an hour.

WALTON And when did it rise?

FORSTER A few minutes ago.

WALTON Not much of a day.
Even less of a life.

Pause.

Shall I turn back now,
and become my father?—
nodding in front of a dying fire,
dreams burned down to cinders,
counting what I have left—a few banknotes—
never to see an unknown shore . . .

FORSTER Is a glimpse of terra incognita
worth any price? You probably think so—
being young and consequently insane—
so all of us have to die.

WALTON *flinches.*

Fair enough: my father told me—
"No man goes to hell before his time."
And our time is apparently now.

FORSTER *looks at the captain, hoping his words have sunk in.*

Unless we make for open water.
Permission to come about, sir?

At that moment, there's a brilliant flash of lightning—then almost immediately, a deafening clap of thunder.
WALTON *stares at something far off, which he saw in the one brief second of light.*
FORSTER *staggers, momentarily blinded.*

WALTON What in the Devil's name is that?
Dead ahead: a team of dogs.
Dragging a sledge across the ice.
And standing on the runners: a man?
Do you see him?

FORSTER (*disoriented*) Only a blinding light.

WALTON Or something *like* a man—an animal?
Slumping over the traces. Look.

FORSTER I see a jagged bolt of light—

WALTON It's an afterimage.

FORSTER —the sky is on fire!

WALTON Rest your eyes, then. Close them.

FORSTER *does so, agitated.*

FORSTER You couldn't have seen a man.
Not out on the ice.
We're a hundred miles from land.

WALTON Any land that *we* know of.
(*Excited at the prospect of discovery*) Terra incognita.

Now there's a very loud cracking sound, like a series of thundering gunshots.

FORSTER I'm blind. And very far from home.
And my captain is insane.
(*As hysteria grips him*) I CAN HEAR THE WATER SEIZING UP.
HOLDING US IN A VISE,
WE WILL BE STOVE IN,
COME ABOUT,
COME ABOUT, SIR!
IF WE TURN BACK, NOW—
IF WE MAKE FOR THE SOUTH—

WALTON But the man on the sledge is heading north.
And the ice he's on is breaking up.
I think we need to lower a boat—

FORSTER THERE IS NO MAN—

WALTON (*peering out, startled*) There are two, I'm afraid.

FORSTER, *dumbfounded, opens his eyes. His vision is coming back—and he's even more frightened, because he's sharing the captain's hallucination.*

WALTON (*continued*) I see another sledge, now.
Where did it come from?
What is it doing?
Racing after the first . . .
But not in time: because a chasm
is opening up between them.
Black water, getting wider . . .
And the sledge on the farther side is
disappearing into the twilight.

Pause.

We could save the man who's closer.

Far off, we hear the barking of dogs.

FORSTER A man can freeze to death,
standing, holding on to the reins . . .
He isn't moving, sir.

WALTON But you *do* see him, Lieutenant.
Then I'm *not* insane?

FORSTER (*reluctant*) And I hear the dogs.
Something's gotten their wind up.

WALTON One is slipping over the edge.
And he's dragging his fellows after him.

FORSTER, *anxious, shouts to the offstage man on the sledge.*

FORSTER Cut the traces, man!

WALTON He can't hear you.

FORSTER Why doesn't he move?
All the dogs will go into the water—CUT THE TRACES!

WALTON Why are you shouting at a dead man?

FORSTER Because I don't know for a fact he's dead.
And God damn me, but I wish he were.
If we attempt a rescue now,
in the little time we have left—

He stops, seeing something new.

WALTON Go on. Or did you see it, too?
Something that wasn't there before—
last light, gleaming on metal?
Our man has pulled out a knife.

Scene 2

Adrift on an iceberg.
Knife in hand, an exhausted VICTOR FRANKENSTEIN *stands at the edge of*
the ice.
He looks down into the water, where the dog he just cut loose has disappeared.
The two surviving DOGS—*suddenly free—back away from* VICTOR. *No longer*
barking, they watch him warily. When he takes a step closer, they growl. VICTOR
stops.

VICTOR What are you thinking? Tell me.
I killed your friend. I'm sorry.
He would have killed you. Do you understand?

Pause.

I used to speak fluent Dog, when I was a child.
And Cat—a little more difficult—
and a smattering of Hill, and Tree, and Cloud—and I would lie down in
    the sun,
in the grass, and be so very still,
I could hear the whole wide world.
Breathing.
In and out—trembling:
Alive.
How was that possible?
Alive.

What could that mean?
"In the beginning was the Word."
What word?

In his agitation, unthinking, he takes a step in the dogs' direction. Baring fangs, they back away.

I've lost you—I thought you were with me.
Because, a day ago, when the trail was cold, and
you were starving,
one of you stumbled and fell,
and the rest of you ate him.
Do you remember that?
One of you I kicked away,
so I could tear at the carcass myself.
Why did you eat your fellow? Why did I?
To stay alive.
In the beginning was the Word.
What was the Word—*eat*?

Behind VICTOR, *at the far edge of the ice floe, Captain* WALTON *is clamber-ing up.*
VICTOR *doesn't sense his presence, at first—but the dogs go wild.*

VICTOR *(continued, to the* DOGS) Is he here? Has he doubled back? (*Afraid to turn around*)
Has he found me? In the beginning—*Devour.*
(*Addressing what he thinks is behind him*) Break every bone in my body,
so the splinters poke through the skin,
you can suck the marrow.
I understand.
Eat.
You have to live.
That was the gift I gave you:
hunger forever.

Resigned, he sinks to his knees.
In spite of their fear of the stranger, WALTON, *the* DOGS *smell* VICTOR's *weakness and begin to move closer, circling.*
Alarmed, WALTON *draws a pistol and shouts at the* DOGS.

WALTON No! Get back! Get away from him!

The DOGS *ignore him.* WALTON *shoots into the air, and the* DOGS, *snarling, retreat.*
VICTOR *can't bring himself to face his savior.*

VICTOR Who are you?

WALTON A friend.

VICTOR Leave me.

WALTON How can I do that, now?
You would perish.

VICTOR You have a vessel?

WALTON For the moment.
Winter coming on, and we are
running out of sea-room.

VICTOR Where are you bound?

WALTON Does it matter?
Anywhere would be safer—

VICTOR (*insistent*) But where?

Pause.

WALTON The men would like to turn back,
before we're trapped, and the ship is crushed.

VICTOR And you?

WALTON I want to go on.
North.
All the way to the Pole,
if there's a way—

VICTOR Ah, yes, well—isn't that the most terrible secret?
There is always a way.
And we find it.
I myself am going North.

WALTON   For what reason?

VICTOR   To seek the one who fled from me.

WALTON   The one in the other sledge?

VICTOR *nods.*

WALTON   (*continued*) Who is he?

VICTOR *doesn't answer.*

What is he?

WALTON's *intuitive guess surprises* VICTOR, *who finally turns to face the captain.*

VICTOR   I said, "Who are you?" You said, "A friend."
But if indeed you were, I could prove my love for you
only by leaving you:
before the doom that shadows me had
overtaken you as well.

WALTON   What are you afraid of? Dying?
"No man goes to hell before his time."

Pause.

VICTOR   My father would have amended that.
He would have said there was no Hell to go to.
He was mistaken.

Scene 3

VICTOR's FATHER *and* MOTHER *enter, followed by* VICTOR's *cousin* ELIZABETH.
FATHER *is reading a paper.* VICTOR *and* ELIZABETH *are children.*

MOTHER   (*too brightly, trying to make conversation*) What is happening?
Anywhere in the world.

FATHER   (*buried in his paper*) The French peasantry are revolting.

MOTHER   Haven't you always felt them to be?

FATHER *gives* MOTHER *a look. Flustered, she turns to* VICTOR.

Don't play with your oatmeal, Victor.

VICTOR (*to* FATHER) How fast is the guillotine—
when it falls?

MOTHER What is a guillotine?

FATHER (*bemused by* VICTOR'*s question*) How fast?

VICTOR Does the head have time to think,
"I am being lopped off?"
Is the blade that keen?

FATHER I don't believe they are killing children—yet.
Though I'm sure they would make an exception,
if you would like to book a passage.

MOTHER Papa!

VICTOR If it were so fast that my eyes could still see,
when they held me up by my hair,
would I look down, and would I mutter,
"Don't drop me into that basket
with the other severed heads?"

ELIZABETH How would you mutter?

VICTOR What do you mean?

ELIZABETH Well, your head would be here,
and your lungs would be there.
You wouldn't have the breath to move your lips.

MOTHER *glares at* FATHER.

MOTHER You *will* insist on reading the morning gazette
at the breakfast table.
The children brood all day,
and then they have horrible dreams at night.

FATHER (*winking at the young ones*) So do I.

VICTOR My porridge is cold.

MOTHER   Good. Elizabeth?

In a huff, MOTHER *exits, followed by the reluctant* ELIZABETH. FATHER *continues to read the paper.*

VICTOR   Papa? Is there a God?

FATHER   No.

He turns a page.

VICTOR   Papa? Am *I* a god?

FATHER   If you like.
I decided it was too much bother.
But you could give it a try.

Folding his paper up, FATHER *exits.*

Scene 4

Back in the present, on the iceberg.

WALTON   Did you? Make an attempt?

Desolate, VICTOR *stares off into the twilight.*

VICTOR   I succeeded.

Pause.

WALTON   Not the most impressive of gods.

VICTOR   Christ, you remember, had a few awkward moments,
while he was dangling . . .

WALTON   You're suffering from frostbite,
and you can barely stand.
You are ill and starving.
Let me take you back to my ship.
I will rub you with brandy,
let you drink some . . .
broth, if you can hold it down—
and when you're on the mend
I would like to hear the end of your story.

VICTOR What of the dogs?

WALTON I'm sorry.
But the supplies on board are low.

VICTOR (*pointing to* WALTON'*s pistol*) Then put them down.

WALTON *looks uneasy at the thought.*

Or leave them. Let them die of cold and starvation.

WALTON, *reluctantly convinced, takes aim at one of the dogs.*
Sensing danger, the DOGS *escape—suddenly racing into the dark.*
WALTON *runs after them.*

WALTON No! Come back!

WALTON *exits.* VICTOR'*s alone on stage.*

VICTOR Oh yes—come back: good dogs.
Come back and die.

The lights change.

Scene 5

Two DOGS *of* VICTOR'*s childhood pursue a screeching* CAT *onstage.*
Chasing them all, but far behind, is VICTOR'*s friend* CLERVAL.
DOGS, CAT, *and* CLERVAL—*yelping*—*run in crazy circles around young* VICTOR
(*who's almost an adolescent, now*).
The menagerie runs off—but VICTOR *snags* CLERVAL *by the collar, stopping him*
short.

VICTOR Clerval—do the animals want you to play?

CLERVAL I don't know.

VICTOR Why didn't you ask them?

CLERVAL *considers this, and then dashes off.*

CLERVAL Rufus! Annabelle—wait!

CLERVAL *is gone. A second later, the* CAT—*with* DOGS *in mad pursuit—runs in*
from another direction.

The CAT *leaps into* VICTOR's *arms.*
Not knowing how their prey has escaped, the stupid DOGS *run off.*
VICTOR *puts down the smug* CAT.

VICTOR A satisfactory morning, then, Mr. Puss—
tormenting the dogs?

CAT It passed the time.

VICTOR They are very silly animals.
You ought to be ashamed.

CAT I'm not.
God gave me a duty. I fulfill it.

VICTOR Papa says there is no God.

He takes out a knife.

So it's entirely possible,
that while I perform my experiments—
I am going to be a doctor, you know—
you may have to suffer unbearably.

CAT (*nervous, but hiding it*) I don't follow . . .

VICTOR No one to stop me.

CAT Ah.

Pause.

There is a god of cats.
He's very large.
Unpleasantly large.
Big.
Some of us believe he coughed up this.

The CAT *gestures around him.*

VICTOR The earth is a fur ball?
That's absurd.

CAT And a talking cat would be . . .

VICTOR Very clever.

CAT But not quite clever enough
to escape your shiny knife.

Pause.

VICTOR The century is turning—
men are doing incredible things.
When they pass an electric current
through a dead frog's leg—
can you guess what happens?

CAT People stare at them, wondering why they would
want to pass an electric current through a dead frog's leg?

VICTOR The leg comes back to life!
It twitches. Dangling on a spike,
attached to nothing, it suddenly—moves!

CAT (*thinking fast*) I already have an electrical current. Inside me.

VICTOR (*agreeing, excited*) Do you think so?

CAT Look!

He demonstrates an impressive array of twitches.

Out of nowhere.
Sui generis.
I don't need to be impaled.

VICTOR But why do we die?
The current stops.
Why does the spark go out?

CAT It's a mystery.

VICTOR That's why I have to cut you open.

At that moment ELIZABETH *enters.*

ELIZABETH (*gently chiding*) Cousin? What are you doing?

VICTOR Explaining fate to the cat.

ELIZABETH (*to rescue the animal*) Shoo!

The CAT, *irate at having been frightened, runs off.*
VICTOR *regards* ELIZABETH.

ELIZABETH (*continued*) Where is your friend Clerval?

VICTOR You like him.

ELIZABETH Oh yes: we are going to run away.

VICTOR He told me he thought you were beautiful.

ELIZABETH Did he? While he was trotting beside you,
hoping you would scruff his fur?

VICTOR Will you marry me?

ELIZABETH I don't think so. No.

VICTOR Why not?

ELIZABETH Because you expect me to.

VICTOR But you love me.

ELIZABETH I don't care.
I will not be a part of your collection.
The tusk of a narwhal.
I am not an albino adder,
or the head of a rabid fox
floating forever in a bottle. Grinning.
Or something that ought to be free,
pinned to a board, for you to study.

VICTOR *points at a dull red stain on her dress.*

VICTOR Did you hurt yourself?

ELIZABETH (*looking down, startled*) No!

VICTOR You're bleeding.

ELIZABETH Am I?

ELIZABETH, *dreading her own understanding, tries to fight down her panic.*

Your mother said I would.
I thought she was only trying to frighten me.
"Regular as the moon—"
so the moon isn't beautiful, not anymore.
I can have a baby, now,
and suffer, having it, and die.

VICTOR *doesn't know what to say.*

ELIZABETH (*continued*) Like my mama did, giving birth to me.
Blood is running down my leg.
Do something.
Please.
I'm afraid.

VICTOR *kneels at her feet. Lifting up the edge of her skirt, he touches her blood with his fingertips.*

ELIZABETH (*continued*) I smell like a butcher's shop.

VICTOR No, not at all: you smell alive.

He buries his face in her skirt. Touched by his lack of revulsion, she strokes his head.

ELIZABETH I tore my mother open.
I'm afraid.

VICTOR Then don't ever marry.

ELIZABETH I may have to.

VICTOR Why? Tell me.

ELIZABETH Because I have always loved you.
I have always wanted to touch your hair . . .
twist it around my fingers,
pull it tight, till you cried out
and I would silence you with my kisses.

Pause.

I don't think you could ever love me like that.
You love me because I'm an animal.
You love me because I bleed.

Upset—at what, she can't be sure—she pushes him away from her.

VICTOR   I don't understand you!

ELIZABETH   I *know*! Why do you think I've always
hated you?

ELIZABETH *rushes off. Bewildered,* VICTOR *watches her go. Then he looks at the
blood on his hands. The serving-girl* JUSTINE *passes by.*

VICTOR   Justine—would you bring me a cloth?

JUSTINE   Yes, sir.

VICTOR   (*feeling he needs to explain*) I cut myself.

JUSTINE   You ought to be careful.

She starts to exit.

VICTOR   Justine—if you were bleeding,
and I asked you why—
would you hate me?

JUSTINE   If I was bleeding, sir?
Where?

VICTOR   It doesn't matter where!
But if I were concerned—

JUSTINE   About me?

VICTOR   Well—curious.

JUSTINE   I could never hate you, sir.

VICTOR   Why not?

JUSTINE   Why not? I would lose my job.

Scene 6

Offstage, a gunshot. Quickly, another.
JUSTINE *vanishes.*
A moment later, WALTON *reenters, shaken.*

VICTOR Done?

WALTON Yes.

VICTOR (*sardonic*) Out of their misery.

WALTON How do they know . . .

VICTOR —that the blow is coming?

WALTON (*nodding*) They were mad with fear
until I aimed—
and then they were nothing.
Before I fired.
They looked up at me—
one of them cocked his head—
he was listening to something—far off . . .

VICTOR So are you. And I think you hear it.
Like the whispering edge of an ancient map:
"Beyond this point are monsters."
And beyond the monsters—what?
Nothing at all.
That's what the dogs could hear:
the pounding of their blood fading out,
wind dying down to nothing.
A very terrible stillness.
You *do* hear it, Mr.—

WALTON "Captain." Robert Walton.
And your name would be?

VICTOR *doesn't answer.* WALTON *tries to provoke a response.*

WALTON (*continued*) You're bleeding.

VICTOR (*looking down*) Am I?

WALTON Your skin is cracked and blistered.
Don't you have gloves?

VICTOR I did—impractical, fine kid leather.
A gift from my wife, to whom I was married
not happily, for a single day.

Pause.

I was going to cook the gloves,
with a little lichen.
But the dogs ate them.

He stares at his fingers.

I have blood on my hands.

He starts to laugh, then tries to stop himself.

WALTON I have blood everywhere.
I was standing too close to the dogs,
when I fired—

VICTOR *(trying to clarify)* No—*(melodramatically)* "I have blood on my hands!"

He laughs again, and can't stop himself.

WALTON Will you let me help you, my friend?
Whatever your name is?
Do you remember it?

Scene 7

VICTOR *is rubbing a glass rod with a piece of fur when his younger brother* WILLIAM *dashes on stage, yelling at the top of his lungs.*

WILLIAM Victor! Victor! Victor! Victor!
Victor! Victor! Victor! Victor!

Distracted by the experiment he's conducting, VICTOR *doesn't even look up until* WILLIAM *is already dashing off.*

VICTOR What?

But WILLIAM *is gone, as* VICTOR'S MOTHER *enters.*

MOTHER Victor, where is the cat?

VICTOR I haven't seen it.

MOTHER Why don't I believe you?

VICTOR Because your life has been a succession
of nagging disappointments?

Pause.

MOTHER What a clever and hideous child it is.
(*Pointing to Victor's materials*) Explain that bedraggled pelt in your hand.

VICTOR It's for an experiment, Mama—
I use it to rub a glass rod, like so—
and then the rod becomes electrical—

MOTHER But *what is it?*

VICTOR It's a scrap of fur. I found it in the woods.

Pause.

MOTHER Do you know the words of the oath
you will have to swear, when you become a physician?

VICTOR "First, do no harm."

MOTHER I was fond of that cat.

VICTOR The cat was subject to fits.

MOTHER And who among us is not?
Your brother runs around the house, screaming
"Victor! Victor! Victor!"

Pause.

VICTOR If I touch you with this rod,
every hair on your head will stand on end.

MOTHER Or, to achieve the same effect,
I can contemplate my life—

a few minutes from now,
when you and your brother are grown,
your cousin is married,
your father is dead—
for no reason but spite—
and I'm alone.

MOTHER *takes the piece of fur from* VICTOR, *looking at it with regret, as she exits.*
WILLIAM *comes galloping back onstage, still yelling.*

WILLIAM Victor! Victor! Victor! Victor!
Victor! Victor! Victor! Victor!

VICTOR *What?*

WILLIAM If you say a word over and over and over,
it doesn't mean anything anymore.
It's just a sound. Have you noticed that? (*Demonstrating*)
The. The. The. The. The.—
what does *the* mean?

VICTOR I don't know.

WILLIAM Then why do we say it?

VICTOR Why do we say anything?

WILLIAM Because, if it's too quiet . . .

VICTOR (*intrigued*) Go on . . .

WILLIAM It's too quiet! Victor! Victor! Victor!

VICTOR (*shouting over him*) William! William! William!

Finally VICTOR *gives up, and* WILLIAM *keeps on gleefully shouting* "Victor! Victor" *as he runs off.*

Scene 8

VICTOR *finishes the memory.*

VICTOR "Frankenstein."

WALTON "Victor Frankenstein."

VICTOR And this is *ice*. And this is *dark*.
And you are not *my friend*.

Pause.

I *had* a friend,
of my childhood . . .

WALTON What happened?
Is he the man?

VICTOR What man?

WALTON You were seeking one who fled.

Unconsciously, VICTOR looks around—as if afraid of something out there in the dark.

VICTOR (*evading*) And you, "Robert Walton"?
What are you after?
The honor of standing, first and alone,
at the top of the godforsaken world?
And then? The cries of "Evohé"?
Women fainting away, as you enter a room?
The thanks of a grateful nation?

WALTON All of that, I thought,
when I first set out—

VICTOR And now?

WALTON I would settle for—

He stops himself.

VICTOR What?

Pause.

WALTON I've put the lives of my men at risk,
for no reason they can understand.

VICTOR Turn back, then.

WALTON Will you come with me?

VICTOR I'm sorry. But I should explain,
about my friend—his name was Clerval—
he isn't the creature I'm pursuing.
Henry Clerval is dead. We were walking
up in the hills, one summer evening—
jabbering on about nothing at all,
when I turned to him, in the twilight,
I put my hands on his neck—
I wonder now if that surprised him—
and I strangled him,
till his eyes bulged out of his head and his
tongue turned black.

Pause.

WALTON I don't believe you.

VICTOR Don't you?

WALTON You want me to abandon you.

VICTOR (*agreeing*) Because "no man goes to hell before his time"?—
its utter rubbish.
My friend was not the first I robbed of his rightful
portion of life. I began with my brother:
(*bitterly mocking*) "William! William!"

WALTON And where did you end?

VICTOR Don't you understand? I haven't ended.

Daunted by VICTOR's *glare,* WALTON *takes a step backward and stumbles,
falling to the ice. But he won't be cowed.*

WALTON Let me *almost* find a way to help you,
let me come this close,
and then turn back.

VICTOR "All my life I have wanted—"

WALTON *is startled that* VICTOR *can echo words he never heard.*

—what? A mate for your troubled soul?

WALTON   Someone who could share my joy.
(*Almost to himself*) Or offer me absolution.

VICTOR   Make one.
Find a new grave, dig it up,
or haunt the morgue, and the butcher shop,
for a bone, a piece of yellow skin,
a patch of greasy hair, a tooth,
an eye sunk into the skull,
two rotting lips. Needle and catgut:
sew the pieces together.

Haunted by what he thinks is VICTOR'*s fantasy,* WALTON *remembers a Bible passage.*

WALTON   "A valley full of bones . . ."

VICTOR   (*recognizing the quote*) ". . . and behold, there were very many—"

WALTON   "—and lo, they were very dry—
and can these bones live?"

VICTOR   Can they?
I wondered.

Scene 9

VICTOR'*s* FATHER *enters, holding a matted, unrecognizable thing.*

FATHER   Victor. Would you bury this?

VICTOR   What is it?

FATHER   Your mother says it's the cat.
The one that ran away—wisely—a year ago.
When she retires, she settles it
in its favorite spot, at the foot of the bed.
I've begun to find that unnerving,

even though I've long accepted the fact
that your mother is quite insane.

VICTOR *takes the cat fur from his* FATHER, *who starts to exit.*

Don't ever marry.

VICTOR Not even for love?

FATHER Do you think I hunted your mother down
for her money?

As FATHER *exits,* VICTOR'S *friend* CLERVAL *enters, holding something wrapped
in a handkerchief. Blood is starting to seep through the cloth.*

CLERVAL Victor?

VICTOR What are you doing with that?

CLERVAL You know what it is?

VICTOR It's a specimen.

CLERVAL Could you enlighten me as to the species?
I only ask, because—

VICTOR Clerval—

CLERVAL Yes, I know, there are mysteries you are intent on solving—
the "What is life?" sort of thing,
and ordinarily I would never presume to inquire
into your methods—

VICTOR I seem to remember telling you never to go in the cellar, Clerval.

CLERVAL You gave me a key.

VICTOR For one reason only:
in case I went down there to work
and failed—after more than a day—to reappear.
But here I am—I have not gone missing.
And yet you decided the time had come
to intrude upon my privacy.

Pause. CLERVAL *holds up the bloody packet.*

CLERVAL Victor, this is still warm.

VICTOR Is it? And how could you have known that
before you went down the cellar stairs?

Pause.

CLERVAL I had a dream about you, last night.
We were on a walking-tour,
up into some highlands I'd never seen before,
deep summer, blazing hot, and when we
came to a tarn, you wanted to bathe.
But I held back—there was something
about the water: how very still it was,
and how dark—and you were laughing at me:
"What are you afraid of?"
And then you took a step closer to me
and you kissed me on the mouth.

Pause.

VICTOR *approaches his friend. Very deliberately, he kisses him.*
CLERVAL *is stunned.*

VICTOR Don't waste a good dream on
something you can have.
Dream about the impossible.

VICTOR *takes the cloth-wrapped thing from* CLERVAL.

This is warm because I passed an electrical
current through it.

CLERVAL Why?

VICTOR Why did you want me to kiss you?

CLERVAL I didn't!

VICTOR Because you were curious.

Pause.

CLERVAL If I were the curious sort,
I might have looked under that bloody tarpaulin

you had thrown over something—God knows what—
in the darkest part of the cellar.

VICTOR (*suddenly very anxious*) Did you?

CLERVAL No.

VICTOR Why not?

CLERVAL Because I was afraid.
The tarpaulin moved.

For a moment, VICTOR *is taken aback.*

Then a rat scurried out from under the cloth.
There was a slick of blood, on its muzzle.
Victor, what was it feeding on?

VICTOR Any number of my hopes.

Scene 10

In a cellar room that VICTOR *uses for his experiments.*
VICTOR *enters, approaching a blood-stained tarpaulin. He pulls the*
tarpaulin off.
A naked CREATURE *slumps in a straight-backed chair. It appears to be dead.*
Stitched together from severed body parts, it looks like the mangled corpse of a
man who was in a terrible accident.
VICTOR *sits in a chair beside the* CREATURE. *He stares at his creation.*

VICTOR Who made you?
I made you.
Bones I stole from the slaughterhouse
and muscle from a dissecting room,
skin I would peel, one bloody sheet at a time,
from my own body,
the brain of a child who was trampled to death
right in front of me, by a runaway carriage—
why did no one ever miss that child,
when I gathered up the remains?
Why did no one claim the cadavers
growing mold in the anatomy halls,

the ones I would whittle away at,
late at night, a lip, an eye,
a finger tucked away in my pocket—
why did it matter to no one, anywhere,
that these bodies had been alive?

Pause.

Did no one lie awake at night,
missing the touch of that hand,
or the weight of those legs, across their own,
or the muscles moving under the skin
of the back, the back arching up:
this man looking down on his love, with delight—
Does no one stare up at the dark
and try to remember what you looked like?

In frustration, VICTOR *hauls the inanimate* CREATURE *to its feet. He struggles to hold it upright, willing it to stand.*

"I look like death."
The spark goes out.
Why does the spark go out?
And why can I never bring it back?

The CREATURE's *silence is terrible.*

WHY DOESN'T ANYONE REMEMBER
ANY PART OF YOU?
A lock of hair, a breath, a single smile . . .
Like you never existed.

The dead weight is too much. VICTOR *roughly drops the* CREATURE *back in the chair—but the chair tips over, and the* CREATURE *sprawls on the floor, in a grotesque heap.*

You *didn't* exist.
I made you.
But I cannot make the spark.

ELIZABETH *appears at the door to the cellar.*

ELIZABETH   Victor? Are you all right?
Did you fall?

VICTOR   What are you doing, Elizabeth?

ELIZABETH   I am standing here, with my hand on the door,
remembering your clear instruction
never to try the lock.

Pause.

But I heard you stumble.

VICTOR   I ran into something.
The cellar is dark, and
my candle is nearly out.

ELIZABETH   Shall I bring you another?

Pause.

VICTOR   No.
My experiment failed. Again.
I am gnashing my teeth.

Pause.

What are you doing now?

ELIZABETH   My hand is still on the door.
Will you let me in?

Far off, we hear the rumble of thunder.

VICTOR   What was that? Was that thunder?

Looking at the fallen CREATURE, VICTOR *has an idea.*

Scene 11

A flash of lightning.
WILLIAM *runs on, holding the string of a kite that is flying high up, offstage.
There's an ominous rumble of thunder.*

VICTOR   (*offstage*) Willie! Bring it back!

WILLIAM (*exhilarated*) I can't! The kite is pulling me into the air!

MOTHER (*offstage*) William Frankenstein!

WILLIAM I can't come down! I'm flying! Look!

MOTHER *hurries on.*

MOTHER Give the string to your brother! *Victor?*

Another flash of lightning.

WILLIAM Hurrah! The storm is on top of us!
That one almost hit!
Victor, hurry!

VICTOR *enters, holding an early version of a battery, a Leyden jar.*
Thunder rumbles. ELIZABETH *and* VICTOR's *friend* CLERVAL *come in.*

VICTOR Willie, the kite is dangerous now.

CLERVAL (*making trouble, to* VICTOR) But why can *your* eyeballs explode?
And no one else's?
I want a turn.

WILLIAM My eyes will explode?

MOTHER Thank you so much for you help, Clerval.
(*to* WILLIAM) Give your brother the kite string—now!

WILLIAM No!

VICTOR It's all right: the part he's holding is silk.
It doesn't conduct—I think . . .

MOTHER You *think?* (*To anyone*)
And what do you mean by "conduct?"

CLERVAL (*aware of* WILLIAM's *game*) Nothing! "Conduct, conduct, conduct,
conduct—"

A flash of lightning, a terrible clap of thunder.

MOTHER I HAVE BURIED SEVEN CHILDREN!
NONE OF THIS IS REMOTELY AMUSING!

Her anger sobers everyone.

Now give your brother the kite,
you little monster. Do you hear me?

WILLIAM, *on the verge of tears, defiantly holds on to the string.*
MOTHER *storms off.*

CLERVAL Willie, your mama's not mad at you.
But she remembers a tree
that used to be right outside your window.

WILLIAM Where that rotten stump is?

CLERVAL That rotten stump was a beautiful oak
your brother and I would climb
all the way to the top,
so high in the air, the wind would rock us,
and we could see the whole countryside—
not to mention, if she preceded us—
your cousin Elizabeth's petticoats.

ELIZABETH By any chance, do you think I didn't
hear the two of you giggling?
I wanted you to look.

WILLIAM What do you mean?

CLERVAL Yes, Lizzie—what?

ELIZABETH I'd offer a glimpse of the unattainable.
You would get dizzy and fall.
That was the plan.

WILLIAM Is that what happened?

CLERVAL What happened was a darkening day like this,
and rain so sudden, the three of us
ran for the door, but the rain was faster,
and just as we tumbled, sopping wet, inside—
there was a scalding light,
and a roar that rattled the windowpanes,

and when we looked out at the tree,
the tree was gone.

WILLIAM Gone where?

CLERVAL Exploded.
Nothing left of it,
but scraps of bark and leaf all over the lawn,
and a blackened stump.

Pause.

WILLIAM, *shaken, hands the string of the kite to* VICTOR.

WILLIAM I found the bones of a robin, once,
and a worm was crawling out of the eye-hole.

CLERVAL The worm was eating the bird?

WILLIAM It isn't funny!
(*To* VICTOR) What will be left of *you*?

WILLIAM *runs off.*

ELIZABETH (*reproving*) A bone. A brittle bit of skin. A tooth—

VICTOR Would you not be womanish now?
Be useful. Here—hold the Leyden jar,
while I attach the string, like so—

He attaches the kite string—above the silk thread he was using to insulate himself—to a metal rod that sticks out of the lid of the apparatus ELIZABETH *is holding.*

CLERVAL And when lightning strikes the kite,
you think "electricity" will come streaming down
like a fluid you can trap in a bottle?

VICTOR I don't think—I know:
an American fellow has already done this.

ELIZABETH Your father says the Americans are revolting.

CLERVAL And is he wrong about that?
Have you ever sat at the table with one?

Suddenly, a blare of light—and directly above them, a shattering clap of thunder.
For a moment, everyone is stunned.
Then VICTOR *realizes the jar is glowing.*

VICTOR   Elizabeth—put down the jar. PUT IT DOWN.

She doesn't move.

ELIZABETH   Am I dead? Is hell Clerval?
(*To* VICTOR) Did I never get to lie beneath you,
in the high grass, in the heat of the day,
and feel the slick of your skin,
and taste your mouth, and hear you whisper
hot in my ear, "Don't move!—
stay still, so very still, if you buck
and I slip any deeper inside you
I am gone"—and I want that,
both of us, into each other,
exploding, so I *do* buck—
and we both cry out,
on the edge, falling into ourselves
and a light streams out of us . . .

Carefully, VICTOR *takes the jar from* ELIZABETH. *She starts to come out of her trance.*

ELIZABETH   (*continued*) Why are you looking at me like that?
I was babbling. What did I say?

VICTOR   (*very gently*) Only—that you were afraid of dying.

He detaches the string of the kite, absently handing it to CLERVAL.

CLERVAL   What happens now?

VICTOR   (*with renewed purpose*) I set us all free.
I make a dead frog leg dance.

VICTOR *exits, with the glowing jar.*
ELIZABETH *and* CLERVAL, *both rattled, watch him go.*
Finally, CLERVAL *shouts out.*

CLERVAL COME BACK!
MAKE ELIZABETH DANCE!

ELIZABETH *stares at* CLERVAL. *Then she slaps him.*

ELIZABETH He doesn't love either one of us.
Could you try not to be so pathetic?

CLERVAL *is speechless.*
Regretful, ELIZABETH *touches his face.*

ELIZABETH (*continued*) Did I hurt you?

CLERVAL Yes.

ELIZABETH I'm sorry.
Or I would certainly like to be.

They regard each other.
Barely aware of what they do, they move into each other's arms.
They kiss—gently at first, and then with a growing, desperate passion.
Another flash of lightning—not as near—and a growl of thunder.
Coming out of their trance, CLERVAL *and* ELIZABETH *step away from each other.*
Confused and upset, ELIZABETH *runs off.*
Watching her go—and dazed himself— CLERVAL *releases the kite. It floats off into the sky.*

Scene 12

The cellar room.
The lifeless, naked CREATURE *again is slumped in a chair.*
VICTOR *enters, in his hands the glowing Leyden jar.*
On the brink of success, he hesitates—fearful of failure. He stares at the
CREATURE.

VICTOR You don't know this, but a general rain
is falling over the countryside.
People are trapped in their rooms,
by a dying fire—if they can afford even that—
watching the flames sink down,
trying not to think of how very little

will ever become of their lives:
they have hopes, but they come to nothing,
they have dreams that die, unborn,
and the ones who love them wait in vain
to be given anything in return . . .

The CREATURE *is silent.*

I have nothing to give—
I have emptied myself into you:
my dream, my hope. And if I fail—
if I turn back now . . .

With a sudden and savage motion, VICTOR *touches the metal rod of the Leyden jar to the* CREATURE'S *chest.*
The CREATURE *jerks. It opens its eyes. It screams.*
The scream is uncanny, terrifying. VICTOR *takes a step backward, staring at what he has wrought.*
The scream stops, just as suddenly as it started. The CREATURE *slumps in the chair again, inert.*

VICTOR   *(continued)* Dead again. Or were you ever alive?
Were you only a frog leg twitching?

Pause.

I have brought you to a door.
Why won't you go through it?
GO THROUGH THE DOOR!

Deciding to put his life on the line, VICTOR *very deliberately drops his hand on top of the Leyden jar.*
As the current runs through him, he touches the CREATURE, *who screams—as* VICTOR *shouts over him.*

The angel—"Revelations"—
what does he promise:
"There shall be time no longer!"
And time is nothing else but death—so
why do we have to wait for the sound of trumpets
at the Apocalypse?

I declare that there will be death
no longer —
And a stream of light, a torrent
will come roaring, headlong,
into our dark world.

At the end of his adrenaline-rush, VICTOR *falls backward, lying where he fell.*
The Leyden jar rolls across the floor and comes to rest.
The CREATURE *stands unsteadily.*
He approaches VICTOR. *Getting down on all fours, he crawls atop his creator.*
He touches VICTOR'S *face, his neck — becoming aware of the pulse at* VICTOR'S
throat.

CREATURE *(softly)* Boom, boom, boom, boom, boom, boom, boom —

Coming to, with a jolt, VICTOR *grabs the* CREATURE'S *hand and forces it off him.*
VICTOR *stares at his creation, horrified and amazed.*

CREATURE *(continued)* I want . . .

VICTOR What?

The CREATURE *shakes his head, unable to be any more articulate.*

CREATURE I WANT.

JUSTINE, *the serving-girl, appears at the cellar door.*

JUSTINE Mr. Frankenstein?

The CREATURE *turns his head at the sound of a woman's voice.*

I heard you cry out.
Have you hurt yourself?
Are you all right?

Before VICTOR *can answer, the* CREATURE *clamps a hand across his mouth.*
VICTOR *fights against the gag, but the* CREATURE *is stronger.*

JUSTINE *(continued)* You left the door ajar.

Appalled, VICTOR *struggles again — but in vain. The* CREATURE *holds him*
down.

You must have been in a terrible hurry.
Did you fall down the stairs?
Would you mind if I had a look at you,
on the cellar floor, in a puddle of blood?

Scene 13

The CREATURE *hides in the shadows.*
VICTOR, *dazed, is still on the floor, where he fell.*
JUSTINE *approaches.*

VICTOR No puddle of blood.

JUSTINE Some other day.

VICTOR I never knew you hated me so much.

JUSTINE It isn't personal.

VICTOR You're in terrible danger.

JUSTINE Of course I am.
I don't mistake myself for a beauty,
it's only—"Here I am. You can have me."
Grab a tit, and *I* can scream—
will anyone come to my rescue?

Now ELIZABETH *appears at the top of the cellar stairs.*

ELIZABETH Victor? No one can find Justine.
Have you seen her?

VICTOR No!
I will be right up.

As VICTOR *stands, the* CREATURE *steps out of the shadows—approaching* JUSTINE, *who doesn't see him yet.*

JUSTINE When you tell a lie, like that,
do you think it leaves a stink in the air?

VICTOR What you smell are some of my chemicals—
in retorts I forget about, until they're
boiling over.

VICTOR *tries—without alerting* JUSTINE—*to step between her and the* CREATURE, *who's very close now.*

JUSTINE Worse than that. Like a fat old rat
had died in the walls—it's sickening.

Before VICTOR *can stop him, the* CREATURE *puts a hand on* JUSTINE's *neck. She gasps, thinking it's* VICTOR.

VICTOR Cold?

JUSTINE (*not looking around*) As the grave.
What is wrong with you?

VICTOR I'm dying. And so are the people I love—
even you, who I hardly know at all—
and every other living soul,
we are racing to oblivion.
And I have been trying to remedy that—

JUSTINE (*dumbfounded*)—by finding a cure—for death.

VICTOR Yes.

The tension finally overcomes JUSTINE, *who starts to laugh.*

JUSTINE I myself was of a mind that death
was a cure for life.

The CREATURE *suddenly silences her, by putting his other hand on her neck.*

CREATURE Boom, boom, boom, boom . . .

VICTOR *unthinkingly takes a step away from* JUSTINE.
She realizes he isn't standing behind her.

JUSTINE Begging your pardon, sir,
but you seem to be—there,
and your hands are here—

VICTOR (*to the* CREATURE) Let go of her.
Let go.

Reluctantly, the CREATURE *takes his hands away.*

CREATURE I want . . .

Fearful, JUSTINE *turns and sees the* CREATURE *for the first time. They stare at each other.*

VICTOR Justine? This is only a dream.

JUSTINE No.

VICTOR All right—but can you pretend it is?

JUSTINE Where did it come from?

VICTOR Here and there.

JUSTINE Where will it live?
It *is* alive?

CREATURE I want to go—home.

JUSTINE Back to the grave.

CREATURE *(contradicting)* Home.

VICTOR *(the scientist, amazed)* There are memories still left
in the brain I gave him—
how is that possible?
Unless—could it be that our memory
is electric?
(To the CREATURE*)* Where is home?

CREATURE A fire. Voices . . .

VICTOR What are they saying?

Pause.

CREATURE "Who made you?"

JUSTINE *points at* VICTOR.

JUSTINE He made you.

Pause.

CREATURE Pain.
Up and down me. All over me.
Why do I hurt?

JUSTINE Because he made you.

Pause.

CREATURE Help me.

JUSTINE If I could, I would.
I would kill you.

CREATURE HELP ME!

JUSTINE *No.* No—

Suddenly JUSTINE *runs away.* VICTOR *starts after her.*

VICTOR Justine!

But the CREATURE *grabs* VICTOR.

CREATURE I want to go home.

VICTOR I don't know where that is.

CREATURE A fire. Voices.

As VICTOR *replies, the* CREATURE *moves away.*

VICTOR Once upon a time.
Those things are gone, now.

ELIZABETH *appears at the top of the cellar stairs.*

ELIZABETH Victor?

He doesn't answer. The CREATURE *looks up at this new voice.*

Something has happened.
Justine is having a kind of—fit,
she fell on the kitchen floor,
and then she vomited.
And I can't help her up—
she won't let anyone near her.

Pause.

You said you hadn't seen her.
But she was stumbling out of the cellar
when she fell.

The CREATURE *remembers* JUSTINE.

CREATURE I said, "Help me."
But she didn't.
"Justine."
If she could, she would kill me.

VICTOR You have it all in a jumble —

ELIZABETH Victor?

Pause.

VICTOR Yes!

ELIZABETH I am coming down.
Is that all right?

VICTOR *doesn't answer.*
ELIZABETH *hesitates, then starts to descend.*
VICTOR *turns to the* CREATURE.

VICTOR Let me move you into the shadows.

CREATURE I hurt!

VICTOR (*as he herds the* CREATURE *into the dark*) I understand —

CREATURE Every part of me.

VICTOR Can you be very quiet?

CREATURE Why did you wake me?

VICTOR I made a mistake.

CREATURE I *hurt!*

VICTOR I will help you! —
but only be still.

The CREATURE *does as he's told.* VICTOR *steps back into the light as* ELIZABETH *appears, looking about at this place she's seldom seen.*

ELIZABETH You don't mind that the walls are wet . . .

VICTOR Not at all. I find the chill keeps me awake.

ELIZABETH Ah. You could work in a room with windows.

VICTOR I could watch the shadows of clouds
moving over the lawn, and get nothing done.

ELIZABETH What is that smell?

VICTOR Another in a series of failed experiments.

Pause.

ELIZABETH Do you remember, when we were younger,
I was afraid of having children?
I'm not, anymore. I'm not.
You don't have to interfere with the servants.

VICTOR You think very little of me.

ELIZABETH I think—there is very little of you I know.

Pause.

VICTOR Do you believe in God?

ELIZABETH I'm not certain.

VICTOR Do you believe *I'm* God?

ELIZABETH You could be.
That would explain a great deal, I imagine:
war, famine, pestilence—
other wanderings of a powerful mind.

VICTOR I do love you—

ELIZABETH Do you? Why? Because I forgive your imperfections?
That isn't love—it's vanity.
You hide yourself away from the people who love you.
No one can find you.

You *are* God.
I can't breathe in this room.
What has happened in here?
Something terrible . . .

VICTOR No—

ELIZABETH Then show me your work.

VICTOR It isn't finished.

Angry, ELIZABETH *turns to leave—but* VICTOR *stops her.*

—and it would upset you to see it now:
when we were children, remember,
I had a specimen I kept covered?
But you had to pull the cover away,
and what was staring back at you?
The fetus of a pig,
in a jar of alcohol—decomposing.
Not a creature out of a nightmare—
only a humble part of nature.
But disturbing—because it was incomplete—
you screamed.

ELIZABETH I thought it was moving.

VICTOR You bumped it—it was sloshing about—

ELIZABETH I told you: I am older, now.
And my childish fears I've put aside.
If there is a "humble piece of nature"
floating in this dark, let me see it.

VICTOR No—not now. But soon . . .
And then there will be no secrets between us.

ELIZABETH Do you think you can live without them?

Again, she starts to exit.

VICTOR Can you? I went back, to retrieve the kite.
I saw you kissing Clerval.

ELIZABETH We were consoling ourselves, for the great
misfortune of finding you beautiful.

Pause.

Change the lock on the cellar door,
or I promise you—I will let myself in,
and overturn every crucible, send all the dead piglets
skidding across the floor, smash every vial and beaker,
—till I find you.
And then you can say, "I don't love you"—
I will leave you alone forever.
Or say it now. *Say* it!

Pause.

VICTOR Will you marry me?

ELIZABETH Victor, what have you done?
What has happened in this room?

VICTOR *cannot answer.*

You didn't lie to me. Thank you.
Yes—I will marry you.
If you can answer one question:
will you hold me to blame, when I fail to
save you from yourself?

VICTOR Yes—I've already forgiven you.

ELIZABETH For crimes I have yet to commit?

At a stalemate, ELIZABETH *storms out.*
A moment later, the CREATURE *steps out of the shadows.*
VICTOR *stares at him, overwhelmed.*

CREATURE Help me.

VICTOR How?

CREATURE I want to go home.

VICTOR (*forming a plan*) High up on a mountainside—
would you like that?—

under so many thousand stars,
you will never count them all.

Scene 14

The CREATURE—*wearing ill-fitting clothes of* VICTOR's—*is following his creator up a winding mountain path. Dusk.*
VICTOR *lights the way with a flickering lantern.*

CREATURE Cold.

VICTOR You can build a fire.

The CREATURE *looks about, uncertain.*

CREATURE Food.

VICTOR There is plenty of game about.

CREATURE (*more insistent*) *Food.*

VICTOR Whatever you catch, you can eat.

CREATURE Rain . . .

VICTOR Stay under the shelter of the trees.

CREATURE Rain. And then I get wet.

VICTOR The fire will dry you out.

CREATURE Beating: "Boom, boom, boom"—Her arms around me.

VICTOR *is startled.*

Somebody held me.

Pause.

VICTOR Your mother. Or a nurse.
That was very long ago.

CREATURE (*agitated*) I WANT—

VICTOR, *reluctant, takes the* CREATURE *in his arms.*
The CREATURE *quiets.*

CREATURE   (*continued*) When I close my eyes . . .

VICTOR   (*giving the name*) *Dark.*

CREATURE   When I open them?

VICTOR   *Light.*

CREATURE   But my eyes are open now.
Why is it dark?

VICTOR   Because it's night.

CREATURE   "Night."
Forever and ever.

VICTOR   Just a few hours.
And then the sun will come up again,
it'll be light, and the air will be warmer—
do you remember the word for that? *Day.*

CREATURE   It was night.
Forever and ever.

VICTOR *suddenly thinks he knows what the* CREATURE *is talking about.*

VICTOR   When you were dead? Is that what you mean?
Then it's true—there is nothing after?
I had hoped you could bring me news of another world.
But there is no other.

The CREATURE *doesn't answer. It's staring into* VICTOR*'s eyes, alarmed.*

CREATURE   There is someone in your eyes.

VICTOR   (*not understanding*) No.

CREATURE   A tiny man, looking out at me.
A demon. With a shining face.

VICTOR   It's you. It's your reflection.

The CREATURE *is horrified.*

CREATURE   Darker! DARKER!

VICTOR   Remember? Close your eyes.

The CREATURE *does so.*

CREATURE   Night . . .

VICTOR   All the long months I was making you—
stitching an arm to a shoulder, hand to a wrist,
threading the nerves, how many thousand,
stretching skin across bone—
I would look at you, splayed across a table
and think you were very beautiful.
Was I wrong? Were you always
as you are now?
Or is it the pain I delivered you into
that made you so very terrible?

Pause.

I have to go.

CREATURE   Come back.

VICTOR   I will.

CREATURE   No—come back *now*.

While the CREATURE'*s eyes are shut,* VICTOR *quietly steals away.*

Colder.
Night. Forever.
(*Remembering*) But I can open my eyes . . .

He does so—and sees that VICTOR *is gone.*

Victor?
Where are you?

He looks all around him, panicking.

WHERE ARE YOU?
VICTOR!

Scene 15

On the iceberg.
The CREATURE *is gone.*
WALTON *watches* VICTOR, *uneasy.*

WALTON You heard it cry out?

VICTOR Yes. And I hear it still: "Victor! Victor!"
If I had turned back—
but I left it there.
And then I made my way home.

WALTON How quickly did you return to it?

VICTOR *looks away.* WALTON *is chilled, realizing what* VICTOR *did.*

WALTON (*continued*) It was alive—it could speak—

VICTOR And when it did, I understood:
I had lost my freedom, forever.

Pause.

Who have you left behind?
Your mother and father—where are they?
Your wife?

WALTON I never married.

VICTOR A sweetheart.

WALTON No one.

VICTOR Why?

WALTON (*evading*) It didn't die—did it?
The creature you dreamed about, and abandoned.

VICTOR No: it's a very disturbing thing about dreams—they want to live.

WALTON (*mocking*) "Victor! Victor!"

At this moment, past and present start to merge.
WILLIAM *runs on, terrified. Both* VICTOR *and* WALTON *see him.*

WILLIAM   Victor! Victor! Victor! Victor! Victor!

VICTOR *grabs the flailing boy, to calm him down.*

VICTOR   Willie? It's all right—

WILLIAM   It was after me!

VICTOR   What was?

Pause.

WILLIAM   I don't know.
I was in the cellar—
I was afraid that something had happened to you . . .

VICTOR   I don't work down there anymore.
The cellar is empty.
Try to go back to sleep.

WILLIAM *sits on the stage.*

WILLIAM   Will you leave the candle burning?

VICTOR *nods.* WILLIAM *stretches out and falls asleep.*
Shaken by this hallucination he seems to be sharing with VICTOR, WALTON
realizes that he needs to assert control.
The groan and creak of ice are loud, as the berg begins to crumble.

WALTON   The ice is starting to break apart.
We need to get down to the cutter.

VICTOR   Go.

WALTON   You are coming with me.

VICTOR   I'm not.

WALTON *draws his pistol, aiming at* VICTOR.

WALTON   And then back to my ship—before it sails without us.

VICTOR   Let it go. Or have you given up on your dream
of finding the Pole?
You can take my supplies, and set out on foot . . .

WALTON   And yourself?

VICTOR   I have a rendezvous, with the one I've been pursuing.

WALTON   The Creature.

VICTOR *nods.*

Is it out there, now, in the dark?

VICTOR   And I cannot leave it behind.

WALTON   Then do what you can to survive.
Come back to my ship—let me help you
regain your strength.
If you perish—what will become of the Creature?

VICTOR   What I fear the most: it will live.

CLERVAL   How did it find you again?

VICTOR   I don't know.
A year had passed. I was free and clear—
or I tried to convince myself that I was.
And then—by the bank of the river—
they found my brother's body.

Now ELIZABETH *enters. She and* VICTOR *sit beside* WILLIAM.
ELIZABETH *touches* WILLIAM's *face. The boy is dead.*

VICTOR   (*continued, to* ELIZABETH) A lock of hair, a breath—
when he slept, he was like a little animal,
a dog by the fire—one of his legs would twitch,
and I'd wonder why he was smiling.

ELIZABETH   Maybe you had been far away, in the dream,
but now you were coming home.
And he was running down the drive,
to meet you.

VICTOR   (*a whisper*) "Victor! Victor!"

VICTOR *starts to cry.*
VICTOR's FATHER *enters.*

ELIZABETH (*continued*) How is my aunt?

FATHER Very poorly.

ELIZABETH I should look in on her.

FATHER Would you, my dear?

ELIZABETH *exits.*

Victor, I have news.

VICTOR (*in a daze*) And the angel said, "There shall be time no longer . . ."

FATHER They have found the monster.

VICTOR (*stunned*) What?

FATHER The creature who took your brother's life.

VICTOR *is horrified by the possibility.*

VICTOR *He* did this?
How could he have survived—
I left him to die—

FATHER Victor, what are you talking about?
The murderer is not a man—

VICTOR I know.

FATHER (*not getting his meaning*)—though how a woman could have done
this—

VICTOR (*startled again*) A woman?

FATHER The serving-girl—Justine.

VICTOR (*with terrible certainty*) Justine is not the murderer.

FATHER I didn't want to believe it myself.
But we found her—delirious—out in the woods,
with your brother's ring on her finger.
She doesn't remember having stolen the ring—
but then how did it get there?

VICTOR Will she hang?

FATHER   Most assuredly.

In the present, the groan and creak of ice, as the berg begins to crumble.

VICTOR   And will my brother revive, do you think—
when he hears the snap of her neck?

VICTOR's FATHER *is bewildered by his attitude.*

FATHER   Victor, the ring had blood on it—
that's how brutally it was ripped away.
The woman is a demon.
Would you have her wandering into the night,
to raven upon other children?

VICTOR   Where is she being held?
I have to speak to her.

FATHER   I forbid it!

The sound of cracking ice is louder. FATHER *tries to explain himself.*

Your mother bore nine children.
She has lost every one of them but you.
Now, in her fevered sleep, she calls for you—
and what do I do if she wakes?
Do I tell her Victor isn't here—
he has gone to visit the murderess?

FATHER, *sad and bewildered, exits.*

VICTOR   (*to* WALTON) The ice is breaking up.
Get down to the cutter.

WALTON   *Did* you visit her?

VICTOR   Yes.

JUSTINE *enters. Both men stare at her.*

WALTON   And were you able to save her?

VICTOR *doesn't answer.* WALTON *makes an urgent plea.*

Tell me.

VICTOR   I will,
for one reason only:
so you can abandon me
without regret.

Pause. VICTOR *approaches* JUSTINE, *in her cell.*

VICTOR   Justine—

JUSTINE   Go away.

VICTOR   —you didn't kill my brother.

JUSTINE   No? Who did?

Pause.

He was watching us, the whole time—
the day of the picnic. He must've been in the woods.
And I think your cousin knew, somehow,
that he was coming closer.

VICTOR   (*terrified of the answer*) Who?

Glad to see VICTOR *in torment,* JUSTINE *waits before she replies. And then she tells her story.*

Scene 16

An empty meadow.
WILLIAM *is gone.*

WILLIAM   (*offstage*) Where are you?

WILLIAM *runs on, out of breath, and looks around.*

Where *are* you?

JUSTINE   (*offstage*) Here—you little goose.

JUSTINE *enters, lugging a heavy picnic basket.*

WILLIAM   Why can't you go faster?

JUSTINE   Because I'm old.

WILLIAM You are. And you never married.
You're an old maid!

JUSTINE That's right.

WILLIAM I'll marry you. If you like.

JUSTINE I wouldn't have you.

WILLIAM Why not?

JUSTINE Because you made me carry this basket.

WILLIAM Isn't that why we have servants?

JUSTINE *plunks down the basket, hard—we hear the clatter of breaking china.*

JUSTINE (*almost admiring*) What a horrid little creature you are.

WILLIAM (*calling offstage*) I'm not the one who just broke all the crockery.
Victor? Am I horrid?

VICTOR (*offstage*) Specifically? Or in general?

JUSTINE Ah—the worm turns.

WILLIAM He does not. What worm?

A nervous ELIZABETH *enters, followed by* VICTOR, *who loosens his shirt against the oppressive heat of the day.*

ELIZABETH Weren't we going to the bank of the stream?

VICTOR Yes, onward! It'd be so much cooler—

WILLIAM But here in this meadow—see?
there are toadstools everywhere.
Justine felt at home.

JUSTINE Now I'm an old maid *and* a witch?

WILLIAM "Oh look," she said, "deadly nightshade!
Shall I make us a pot of tea?"
Then she put the hamper down—like this.

He gives the basket a thump, so the others can hear the broken dishes.

VICTOR If Justine is an adept in the black arts—
is it wise to be tattling?
She could find a piece of mandrake root
and carve it into a likeness of you—
did you know the root screams, when you
pull it up?

WILLIAM Oh, tosh! *You* don't believe in magic.
"It's only laws of nature
that ignorant people don't understand."

VICTOR Explain one word of what you just said.

JUSTINE He can't—he's a little parrot.

WILLIAM I am! And I'll fly so far away,
you'll both be very sorry.

WILLIAM *runs off, flapping his arms like wings.*

VICTOR (*calling after him*) Oh yes, we'll shed great crocodile tears.
(*To* ELIZABETH) To the river then, milady?
So we can lie down beside it and weep?

Lost in thought, ELIZABETH *doesn't respond.*

Elizabeth? Is something wrong?

ELIZABETH Do you smell it?
Something dead, in the woods.

VICTOR Then shall we leave it behind?

Uneasy at ELIZABETH's *mood,* VICTOR *starts to move off. As* JUSTINE *picks up the picnic hamper,* ELIZABETH *speaks to her, quietly urgent.*

ELIZABETH Justine . . .

JUSTINE *stops.* What was it like?

JUSTINE (*knowing very well*) I don't know what you mean.

ELIZABETH His hand on you.

JUSTINE *doesn't respond.* VICTOR *can guess what is happening, but can't quite overhear.* ELIZABETH *forces herself to go on.*

That day in the cellar—
Victor made advances . . .

JUSTINE Months ago—
and nothing happened.

ELIZABETH Then why did you run from him?—
as if the very Devil were after you?

JUSTINE *puts down the basket again.*

JUSTINE All right:
his hand was cold—
the one he put over my mouth
when he bent me over.
Bone-cold, and rough—

ELIZABETH (*beginning to doubt*) Victor's skin is smooth—

JUSTINE —and rank, like a gutted animal—

ELIZABETH He didn't—bend you over.

JUSTINE No—I did that on my own.
I reached behind me
and spread myself, wide open,
like a mouth.
Could you hear the words of my wet mouth?—
when I cried out: "I WANT!"

Pause.

ELIZABETH What has Victor done to you,
if he hasn't touched you? Tell me. Please.

JUSTINE *doesn't answer.*
ELIZABETH *suddenly grabs her.*

ELIZABETH There was something down there, in the dark—
I know the smell of blood.
What was it?

JUSTINE What do you think it was? A monster.
And it was very beautiful.

ELIZABETH *stares at* JUSTINE, *trying to guess if she's telling the truth. Then she hurries off, unable to look at* VICTOR.

ELIZABETH *(calling out)* William? Willie!

JUSTINE *watches her go, as* VICTOR *approaches.*

VICTOR What did you tell her?

JUSTINE Everything.

VICTOR Why?

JUSTINE For the relief of confessing to someone
who couldn't afford to believe me.

VICTOR You've done nothing wrong.

JUSTINE That isn't true.
I saw what you had made,
and people should have been warned.
But I held my tongue.
I was waiting for you to speak—

VICTOR And exactly what was I to say?
That I had made a mistake
I was sorry about, and had gotten rid of it?

JUSTINE *(surprised)* When?

VICTOR A year ago. You knew it was gone.

JUSTINE I thought you were hiding it.

Pause.

Then all this time, I've been afraid—for nothing?
Why didn't you tell me?

VICTOR I hadn't been aware that I was to
answer to you, Justine.

Pause.

JUSTINE I had a hope—it's gone now—
but when I was a girl, I had a hope

that the Revolution would never end,
it would roll across the Channel
like a great bloody wave come crashing down
and sweep all of you before it.
All of you with money enough
to know not what you were doing.

Pause.

VICTOR You would like us all to die?
Even the little ones?

JUSTINE They grow up.

ELIZABETH (*offstage*) Victor? Are you coming?

VICTOR (*shouting*) Yes! I'll meet you by the river.

ELIZABETH (*offstage*) With the basket? If the food can be salvaged?

JUSTINE *picks up the picnic basket, gives it a clattering shake.*

VICTOR (*quietly*) Possibly not.

JUSTINE (*shouting*) Justine will go back to the house for more!

VICTOR *takes the basket away from* JUSTINE.

VICTOR Let me.
Why don't you go on to the river—
see what my brother is up to?
He is fond of you, you know—
whatever you think of his relations.

JUSTINE *says nothing.* VICTOR *exits, with the picnic basket.*

JUSTINE (*calling out*) William? Willie!
Come out, come out, wherever you are!
(*To herself*) Or stay in your hidey-hole and rot.
(*Calling out*) You little monkey—we're tired!
Your cousin wants her tea!
I want—

She wonders what it is she wants.

—to do nothing.
Would that be possible?
For a day or two, a week—
if I could simply—not move—

ELIZABETH (*offstage*) Justine? Is Willie there with you?

JUSTINE No!

ELIZABETH (*offstage*) Then I'm going down to the river! (*Calling*) Willie!

JUSTINE I'll meet you!

ELIZABETH (*offstage*) Hurry!

JUSTINE (*not hurrying*) I'm racing.

As JUSTINE *starts to move off, her exit is suddenly blocked by the* CREATURE.
JUSTINE *takes a step backward.*

CREATURE Justine.

JUSTINE (*terrified*) Hello.
How have you been?
Where have you been?
I thought I dreamed you.

CREATURE Kill me.
You said you would.

He takes a step in her direction, she stumbles back and falls.
He leans over her.

CREATURE (*continued*) *Kill me.*

JUSTINE *No.*

Suddenly, far off, we hear ELIZABETH *scream.*

JUSTINE (*continued*) What have you done?
My God—William . . .
(*She cries out*) WILLIAM!

The CREATURE *strikes her.* JUSTINE *falls back and lies still.*

The CREATURE *feels her pulse.*

CREATURE (*softly*) Boom, boom, boom, boom . . .

Satisfied that JUSTINE *is alive, the* CREATURE *takes out the ring he stripped off* WILLIAM's *body.*
He slips it onto one of JUSTINE's *fingers.*

CREATURE (*continued*) Your little master had a gold ring.
You wanted it. He wouldn't give it to you.

ELIZABETH (*offstage*) HELP ME! SOMEBODY HELP ME!

Scene 17

JUSTINE's *cell.*
She's just told her story to VICTOR.
The CREATURE *is gone.*

JUSTINE (*of* ELIZABETH's *cry*) But it was too late for that.

Pause.

VICTOR Where is the Creature now?

JUSTINE I'd guess—in hiding,
till tomorrow night.
And then, from the shadows, it will watch me hang.
I die at midnight.

VICTOR Why didn't you tell the authorities the truth?

JUSTINE That "it wasn't *me*, Your Worship—
it was an 'orrible monster"?

VICTOR I can corroborate your story.

JUSTINE And if they ask for proof?

Pause.

You dismantled your laboratory,
I would imagine you burned your notes—

VICTOR *did—he flinches.*

—the Creature is gone, a child is dead,
and I was the one they found
with a stolen ring on her bloody finger.

Pause.

VICTOR Do you think my brother suffered?

JUSTINE Yes. I'm certain.
The Creature wants company.
He also wants an answer to his question.

VICTOR What are you talking about?

JUSTINE When he saw me stirring—after he hit me—
he waited till I opened my eyes,
and then he bent down close to me,
and he asked me: "Why am I alive?"
I couldn't tell him.
He smiled.
You could have given him better teeth.

A distant bell begins to toll the hour. ELIZABETH *and* CLERVAL *enter, approaching* JUSTINE's *cell—unnoticed at first.*

JUSTINE (*continued*) I never knew myself, why I was here—
and that would trouble me.
But by tomorrow night, I will never
have to wonder again.

VICTOR Where do you think the Creature will hide, until then?

JUSTINE You won't find him.

VICTOR Up in the mountains?

JUSTINE I think you should leave me alone, now.
Guard!

ELIZABETH Victor?

VICTOR, *startled, spins around.*

VICTOR What are you doing here?

VICTOR (*continued, now noticing* CLERVAL) And Clerval. Something has happened.
Tell me.
Is my mother dead?

ELIZABETH No. But she is very weak.

CLERVAL The doctor said she may leave us tonight.

VICTOR Is she going on a trip?

CLERVAL I don't know. It's possible:
to a better place—

VICTOR And where exactly would that be, Clerval?
If you could draw me a map . . .

CLERVAL *stiffens at this rebuff.*

Did my mother call for me?

CLERVAL *and* ELIZABETH *hesitate.*

DID SHE CALL FOR ME?

ELIZABETH Yes. We couldn't find you.
Then your father said you might be here.
Conferring with the murderess.

Pause.

VICTOR I have to go away.

ELIZABETH Now?

VICTOR Up into the mountains.

ELIZABETH Your family needs you.

VICTOR Tell them I will be home by tomorrow sunset.
Or not at all.

ELIZABETH Victor, why are you doing this?

VICTOR On our wedding night, when we embrace,
my brother's blood will be on my hands.

I will leave a smear of red on your skin.
And you can pretend it isn't there—
let it dry and flake away, like rust—
but if I let one more person die—
my hands will be so slick with gore,
I won't be able to hold you.

ELIZABETH *has no answer to this.*
*The figures from the past—*JUSTINE, ELIZABETH, *and* CLERVAL—*begin*
to recede.
WALTON *faces* VICTOR.

WALTON   You went up into the mountains.

VICTOR   Yes.

WALTON   And did you find the Creature?

VICTOR   He found me.

The ominous thunder of breaking ice grows louder.
In the shadows, the CREATURE *appears.*
The CREATURE's *look is intent—that of a hunter who has found his prey.*
A wind begins to howl.
The lights fade out.

End of Act I.

Act II

Scene 1

In the mountains.
VICTOR, *alone, is searching for the* CREATURE.

VICTOR   WHERE ARE YOU?
WHY ARE YOU HIDING FROM ME?
I KNOW YOU'RE HERE—I CAN SMELL YOU!
EVERY PART OF YOU, ROTTING FLESH FALLING OFF OF
BLACK GUMS AND FESTERING BONES,
AND THE STENCH OF MY BROTHER'S BLOOD . . .

The CREATURE *appears, behind* VICTOR.

CREATURE Shall I tell you how he died?

VICTOR *can't bring himself to turn around.*

VICTOR No.

CREATURE (*relentless*) This is how he died.

Scene 2

By a stream.
WILLIAM *enters, looking down into the water.*
Unnoticed, the CREATURE *appears behind him, watching him.*

WILLIAM (*calling offstage*) Justine! Come and look at me in the water.
I don't have fingers—see?

He checks his reflection, as he waves his fingers about.

I have big long feathers, beating the air
till I'm so high up,
the trees are little green puffs
and you people are specks,
you and Lizzie and Victor:
(*imitating*) "Willie, come down!"—
But I *won't* come down—

The CREATURE *approaches.* WILLIAM *sees its reflection beside his own, in the water.*
Startled but not afraid, WILLIAM *turns to face the* CREATURE.

WILLIAM (*continued*) What happened to you?

CREATURE I was dead.

WILLIAM Oh.

Pause.

I don't believe in ghosts.
Not in the daytime.
Are you hungry?

The CREATURE *nods.*

I think we have cold chicken, if you don't mind
the odd bit of broken plate—
Justine let the hamper drop.

CREATURE   "Justine . . ."

WILLIAM   Do you know her?

CREATURE   (*dimly remembering*) "Help me," I said—
but she wanted to kill me.

WILLIAM   Yes, that would be Justine.
Where on earth did you meet her?

CREATURE   I don't remember.

WILLIAM   Maybe you hit your head.
Have you been attacked?
Is that what happened to you?

CREATURE   If I show my face—if they see me—
they shout at me, they throw rocks at me—
they beat me.
I live in the woods.

WILLIAM   But what do you eat?

CREATURE   What I can find:
roots, acorns, berries.

WILLIAM   And in the winter—where do you go?

CREATURE   (*almost patient*) Where do I go?
I live in the woods.

WILLIAM   But everything is dead.

CREATURE   Except for me. And I want to be still,
like the rest of the world,
but my heart keeps beating: "boom, boom . . ."
I lie awake all night,
with a rat in my stomach
trying to claw its way out,

and the wind is so cold,
sometimes I let the snow cover me over—
"this is my shroud."
But it isn't.
I always rise again: why?
So I can suffer one more day.

WILLIAM "Man was born to suffering."

CREATURE Which man?

WILLIAM I don't know. It's in the Bible.
Mother reads it to me when I've been bad:
I can quote whole passages.
Victor says it's rubbish,
but Mother says that's why she likes it—
God seems to hate almost everyone,
and Mother is sympathetic.

CREATURE "Victor?"

WILLIAM My brother—Victor Frankenstein.
He's a doctor. He could help you.

CREATURE Where does he work? In a cellar?

WILLIAM How did you know that?

CREATURE I was born there.

WILLIAM *is finally frightened—he thinks the* CREATURE *is mad.*
He turns to run, but the CREATURE *suddenly grabs him by the throat.*

CREATURE (*continued*) Your brother tortured me to life—
and then left me out on a hillside.
He thought I would starve,
or animals would attack me,
or winter would end me.
He didn't know how well he made me.
I am about to show him.

WILLIAM, *terrified, tries to be brave.*

WILLIAM You're hurting me.

CREATURE Am I?

WILLIAM Please—let me go.

CREATURE Does your brother love you?
Does he?

WILLIAM *is afraid to answer "yes."*

Maybe he can give birth to you,
when you're dead.
You and I can be brothers.
You can teach me how to pray.

WILLIAM *tries to oblige.*

WILLIAM "The Lord is my shepherd—
I shall not want . . ."

CREATURE Go on.

WILLIAM "He leadeth me beside the still waters . . .
he restoreth my soul . . ."

CREATURE I don't know what that is: "the soul."
Do you?

WILLIAM I think it's rubbish.
A worm crawls out of the socket
where your eye had been. That's all.

Nodding agreement, the CREATURE *strangles* WILLIAM.

CREATURE Can your brother not know that you worship him?

WILLIAM*'s struggle is feeble and brief.*

How can he help but love you?

The boy is dead. The CREATURE *eases the body to the ground.*

CREATURE (*continued*) But I will have my own disciples.
(*Pointing at the body*) SEE WHAT I HAVE CREATED!

Noticing a ring on WILLIAM's *hand, the* CREATURE *bends down and wrenches it off the finger.*

CREATURE *(continued)* . . . and how I accept your offering.

Scene 3

In the mountains.
Back with the CREATURE, *who's finished his story.*
WILLIAM *is gone.*
VICTOR *is disgusted by the* CREATURE *and by himself.*

VICTOR Get out of my sight.

The CREATURE *approaches* VICTOR, *who stands his ground, afraid he's about to be killed.*

CREATURE All right—

The CREATURE *reaches out and covers* VICTOR's *eyes with his frightening hands.*

—I am gone.
Do you like it there, in the dark?
Alone? Pretending I don't exist?

CREATURE *(continued, as he removes his hands)* "Light."

He covers VICTOR's *eyes again.*

"Dark."

VICTOR *thrusts the* CREATURE's *hands away from his face.*

"Day."

Staring at the CREATURE, VICTOR *shakes his head.*

VICTOR Night.

Pause.

You speak very well.

CREATURE I remembered letters—words—
from . . . whatever I was, before.

I had little enough to do in the woods,
so I set about improving myself.
I stole a few books—the Bible, *Paradise Lost*—
and I taught myself to read.
I thought there might be an answer . . .

VICTOR To what question?

CREATURE Why did you abandon me?

Pause.

VICTOR I wanted to save the world from death—
but all I gave you was life,
and I saw that I had saved you from nothing:
hunger, thirst, longing,
terrible loneliness like a cancer—

CREATURE You mean you had made me human.

VICTOR And I had hoped for something better.

CREATURE Why didn't you simply destroy me?

VICTOR *pulls out a dagger, being careful not to let the* CREATURE *see it.*

VICTOR Can you be destroyed?

Without warning, VICTOR *suddenly plunges the dagger into the*
CREATURE's *heart.*
The CREATURE *stumbles and falls to the ground. He shudders, and is still.*
VICTOR *stares at the body, appalled and elated by what he's done.*
Desperate to exonerate JUSTINE, *he stumbles off.*
A moment later, the CREATURE *opens his eyes.*
The horror of being alive rushes back.
He screams.
Crawling on his knees, he looks about him.
He starts to weep.

Scene 4

JUSTINE's *cell.*
JUSTINE *stares through the bars of her window.*
VICTOR *enters.*

VICTOR Justine, I have been to the judge —
I told him everything.

JUSTINE Did he believe you?

VICTOR That I had made a creature
and brought it to life?
He called me a lunatic.
"Sir, I am not disputing that," I replied,
"but I have proof of my claim —"

JUSTINE What proof?

VICTOR The Creature's body.

Despite her despair, JUSTINE *is surprised.*

I went up into the mountains
and I found it. And I killed it.

Pause.

JUSTINE Have you told your cousin yet —
about this monster you created?

VICTOR *hesitates.*

VICTOR She'll find out soon enough,
when they bring the body down,
and arrest me.

JUSTINE Will she forgive you?

VICTOR (*evading*) Does it matter?
I will never forgive myself.

JUSTINE Maybe you don't have the right to.

CLERVAL *appears in the doorway of the cell.*

CLERVAL Victor?

VICTOR What is it, Clerval?

CLERVAL I've come to take you home.

VICTOR I don't think they will let you.
Justine is innocent. I have confessed to the crime—

CLERVAL You have a brain fever.

VICTOR (*alarmed by* CLERVAL's *tone*) No—my mind has never been clearer—

CLERVAL Then why did you lie to the judge?
You babbled on, he said, about a
corpse you had—animated—

VICTOR Yes—and then, too late, returned to the dust—

CLERVAL Then where is the body?

VICTOR *stares at* CLERVAL, *uncomprehending.*

The bailiff's men have searched the mountainside—
and I accompanied them.

VICTOR (*more and more afraid*) Near the timberline—at the base of a cliff—

CLERVAL And spreading out, far beyond it:
we looked everywhere.

VICTOR (*dreading the answer*) And found nothing?

CLERVAL What was there to find?

Pause.

VICTOR You truly believe I'm insane.

CLERVAL No. I think grief has overcome you.

JUSTINE *edges into hysteria.*

JUSTINE Yes, and me as well—
so I went on a rampage:
"grief overcame me."

She starts to laugh — it's frightening. VICTOR *grabs her.*

VICTOR YOU DIDN'T KILL MY BROTHER!

JUSTINE Then why did I have his ring on my finger?

Pause.

I would have pawned the ring,
and taken the money and run away.

Pause.

I didn't want to be a servant the rest of my life,
but I had no savings.
And what else could I have been?
A fishwife? A ladies' companion? A trollop?
I was trapped, and I thought that I could escape.
But first I needed capital:
so I killed a child.

VICTOR YOU DIDN'T! THAT WAS THE ACT OF MY CREATURE!

Pause.

JUSTINE What creature?

VICTOR *stares at her, not knowing how he can prove his guilt.*

Scene 5

At the back door of VICTOR's *home.*
ELIZABETH *enters, with a lit candle.*
She peers out into the dark, afraid.
VICTOR *enters.*

VICTOR Elizabeth?

ELIZABETH Something is out there.

Pause.

VICTOR It doesn't want you.
Go back to bed.

Pause.

ELIZABETH Clerval said you were hallucinating.

VICTOR No. You hear it yourself, in the garden,
just beyond the candlelight.

Pause.

ELIZABETH I think we should marry. Soon.

VICTOR You don't know what I've done.

ELIZABETH All right: then tell me.

Pause.

We have lived together, side by side in this house,
since we were very young,
and you have never loved me.
You have cared about me, you have wanted to fuck me—

VICTOR Elizabeth!

ELIZABETH Yes! I'm sorry, but I know the word.
I know many words.
Why would you never let yourself love me, Victor?

He doesn't answer.

Because I can die?

Pause.

And so can Clerval, who adores you,
and whose affection you despise.

Pause.

Clerval and I will grow old,
our flesh will sag, our eyes cloud over,
we will sit at the table, gumming our porridge,
forgetting the word we wanted, farting—
thunderous, uncontrollable, uninterrupted
sulpherous farting—

till even the dogs by the fire trot off in dismay:
how could you love us?

A bell begins to toll the hour.

VICTOR Midnight.
Then Justine is dead.

VICTOR *listens, haunted, till the sound of the bell fades away.*
Overwhelmed by guilt, he finally tries to confess.

VICTOR *(continued)* I will tell you what I did:
I had a child.
You were right to be frightened.

Pause.

It quickened—I felt it stirring in me—
and then it tore me open.

Pause.

ELIZABETH (*putting things together*) In the cellar.

VICTOR Yes.

ELIZABETH A year ago.

He nods.

And in all that time—where has it been?

VICTOR Out there. Waiting . . .

ELIZABETH For what?

VICTOR I don't know.
But it finally sought me out.
In terrible pain—

ELIZABETH (*from experience*) Because of its solitude.

VICTOR *begins to see how completely he had misunderstood.*

VICTOR I thought it was asking for something else—
to be put out of its misery.
I tried to kill it—

ELIZABETH   Again.

VICTOR   I thought I had.
But the body has disappeared.

ELIZABETH   No—it is right out there. Waiting . . .

VICTOR   To butcher anyone I love.

ELIZABETH   Ah. Well, then—at least *I'm* safe—

In desperate protest, VICTOR *grabs* ELIZABETH.
He kisses her, with shocking force. She struggles to escape him.
Finally, she goes limp—and VICTOR *is overcome with shame.*
He lets her go; she trembles.

ELIZABETH   (*continued*) Find it. Bring it back to the house.

VICTOR   Are you mad? It killed my brother.
And an innocent woman hung for the crime.

ELIZABETH   Then bring the Creature home
before it claims another victim.
Learn from it about desolation.
Teach it what you know of regret.
I told you before—I cannot save you.
But maybe the Creature can.

Pause.

VICTOR   It will hide from me—if I try to find it.

ELIZABETH   What if we set a kind of trap?
Wouldn't it take a malign delight
in being the Uninvited Guest—

VICTOR   At a party?

ELIZABETH   At our wedding.

Scene 6

In the mountains.
VICTOR—*with a skeptical* CLERVAL—*is tracking the* CREATURE. *The offstage* DOGS *are barking in confusion.*

VICTOR The dogs have lost the scent.

CLERVAL It was here?

VICTOR I stabbed him. He fell—by that rock.

CLERVAL Victor, I helped to search this area.
We found nothing. No blood—

VICTOR Because it has no blood in its body.

Pause.

CLERVAL I was in the lead. I came upon
this clearing—and I was startled.
Because I had never been up here—
but this was the place I dreamed about.
Do you remember me telling you?
With a deep black pool, at the foot of a cliff.
You wanted to go for a swim, but I was afraid—

VICTOR And then I kissed you.

VICTOR *approaches* CLERVAL.

What are you afraid of, now?

CLERVAL Being the bachelor friend of the married couple.
For the rest of my life.

VICTOR You know you will always be welcome . . .

CLERVAL How even more truly terrifying.

Pause.

VICTOR Did you ever want to have a child, Clerval?

CLERVAL No. I wasn't sure I would need one.
There was always you.

CLERVAL *wants to say more.*
But the offstage DOGS *have begun to bay, and* VICTOR *is distracted.*

CLERVAL (*continued*) Does Elizabeth believe in your Creature?

VICTOR She hopes it will come to our wedding —
that I might finally offer it shelter.
But if it does appear at our door,
I think it will want much more than that.

CLERVAL *begins to suspect the truth.*

CLERVAL Then — we aren't hunting it down.

VICTOR No.

CLERVAL But it may be hunting us.

VICTOR *doesn't deny this.*

The Creature cannot die.
You can.
You want it to end your suffering.

Pause.

Come back to the village with me.

VICTOR *tears himself away from* CLERVAL's *sympathy.*

VICTOR No.
(*Shouting to the unseen* CREATURE) I AM HERE!

VICTOR *starts to run off* — CLERVAL *grabs him.*

CLERVAL Victor —

VICTOR Clerval, let go of me.

CLERVAL *lets go.* VICTOR *stares at him.*

Listen to me: let go.

VICTOR *suddenly dashes off, leaving* CLERVAL *alone.*

CLERVAL (*shouting after him*) Your mind is unbalanced!
Victor — let me help you!

CLERVAL *starts to run off—and almost collides with the* CREATURE, *whom he has never seen and never completely believed in.*
CLERVAL *recoils, then tries to hide his fear. The* CREATURE, *who has spied on* VICTOR's *family, recognizes* CLERVAL.

CREATURE Why did he give me a cock?

CLERVAL I don't know.
So you can make little monsters?
I couldn't begin to guess—
do you use it to urinate?
I don't know.

Pause.

CREATURE Did he ever love you?

CLERVAL Perhaps—as a friend.
All he cares about now is you.

Pause.

CREATURE When I killed his little brother—
when I made them hang the serving-girl—
my cock got hard. It was like a club.
Why have I got a cock?

Pause.

Tell him I need a wife.

CLERVAL I didn't understand you could simply
order a mate from his workshop.

The CREATURE *comes nearer.*

CREATURE Someone to hold me, late at night,
when the rain comes down and puts out the fire . . .
Call him to me. Now.

CLERVAL, *deeply frightened, shakes his head.*

I know how to propose—
I was in the shadows, watching him.
He taught me.

Pause.
As VICTOR *grabbed* ELIZABETH, *the* CREATURE *suddenly grabs* CLERVAL.
He kisses him, with ferocity.
CLERVAL *fights to get away, but the* CREATURE *holds him by the neck.*

CREATURE (*continued*) I want a wife.

CLERVAL And after he made you one—
a virgin-fiend—
would you let him live?

The CREATURE *throws* CLERVAL *to the ground.*

CREATURE If you scream, will he come to your rescue?

CLERVAL No.

The CREATURE *suddenly hits* CLERVAL, *who cries out, before he can stop himself.*

VICTOR (*offstage*) Clerval?

CREATURE You were lying. Scream again.

He hits CLERVAL *again—but* CLERVAL *is able to stifle his cry.*

Cry for help—or you are a dead man.

CLERVAL *crawls away from his attacker, dragging himself offstage.*
The CREATURE *exits, pursuing him, grimly deliberate.*
VICTOR *enters, looking around.*

VICTOR Clerval, I heard voices—where are you?

Suddenly he is very afraid.

Clerval?

The CREATURE *enters.*

CREATURE I asked him to give you a message.
But he refused.

VICTOR What did you do to him?

The CREATURE *doesn't answer.*

CLERVAL!

CREATURE He cannot hear you.

VICTOR *slumps, devastated.*

VICTOR I am the one who harmed you.
Why are you slaughtering innocent people—
one after another—man, woman, and child?

CREATURE So you will do my bidding.

VICTOR And if I refuse?

CREATURE I can always spare you.
And watch your conscience devour you.

VICTOR I will kill myself.

CREATURE You don't have the courage.
Isn't that why you sought me out?

Pause.

You are getting married.

VICTOR Yes.

CREATURE I would like a wife as well.
Make me one.

VICTOR You can rot in hell.

CREATURE I am already rotting. Here on earth.

Pause.

I am alone, and miserable.
Your kind will not associate with me.
But if you brought to life a woman
as horrible and deformed as myself,
she would not deny herself to me.
We would disappear into the wild
and you would never behold us again.
Our lives will not be happy,
but we will be harmless, and—
in each other—content.

VICTOR Or the two of you could band together
to desolate the world.

CREATURE If I have no ties of affection,
hatred and crime must be my portion.
But if I had the love of another,
why would I need to avenge myself?

VICTOR It took me almost a year to make you.
Can you wait that long?

CREATURE No.

VICTOR I had to assemble you, part by part—

CREATURE Why? Dig up a single body.
One that has only begun to cool.
Justine.

VICTOR (*horrified*) No . . .

Offstage, the DOGS *begin to howl.*

CREATURE The dogs have found your friend.

Pause.

VICTOR Where is he now? You said it was night . . .

CREATURE Without end. Forever and ever.

VICTOR Cold?

The CREATURE *doesn't answer.*

Peaceful?

CREATURE Nothing.

VICTOR And you were alone.

CREATURE Completely.

VICTOR Was that agony?

CREATURE It was nothing.

Pause.

VICTOR Then why is it agony now?

Pause.

CREATURE Maybe Justine can tell you.

VICTOR (*still fighting this demand*) No.
Let the woman sleep.

CREATURE Is she asleep?
Then she must have been buried alive.
Dig her up.

VICTOR I will not do it.

VICTOR *forces himself to turn his back on the* CREATURE, *dreading its anger,
and stumbles away.*
The CREATURE *stares after him. He smiles a terrible smile.*

Scene 7

VICTOR's *home.*
ELIZABETH *is comforting* VICTOR's FATHER, *who is weeping.*
VICTOR *rushes in—and learns that his mother is gone.*

VICTOR That man in the hall—

FATHER —is the undertaker.

VICTOR (*aware of this*) Send him away. GET RID OF HIM!

VICTOR's *outburst is shocking. No one moves.*

My mother is dead. When?

FATHER Do you care? An hour ago.
Victor, where have you been?

VICTOR Was she strangled?
Was she torn apart?

FATHER She died of a broken heart.
In her sleep.
She wanted to say good-bye to you.

VICTOR *speaks, from ghoulish experience.*

VICTOR Your undertaker drinks too much.
At the end of the day, when he staggers off,
he forgets to lock his doors.
So vandals wander into his charnel-house
and desecrate the bodies.
They take souvenirs.

ELIZABETH Don't speak of these things.

VICTOR A finger, if the ring is stuck—
a glass eye someone could sell again,
a tooth with a golden filling—

ELIZABETH Stop it!

VICTOR Smash the jaw with a crowbar—

FATHER Victor—why do you hurt us this way?
Why are you hurting yourself?
Your mother loved you.

VICTOR Then I should have saved her.
I didn't.

He stares at his FATHER *and* ELIZABETH.

And now I may have waited too long
to save you . . .

Without another word, VICTOR *dashes off.*
VICTOR'S FATHER *and* ELIZABETH, *deeply upset, watch* VICTOR *go.*

Scene 8

The graveyard. In a thunderstorm.
VICTOR *enters, pushing a laden wheelbarrow. Tied to one of the handles is the*
string of a kite stretching taut into the dark sky.
JUSTINE'S *body lies in the barrow, hidden by a tarpaulin.*
One of her arms dangles over the side, uncovered, wet and gleaming.
VICTOR *wheels the barrow into place. Then he takes in the storm—lightning*
flash, almost simultaneous crash of thunder.

VICTOR I have a power no murderer ever had:
I can give you back what I stole from you.

Pause.

But do you want it?

Pause.

Justine, where are you now?
Up above, playing airs on a little harp?
Or below, in a lake of fire, dragging
your burning body to shore?
Or was my Creature telling the truth?
Is there nothing at all —
and are you content?

Another dazzle of lightning, clap of thunder. VICTOR *looks around, expecting to see the* CREATURE.

He is in this graveyard, now — he must be:
hating me for giving him life —
but waiting for me to commit the same crime against you.
And if I falter . . .
I know he will slaughter Elizabeth,
and drop her broken body at my feet —
that will be his wedding gift.

Pause.

VICTOR (*continued, to* JUSTINE) Then you have to be mine, to him.
Forgive me, Justine.

He begins to wrap the cord of the kite around the dangling hand of JUSTINE.
The wind picks up.
The kite flies higher, tugging JUSTINE'*s hand and arm up into the air.*
A lightning bolt hits the kite. As thunder booms, the kite string glows.
JUSTINE *sits up in the wheelbarrow, shedding the tarpaulin that had covered her.*
Arm still held aloft by the kite, JUSTINE *stares out — a look of horror on her face.*

JUSTINE I want —

VICTOR What? Tell me!

She sags.

JUSTINE I want—to go—

VICTOR Where?

JUSTINE Home.

Another lightning bolt hits the kite.
JUSTINE *rises up, more nearly alive.*

JUSTINE (*continued*) I WANT!

VICTOR Where is home?

JUSTINE THE DARK—FOREVER!

VICTOR (*already regretting what he's done*) Can you find the way?

JUSTINE I CAN SEE IT—
BACK THROUGH A DOOR,
OH, LET ME, PLEASE—
THE DARK, FOREVER AND EVER—
WHY AM I CAUGHT IN THIS NET,
WILL SOMEBODY CUT THE,
SET ME FREE! THE CORD!
I WANT!
I WANT!—

JUSTINE *falters again, not quite alive.*
VICTOR, *making a sudden decision, grabs the string of the kite and starts to work it free from* JUSTINE'S *hand.*

VICTOR Go back, then.

CREATURE (*offstage*) NO!

VICTOR *flinches, but only works faster.*

VICTOR Go back to the dark.

The CREATURE *rushes in.*
He wrestles with VICTOR, *who jerks the final loop of string from* JUSTINE'S *hand.*

JUSTINE *crumples.*
As creator and creation fight for the kite, it is hit by lightning one more time.
Both the CREATURE *and* VICTOR *stagger from the shock.*
In that moment, VICTOR *wrenches himself from the* CREATURE'S *grip, and—*
very deliberately—lets go of the kite string.
The CREATURE *watches it soar into the night sky and disappear.*
Exhausted, VICTOR *sinks to his knees.*
The CREATURE, *desolate, moves to* JUSTINE, *putting his hand to her neck, to feel*
for a pulse.

CREATURE Nothing.
Nothing.
NOTHING!
I WANTED—

Pause.

VICTOR —not to want anymore.

The CREATURE *stares at* VICTOR.

CREATURE I am going.

VICTOR Where?

CREATURE Does it matter?
I will be with you
on your wedding night.

The CREATURE *moves off, leaving* VICTOR *alone with* JUSTINE'S *body.*

Scene 9

On the iceberg.
VICTOR *has almost finished his story.*

WALTON You didn't believe him . . .

VICTOR Yes—I did. Completely.

Pause.

WALTON Then why did you marry?

Pause.

You said your wife had given you
a pair of gloves.

VICTOR My wife of a day.
Less than a day—one night.

WALTON Did she understand that she was
putting herself in jeopardy?

VICTOR *doesn't answer.*

She *is* dead . . . ?

VICTOR Something is drifting across the sky—
see that shadow, on the horizon?
Is it a cloud moving off? Or a sail?

WALTON (*concerned*) Where?

VICTOR *points.* WALTON *looks out.*

My ship is coming about.
My men are defying the orders I gave them.
Making for open water.

VICTOR The wind has dropped. Get down to the cutter.
You could still overtake them.

WALTON Come with me.

VICTOR *shakes his head.*

All my life I have wanted a friend.
And I have finally found him, in you.
The darkness in your heart
is a part of my heart, as well,
and has led me here.
If my men were driven to mutiny,
it is only because I abandoned them.

VICTOR Then take command of your ship, again.
Help them find a way home.

Pause.

I had a friend. I killed him.
I will never have another.

Pause.

WALTON *knows he will have to leave. But he tries a final gambit.*

WALTON Finish your story, and I will go.
What happened to Elizabeth?

VICTOR *hesitates.*

Tell me, and I swear to you:
I can keep them alive, forever—
the people you never wanted to die—
I can say, "Once upon a time . . ."

Scene 10

ELIZABETH *enters, in her nightgown, a candle lit in her hand.*
VICTOR *stands, looking out at the night.*

ELIZABETH Victor? Is he out there?

VICTOR I don't know, anymore.
He may be gone.
But he will come back—
on our wedding night. He promised.

ELIZABETH What if we marry in secret?

VICTOR Somehow he would hear.

ELIZABETH What if we marry now?

ELIZABETH *lets her robe fall from her, revealing her nakedness.*

VICTOR Do you know how beautiful you are?
And how your beauty hurts?

Pause. He kneels in front of her, kissing her. She strokes his hair.

ELIZABETH Could that be how your Creature felt—
when he opened his eyes,
and he found himself back in the world?

Pause. Behind VICTOR *and* ELIZABETH, *the* CREATURE *appears, listening.*

ELIZABETH (*continued*) That first winter had to be terrible.
But I wonder if the spring was worse—
to feel a warm breeze, or the sun on his skin—
look up, and all the new green glowing—
snow melting off into streams he could drink from,
cold, and clear as the sound of water
running over rocks, and the cries of birds,
and the smell of grass . . .

VICTOR . . . lie down on his back, and be still,
and know the whole wide world was trembling—
breathing in and out:
alive.

Pause.

ELIZABETH What could that beauty have been like—
to a thing so completely alone?

ELIZABETH *gently disengages from* VICTOR, *who is stricken by what she said.*

ELIZABETH I am going to bed.
Come and marry me.

Picking up her robe, ELIZABETH *moves off. When she's almost out of sight, the* CREATURE *steps out of the shadows, blocking her way.*
ELIZABETH *stares at the* CREATURE.
Then she offers her hand—he takes it.
Hand in hand, they disappear into the dark.

Scene 11

VICTOR *ends his story.*

VICTOR She was lying on the bed, where he left her—
I thought, for a moment, that she was asleep.

But then I took a step closer,
and I saw that her mouth was open
in a scream that he had stifled . . .
How could I look at that and live?

Pause.

Because, my creature taught me, life is obstinate —
and holds us tighter when we hate it most.

Pause.

Since that night, I have sought revenge.
And my pursuit has led me here.

Pause.

WALTON But — even if you found him —
you tried to kill him before . . .

VICTOR And I failed.
I will have to destroy his body.
I brought a supply of lamp oil.
I will douse him and set him aflame.

Suddenly, with an explosive crack, a crevice opens up in the ice.
WALTON *knows he's run out of time.*

WALTON HE ISN'T HERE!

VICTOR He is always here.
Go, now. Save your crew.

WALTON Am I God?

VICTOR In this alone: that you can suffer with your men.
Beside them.

WALTON Is that enough?

Pause.

VICTOR Get down to your boat and cast off.
And while you are rowing, watch the dark for a fire.

Accepting his duty, but desolate, WALTON *exits.* VICTOR *watches him go.*
Then he opens one of his knapsacks, carefully laying out a flask of oil, and a flint
and steel for making a spark.
As he does this, the CREATURE *appears.*

CREATURE You want to burn me alive?

VICTOR *whirls about and sees the* CREATURE *approaching. Before he can move,*
the CREATURE *is on him, knocking him to the ice.*
Then the CREATURE *picks up the flask.*

CREATURE *(continued)* What does that feel like, I wonder?

Savagely, he splashes lamp oil on VICTOR.

CREATURE *(continued)* One day, the winter you left me—
when the cold was like a whip,
and the tears were freezing on my cheeks—
I found a fire, still smoldering,
that some wandering beggars had left behind.
And the warm was such a relief,
I wanted to hold it in my hands.
I bent down and picked up a glowing ember.
And screamed: could the fire be both at once?
Pleasure, and also unbearable pain?
Later I came to realize
that that was the nature of life.

Putting the flask of oil aside, he strikes the block of steel with the flint, producing
a shower of sparks.
VICTOR *scrambles away from the* CREATURE, *terrified of being ignited.*

CREATURE *(continued)* Even so my revenge:
I destroyed your hopes,
but what was I left, of my own?
I still desire love—
and I am abominated forever.

He stares at VICTOR.

Stop cowering. Are you that afraid of dying?

VICTOR Why do you think I made you?

CREATURE But—if you aren't alone—
if I accompany you . . .

The CREATURE *picks up the oil again, now pouring it over himself.*
Knowing the CREATURE *will be destroyed,* VICTOR *begins to accept his fate.*

VICTOR So this will be my legacy:
two heaps of ash. And then
the wind will sweep them into the sea.

Pause.

Will I have thoughts, in the darkness?
Will I dream?

CREATURE Are you certain you want to?
Or is it not because of your dreams
that you and I are here?

A loud splintering crash, and the crevice widens, separating VICTOR *from the*
CREATURE.

CREATURE *(continued)* No! *NO!*

VICTOR *watches the* CREATURE, *across the abyss.*

Come back.

The CREATURE *reaches out a hand.*
VICTOR *hesitates—but only a moment.*
Then he reaches out, to grab the outstretched hand.
VICTOR *jumps—and barely makes it across, as the* CREATURE *hauls him in.*
With a shudder, the ice where VICTOR *had been drops into the dark.*
The wind picks up.
VICTOR *and the* CREATURE *regard each other.*
The CREATURE *tries, a final time, to start a fire with the flint and steel.*
A few glints—but they die in the wind.

CREATURE The spark goes out.
Why does the spark go out?

VICTOR *holds out his cupped hands, to make a windbreak.*
The CREATURE, *understanding, strikes the flint behind the shelter of*
VICTOR's *hands.*
A shower of sparks in the dark.
Then—a second of blinding light: the CREATURE *and* VICTOR, *blazing—*
Blackout.

End of Play.

Fredric Jameson

On Neal Bell, *Monster*

> Is the thing seen or the thing heard the thing that
> makes most of its impression upon you at the theatre.
> How much has the hearing to do with it and how little.
> Does the thing heard replace the thing seen. Does it
> help or does it interfere with it.
> —Gertrude Stein, *Lectures in America*

It seems fair to say that, in whatever provisional "systems of the fine arts" emerged under modernity, language, in particular poetic language, occupied the place of the dominant. But this raises interesting general problems in a postmodern situation generally characterized by the dominance of the image, or of spatiality. In particular, what becomes of language itself in the new situation? Modernist language, "poeticity" or poetic language, promised a utopian transformation of ordinary degraded or media speech which is clearly no longer on the agenda: poetry today is therefore yet another fallen part of the cultural world in general. As for the novel, its tendential symbiosis with film has produced a narrative generic in which language becomes indistinguishable from profilmic background— it would be abusive to identify this "generic"

The *South Atlantic Quarterly* 99:2/3, Spring/Summer 2000.
Copyright © 2001 by Duke University Press.

with the older term *realism*. Novelistic language, then, does not revert to description so much as it organizes scenarios and supplies directions for shots. Does language, however, know its own version of "special effects"?

In fact, although "plays are not prose" (Gore Vidal), the theater is the place one forgets to look. The old fantasies of a revival of verse drama having been swept away, "heightened speech" in drama followed them into oblivion, leaving yet more "special effects" on the one hand, and a unique practice of language on the other. About this last, in the newer experimental drama today, one is tempted to think that it is beyond the usual generic categories, unless one considers that this kind of theater has become a genre in its own right: the genre which stages the very emergence of language itself.

I want to think about this genre in two ways: in terms of light and in terms of projection. Both are artificial: light first of all, not merely because it brings out all the makeup on the actors' faces, but because it exists in its own right. Light in the theater is no longer the transparent medium of everyday life; nor can it be rationalized as some sublime transnatural illumination. We see it first and foremost, and only then the things it lights up: it is the first artifice we are here to enjoy, and even though it has its "sources" (clearly visible on the ceiling), light has been projected in and for itself, it exists artificially. So does the human voice, strangely enough, whose analogous projection by the actors does not have to signal stylization at all, but rather merely that the conversational voice has been separated from its context and transferred to a place in which it exists autonomously, and all by itself: an artificial place of voices such as exists nowhere in real life. The artificiality is not to be located in the diction or the expression, but rather in that new space in which the voice floats after it has been projected.

Oddly enough, this new space, separated from everything else, allows the new theater to develop its mysterious connections with the very roots and sources of language itself, in conversation. In Neal Bell's plays the dramatic situation is not particularly one in which something dramatic happens, but rather in which people begin to reinvent their replies to one another; not one in which something significant gets said, let alone expressed, but rather one in which that peculiar business of talking to someone else begins to take place—to take place again, one might be tempted to say, if any memory remained of the earlier times. Gilles Deleuze has a wonderful diatribe against "communication": "There's always something crazy and schizophrenic about a conversation taken in itself . . . all conversations are schizophrenic, conversation is a model of schizophrenia, rather than the other way round." So also here: these nascent conversations are neither communications, nor are they some "failure to communicate." They are the first feeble reemergence of that utterly useless and gratuitous thing, the "exchange" of words. This is the sense in which all of these plays are "about" language, in its most vulnerable state, as anyone might muster it. The "dramatic" situation is nothing but a pretext for that emergence, which, as democratic and everyday as it may be, is very far from what used to be called "realism."

But now we come to a new twist or wrinkle: for Bell has here used this "genre" for a very old and very new function, namely to "stage" a novel, something playwrights did all the time in the nineteenth century, but which today would seem rather to be the task and responsibility, the honor and exclusive right, of film, partly for the reasons and affinities noted above. To offer a play version of Frank Norris's *McTeague*—a novel which is to be sure one of the unacknowledged treasures and summits of American literature— is to enter at once into competition with Erich von Stroheim, and perhaps the final desperate duel to the death in Death Valley offers Bell's own allegory of that struggle. Here Bell contends with innumerable film versions, under which Mary Shelley's novel is itself already buried: Are we merely to suppose that it is a tale thrilling enough to listen to over and over again?

In fact, however, Bell here picks up the most filmic "special effect" of the novel, itself, which virtually none of the *Frankenstein* films tried to stage, and that is the final deadly pursuit over the ice—a polar version, perhaps, of the expiration of the pseudo-couple in the suffocating last pages of Norris. This "image," if we may call it that, to underscore everything incompatible with the theatrical form, is then augmented by the ship itself, the witnesses, on the point of being caught forever in the ice floes. But this is clearly an affront to stagecraft and an offense to the "aesthetic" of special effects: a situation in which everything material must be conjured up by language and a radically "poor" or impoverished theater; yet in which what is to be thus conjured up is itself a radical simplification and impoverishment of Being, the end of the world in ice, a nothingness that Bell conveys with a spark and a final glimpse of burning bodies aflame.

Still, the arctic frame means that this will be a theater of flashbacks, that is to say, of illuminated "scenes" whose content is very specifically that artificial light evoked above. Yet the flashback is also sealed in the closure of the past and of death, and if the text is to be interrogated for Bell's reinterpretation of the Shelley novel, it would clearly be in this direction we would have to look: Thanatos rather than Eros, Victor and the Creature both longing for extinction. But this was always the undecidable core of the original text—how the longing for the mate could prove to bear within itself the lust for mortal vengeance, and how the asexual production of life is at one with hatred and the duel to the death. It is this undecidability that keeps alive the text that cannot solve it, so that it can only be replayed, over and over again.

Yet Bell needs to differentiate his play, not just from one text, but rather from two: since Mary Shelley's source of 1817 has long since been overshadowed by James Whale's film (1931), leaving at most the misapprehension that the Shelley original is a kind of *tale*, whereas in fact it is a relatively aimless and undistinguished *novel* (which does, however, contain at least one immortal sentence: "It was already one in the morning; the rain pattered dismally against the panes, and my candle was nearly burnt out, when, by the glimmer of the half-extinguished light, I saw the dull yellow eye of the creature open"). Whale anticipated Nazism by reorganizing his fable around the dual structure of Fritz Lang's *M*, the antisocial loner over against organized crime (in this case, the lynch mob of the German small town). Mary Shelley's episodic narrative, with its clusters of parallel episodes, its comprehensive tourisms (from Italy to the Orkneys, from the Mont Blanc to St. Petersburg and beyond), and its romantic emphasis on "friendship" (including sexual intimacy but subsuming it), could be inflected optionally in any number of ways, of which these are only two. One imagines, for example, a reading on the order of Edmund Wilson's reinterpretation of *The Turn of the Screw*, in which it is the narrator who is the villain, and the "creature" is a mere figment of his imagination. At any rate, I cannot be the only reader for whom the eponymous narrator comes over as an insufferable prig who loses interest in his creation the moment he succeeds (one motif, reduplicated in Walton's frame narrative, is the Balzacian "recherche de l'absolu," the obsessive scientific discovery—in this case, the infusion of life). No wonder the monster hates him! I doubt if contemporary readership, well trained in the stigmata of various forms of victimization, will have much sympathy with the creator's physical revulsion from his creation.

Bell turns all this into a story about death, infusing the interpolated narratives and minor characters with existential liveliness and cross-cutting throughout the play between the Arctic venue (and Frankenstein's dialogue with Walton) and the sad and tragic episodes of the original. The new focus—

the death obsession—in fact makes Victor a far more interesting and attractive figure, doing away with the incomprehensible and Byronic mood swings of the romantic text and generating dialogue in the place of monological lamentation. The centrality of the Artic secures that centrality of landscape that interested Stein in drama, while the self-immolation of the ending combines the act itself with the ultimate experience of light and darkness.

Jody McAuliffe

Interview with Neal Bell

JODY MCAULIFFE *What got you interested in theater in the first place?*

NEAL BELL I guess it was seeing theater when I was a kid. I grew up in Norfolk, Virginia, and Norfolk had a vigorous little theater movement that grew out of the Federal Theater Project in the thirties when the Federal Theater was founding small regional theaters all over the country. When I was six years old I saw a production of *Cinderella* and was trying to figure out how they could possibly do live on stage what I had seen in the animated version, and was prepared to be completely bored out of my mind, then discovered through the magic of theater—somehow or other, just by using my imagination—that all the things that seemed so easy to do in the animated version they did on stage. That was pretty much it. I started doing plays in my backyard. Although I don't remember any of this, I've been told this by my aunt, my one surviving relative. My little cousin and I used to put on plays in my backyard by using a sheet as a curtain.

Very Brechtian.

The *South Atlantic Quarterly* 99:2/3, Spring/Summer 2000.
Copyright © 2001 by Duke University Press.

Oh, yeah, I'm still doing it. It's still pretty much the level of the stagecraft.

Well, your work relies very much on the audience's imagination.

I think I've never lost that.

It's a good thing not to lose.

Well, it's one of the interesting things about the amateur theater movement in this country. Because they didn't have the resources of the supposed cosmopolitan centers, they were able to challenge and stretch the audience's imagination just because they had to, not because they had an aesthetic plan. It just worked out that way.

It's been awhile since I've seen On the Bum, *but there's that spirit in that, too, isn't there?*

I think *On the Bum* is my tribute, in some ways.

What was your first play?

My first play was an outrageously direct rip-off of *The Glass Menagerie* substituting my family for Tennessee Williams's family. Which was in response to an eleventh-grade English classroom assignment. And then the winner (it was a contest) was to have his play read out loud in class. And it turned out that I won, and the play that I wrote was read out loud. Everybody recognized the thinly disguised versions of my family as my family, much to my family's horror.

What kind of theater attracted you—clearly Williams?

Well, I loved *The Glass Menagerie*, which we had studied in high school. I remember when I was older than the *Cinderella* stage, one of the plays that knocked me out in high school was Jean Anouilh's *Antigone*, which they did in a theater in the park in Norfolk. I was always afraid to go back to that play because I have no idea whether it's as good as it seemed to me at the time.

He has a magical touch—very imaginative, very poetic.

I found this completely thrilling, challenging. The other thing that grabbed me was musicals.

Really? Which ones?

It was a Little Theater production of *Wonderful Town*, the Bernstein. I don't think I'd ever seen a musical before, it seemed like a whole new world was opening up. I'd never seen that kind of explosion of energy and excitement. When the cast started conga-ing down the aisle—

You were lost—

I was gone. I was so thrilled that I used to have dreams. I didn't know that there was a movie version of it. In fact, I thought there wasn't, but I used to wish that there was a movie version of it so that I could see it over and over again.

What kinds of works or artists have influenced you as a writer?

That's an enormous question.

I know.

I'd always wanted to be a writer. That again I don't remember, but when my brother and I were digging out my parents' attic prior to selling the family house, we found an essay that I'd written in third grade in which I said— it was supposed to be what do you want to be when you grow up. I said I wanted to be a science fiction writer and make a lot of money. So I achieved one of those goals. I did actually in my twenties write a science fiction novel that was published as a paperback original.

And what was the name of it?

Gone to Be Snakes Now. When I started narrowing in on theater—which was basically when I got to college—Brecht made an enormous impact on me. Beckett. And then as I started digging deeper into world playwriting, the Germans in general grabbed me. I loved Wedekind, Büchner. In fact, when I first started teaching playwriting I made a suggested reading list of plays that I thought were worth reading, they were almost all European, almost all nineteenth century or earlier, which my class found puzzling.

I'm with you there.

They wondered why I didn't have any Americans. Actually, at a certain moment, I felt a little uncomfortable about the fact that I seemed to have this, not a prejudice against American playwriting, but it did seem that the kind of writing that interested me was happening elsewhere by and large. The other big push, the thing that got me into the theater, was the explosion of talent off-Broadway in America in the sixties.

Anything in particular?

Well, I loved early John Guare and Sam Shepard. I saw a great production of *La Turista*, which was one of the indelible experiences of my life. Also a wonderful production of John Guare's *Muzeeka*.

That's a neat play.

It's a wonderful play, and it was a great production. Again on an almost bare stage. I mean, it's written to be done that way, with just a bunkbed as every part of the scenery. But I was totally entranced by that. People of my generation who inspired me were doing wonderful work at the time. One of the sadnesses of my life as a lover of that particular moment is that people have forgotten those writers or forgotten the energy of their early work. I had the experience of trying to teach some of Shepard's earliest one-acts, and the people just didn't get it.

One of my students is directing Cowboy Mouth, *which I am thrilled about.*

It's great. When I saw that play and plays like it, there was so much work like it going on that one had a context in which to understand it.

It doesn't seem like some strange thing.

Yes, it's not this completely anomalous, quirky experiment. It's part of an ongoing attempt to push theater further—to make it do things that it hadn't done before. And just to briefly get back to my comment about the reading list and European classics, the premodern works, I think one of the things that I found so telling about them was that they weren't bogged down in the sort of method realism, which is the one thing I have trouble with in American writing. A large trouble, because it seems to have been the largest commercial success as a movement in this country, largely fostered, I think, by the success of television, so that for most people the idea of what drama is is based more on television than on what the possibilities of theater actually are.

How do you begin a play—is it different for each play or do you have a kind of process that you repeat?

It's pretty much different for each play. It takes me a certain length of time to find out what it is that's nudging me or bothering me that I want to write about. I do believe in this thing which I guess is a cliché by now, but I think it's true that you write to find out what it is that you're writing about. That, in other words, you write to explore some part of yourself that you're not completely clear about. Because I think that if you were clear about it, then you would write something that was arid and overexplained and already solved. So it seems that I have to wait a certain length of time until I finally get nudged enough that I start to write something.

Did you choose to adapt Frankenstein *and then find out something about it that you wanted to find out about?*

It was actually both. A director that I'd worked with on another adaptation, Michael Greif—I had worked with Michael on an adaptation of *Therese Raquin*—we had a good time, and he thought maybe we should try it again.

*Was that the first adaptation you did—*Therese Raquin?

Well, actually the first adaptation I did years ago was of *Philoctetes*.

That's a play I directed Heiner Müller's version of.

It's such a great play.

It's a wonderful play.

This is one of my lost works. I keep thinking I should dig it out and show it to people. It was sort of a brutal condensation, with the brutality of the condensation being in some sense my attempt to mirror the brutality of the play, the source material, because it really is a terrifying play.

So that was never produced?

It was produced at Iowa.

When you were in graduate school.

Then I actually did an adaptation of *The Wind in the Willows* at Iowa for a children's theater group, and that was it for a long time.

Until Therese Raquin.

Yes.

I think that you're gifted at adaptation, and I wonder what is that process compared to playwriting.

One of the things it does is help me with plot. I find plot tremendously difficult, and one of the obvious advantages of working with a preexisting text is it does give you a structure to work with, whether you end up with that structure or not. I think part of my fascination with adaptation came from again one of the cardinal theater experiences of my life, which was seeing a production of a play called *Subject to Fits* when I was an undergrad, which was Robert Montgomery's response to Dostoevsky's *The Idiot*. It was a truly thrilling piece of theater based on a novel that I didn't know at the time. The play itself, in and of itself, just worked like gangbusters. I went to see it five times. And what was amazing to me afterward—I finally read the novel—I was amazed that the guy had gotten the entire novel into a two-hour play by somehow distilling the essence of it, fragmenting the chronology of it, doing all kinds of theatrical things to it, but yet just preserving utterly the spirit of the novel. So that's always been kind of a yardstick to me, that particular adaptation.

What was it about Frankenstein *that intrigued you?*

Well, I've always loved horror movies and the horror genre.

The play is very scary.

I would like it to be.

As I imagine it.

I certainly intended it to be.

Those scenes in the cellar, they're quite haunting.

Michael Greif suggested, I think, for no particular reason, that I look at the novel *The Phantom of the Opera*, although I think somebody's already done that.

Yeah.

No, he was thinking about a straight play adaptation. I don't think he'd read the novel, and it was sort of dismayingly bad. But then I thought, well, what about other nineteenth-century novels, probably just because they're in the public domain. I thought that I had read *Frankenstein* and proposed it to him.

He said, look at it and let's see. And then when I started reading it I was pretty sure that I hadn't read it before, and it was a revelation to me because it is so completely different from—

The Boris Karloff movie.

Yes, and all the parodies of it, the thick cultural encrustation all over it. Encountering the original thing itself was amazing, because it really is terrifying, and not terrifying because there's a monster running around killing people; because of the moral problems it's dealing with—

As far as Victor's concerned—

Yes.

His godlessness.

Just the whole idea of responsibility.

Abandonment, too.

What seemed to me to be the largest idea in the novel is responsibility for one's creation. It's not what the movie had suggested, namely, that there are some things man is not meant to know or that in taking godlike powers you invite destruction. I think that may have been what Mary Shelley meant, but I don't think so. I do really think that what she was talking about was if you create something then you take responsibility for it.

Which Victor finally does in the double immolation. He finally accepts, and while accepting his fate, he also accepts responsibility for the creature.

Right, exactly.

And finally takes care of him.

That's one departure I made from the novel. Because in the novel, Frankenstein the doctor dies, and the creature escapes into the Arctic, which is an even bleaker ending.

It's more horrifying. And you changed the ending because you wanted him to take responsibility?

Exactly.

You wanted that action to happen.

Yes.

How much writing do you do in production? I know from my experience direct-ing your play McTeague *that when you turn a script in that it's virtually finished and you like to do what you call tinkering.*

Yes. I do think that there's a part of the process which involves the transition from the page to the stage. I've written for a long time and have been lucky enough to have a fair number of productions, but there are still things that I need to learn about what works and what doesn't work when you move from words in your head to words that are actually spoken and how they affect somebody listening in the audience. So there's always that kind of adjust-ment. I feel that you get in trouble if you don't have a fairly strong backbone in the play itself and in the version that you're working with from the be-ginning. The one complete and utter disaster that I had in the theater years ago was with a play called *Gradual Clearing*, which was about the blacklist-ing era, the McCarthy period. And it had a lot of things that I like a lot in it, but the play was not ready to be done when it was done. And the produc-ing organization was producing it largely because they liked my work and they wanted to do me a favor, but it turned out not to be a favor because the thing wasn't working. And the more I rewrote it in rehearsal the muddier and more obscure it got. It just got away from everybody, and I think that was because the backbone of the play wasn't there enough—

To withstand the process—

Yes, the questioning, which is so much a part of the rehearsal process.

Do you have a notion of what effect on the audience you hope your plays will have.

That is an interesting question because I don't, and sometimes people have angrily asked me, "Well how do you think the audience is supposed to react to this?" And I'm not sure. In general, I think the plays should shake people up and unsettle and disturb them, which doesn't necessarily mean depress them or horrify them. *The Importance of Being Earnest* is a disturbing play, and it's as funny as anything ever written, but a play should make you reex-amine your preconceptions. And if it does that, then it's done a basic duty. And then beyond that, it seems that people's reactions are going to be very individual.

Have you ever directed your own work?

I haven't, and I never intend to.

Can you say why?

I think because it's so important to have an objective version of what's going on. I guess nobody's version is objective, but it's important to have another version of what's happening on stage being relayed to you that's not the one that you yourself are taking in. Because so much of the interior life of the play is still in your head as the author, and I think it's very easy for a writer who's directing his own work to think that because it's in his head—

That it's coming out—

And there's nobody there to tell him, "No, it's not."

Except the actors, and they really can't.

The actors sometimes, but sometimes the actors are happy to collude with the writer also, because they think that if they're good enough they can convey subterranean depths of subtext that nobody is getting, that they're privy to because they've been having conversations with the author. In the happiest collaborations I've had with people like yourself, I feel like it's just necessary, that I've learned things from the director that I would never have learned about the play.

It's hard to know what you wrote yourself, in some aspects.

No, I know, it sounds like a sophism—you write to find out what you're writing about, but I do think that's true to a certain extent. You don't know exactly what it is that you've got.

I think if you do, it goes back to what you were saying, it's pedantic or over-explained.

When you directed *Somewhere in the Pacific* at Manbites Dog and I saw the first preview, something happened to me while I was watching it. And I don't know exactly what that was, but I knew that was exactly what I wanted the play to do.

Some feeling that you had.

Yes, I was not aware of time passing.

Good.

That I was in some other world for a while, and then I came back out of that world.

It's true, and I wasn't either. It seemed like it happened in a flash, afterward.

Right. And I think that's the territory that theater tries to get to.

Part of that, by the way, I think is structurally built into that play.

Well, I think that's what you aim for.

Yes, that the form will realize the intent.

Yes.

Do you have any thoughts or comments on your evolution as a writer?

I think that's completely unanswerable.

Maybe, yes. Do you have favorites among your plays?

I do. Two of the ones that you've directed are two of my favorites.

McTeague.

And *Somewhere in the Pacific.* One of the things I used to feel bad about was that every time I started a play I felt like "I don't know how to do this," as if I hadn't learned anything from the previous play. And I thought I must be the only person who's ever felt like this.

Oh, boy, no.

This was years ago. I was rereading Moss Hart's wonderful autobiography, in which he said that he felt exactly the same way, that every time he started writing a play it was as if he'd never written a play.

That's a really modernist notion, too.

And I think it's true. You learn more craft so you're better able to deal with the questions when they come up, but the questions, as Moss Hart said, are always different ones, and you don't know the answer. You throw your craft at it and see if anything happens.

Do you consider yourself a political writer?

I think in the larger sense. And I don't want to sound glib or slick, but it just seems like all writing, but especially theater writing, is so much about the society that's witnessing it, and it either takes the politics of that audience into consideration or ignores them. Both of those decisions are political decisions. Again, because theater, when it works, is about creating a kind of communion between the members of the audience and the people onstage, that it is itself a sort of political act. And then you can define the outside politics against the sort of purity of that political act, whether they help it or hurt it.

How does the American theater look from your perspective?

Well, I think it's in a funny place right now, again having come of age in these glorious days of the off-Broadway explosion. My impression is that there are more talented people out there than ever, that the theater has continued to nurture in one way or another people who keep building on what seemed like the promise of a new day back in the sixties. And what's changed is the audience, the institutions, all the means of supporting the theater, which have become more conservative. Venues have closed. Theaters do fewer plays. The audience has shrunk. So there's that kind of contradiction at the heart of everything right now. I don't think theater will ever die. I think there are the people out there to do the greatest theater that we've ever seen. And yet the opportunities to do it become more and more difficult. That's why it's so amazing to me, for example, that a little theater in Durham, North Carolina, Manbites Dog, will do as wonderful a production of a play of mine as I'll ever see in my life. And that theater wouldn't have existed twenty years ago. So I have to say that in my case, that's a good thing.

What are the differences in your experience in the regional as opposed to the New York theaters?

I think that's also changed. I think the regionals have gone through a series of evolutions. First they were an alternative to New York, and then they were a rival to New York, and now I think they're trying to define a new role for themselves. The theaters that continue to try to be New York seem to be very tired, and seem to be doing the same old thing over and over again. And I sometimes wonder if institutional theaters have a natural lifespan.

Well, you wonder especially in the case of regional theaters that were created by very specific people. And what do they have to do to survive?

Because at a certain point, they seem to exist only because they're surviving. Not because they still know what their mandate is or have a particular passion beyond just surviving.

That's the problem of almost any institution.

It seems like. And that's why I suspect that the future of the theater is going to involve a movement into much smaller theaters all over the place.

Like Manbites Dog.

That's my most optimistic hope, that there will be more theaters. Again, they'll be more diffuse than theater used to be, and that's not necessarily a good thing.

Interviewer's Note

Other works by Neal Bell include *Two Small Bodies, Raw Youth, Breaking and Entering, Cold Sweat, On the Bum, Ready for the River, Sleeping Dogs, Out the Window, McTeague, Therese Raquin, Somewhere in the Pacific,* and *Terminal Choice.*

Nilo Cruz. Photo: Miguel Ariza.

Nilo Cruz

Two Sisters and a Piano

Two Sisters and a Piano, commissioned by the McCarter Theatre and developed in part with the support from the Sundance Theatre Laboratory, received its world premiere at the McCarter Theatre in Princeton, New Jersey, on February 19, 1998, with the following cast—Yvonne Coll (Maria Celia), Marissa Chibas (Sofia), Bobby Cannavale (Lieutenant Portuondo), and Gary Perez (Victor Manuel); and creative contributors—Brian Kulick (Director), Mark Wendland (Sets), Anita Yavich (Costumes), Mimi Jordan Sherin (Lighting), J. R. Conklin (Sound), Cheryl Mintz (Stage Manager), Mark Bennett (Composer), Janice Paran (Dramaturg), and Mara Isaacs (Resident Producer).

The play received its West Coast premiere on the Second Stage of South Coast Repertory in Costa Mesa, California, opening April 27, 1999, with the following cast—Adriana Sevan (Maria Celia), Jill Remez (Sofia), Carlos Sanz (Lieutenant Portuondo), and Javi Murillo (Victor Manuel); and creative contributors—Loretta Greco (Director), Robert Brill (Sets), Alex Jaeger (Costumes), Geoff Korf (Lighting), Rob Miller (Sound), and Randall K. Lum (Stage Manager).

The *South Atlantic Quarterly* 99:2/3, Spring/Summer 2000.

It was presented by the Joseph Papp Public Theater in New York on February 15, 1999, with the following cast—Adriana Sevan (Maria Celia), Daphne Rubin-Vega (Sofia), Paul Calderon (Lieutenant Portuondo), and Gary Perez (Victor Manuel); and creative contributors—Loretta Greco (Director), Robert Brill (Sets), Alex Jaeger (Costumes), James Vermeulen (Lighting), Fabian Obispo (Sound), Shirley Fishman (Dramaturg), and Buzz Cohen (Stage Manager).

Characters

MARIA CELIA, *the older sister*
SOFIA, *the younger sister*
LIEUTENANT PORTUONDO, *a man in his thirties*
MILITIA GUARD #1, *a man in his thirties. Played by actor playing* VICTOR
   MANUEL
VICTOR MANUEL, *a man in his thirties*

Time and place: Cuba, 1991. A spacious colonial house. (Note to designers: The set and lights should have a feeling of openness. It should not feel claustrophobic.)

Prologue: The Search

A Victorian sofa with a side table stands to the center left area. A baby grand piano stands to the right of the center. Music plays, then in full darkness we hear the loud sound of a metal prison door closing. Shadowy lights fade up to reveal a few militia guards in green uniforms, at the Obispos' house doing a search. The electricity has been cut off. The guards hold flashlights, which they aim at different parts of the stage. The sound of furniture turning over, glass breaking, objects falling on the floor. MILITIA GUARD #1 *pushes* SOFIA *and goes after* MARIA CELIA.

MILITIA GUARD #1 Tell us where you hide them.
Tell us where you keep them.

LIEUTENANT PORTUONDO *(at the same time)* Come on, tell us.
Come on . . .

MARIA CELIA I don't know what you're talking about!

SOFIA She's not hiding anything!

MILITIA GUARD #1   Liar . . . You're lying. We want all the papers you're hiding.

SOFIA   She's not hiding any papers.

LIEUTENANT PORTUONDO   Just tell us where you keep them, bitch! Go get your papers.

SOFIA   Don't hurt her or I'll hit you with this chair.

LIEUTENANT PORTUONDO   Just tell us where you hide them.

MARIA CELIA   Hide what! Hide what!

SOFIA   She's got nothing!
She's got nothing!
She's not hiding any papers!

MARIA CELIA   (*at the same time*) I don't have any papers.

MILITIA GUARD #1   You shut up, bitch!

MARIA CELIA   I already told you . . .

SOFIA   She already told you . . .

MILITIA GUARD #1   You shut up, you big mouth, or I'll cut off your tongue! I'll cut off your tongue!—Where do you keep your writing?

MARIA CELIA   I've got nothing! . . . I've got nothing hidden, *compañero*!

LIEUTENANT PORTUONDO   Let's start the inventory, Mena.

MILITIA GUARD #1   Who does inspection here every week?

MARIA CELIA   Polita . . . Polita Mirabal.

MILITIA GUARD #1   (*to the other guard*) Polita Mirabal . . . Polita Mirabal.

LIEUTENANT PORTUONDO   The girls have had enough.

MILITIA GUARD #1   Yeah, they've had enough. A bunch of weaklings. We got two lesbos in here. A writer and a pianist. Which one is the pianist?

SOFIA *raises her hand.*

Play something on the piano. I have a headache.

(*Gives* LIEUTENANT PORTUONDO *a file*) See if you can figure out these papers. It's a bunch of rice and mangoes. (*Walks around, inspects the place with the flashlight*) This is a big house for just two people. Who else you've got living here, ghosts?

LIEUTENANT PORTUONDO   I can't figure out this shit either.

MILITIA GUARD #1   We'll leave it blank. What's the pianist doing? I told you to play something.

SOFIA *goes to the piano.*

Let's start the inventory. A piano.

LIEUTENANT PORTUONDO   Piano, check.

MILITIA GUARD #1   A sofa.

LIEUTENANT PORTUONDO   Sofa, check.

MILITIA GUARD #1   A small oak table.

LIEUTENANT PORTUONDO   Oak table, check.

MILITIA GUARD #1   A radio.

LIEUTENANT PORTUONDO   Radio, check.

SOFIA *plays the piano.*

MILITIA GUARD #1   Brass lamp.

LIEUTENANT PORTUONDO   Brass lamp, check.

Lights start to fade up on MARIA CELIA *standing on the rooftop.*

MILITIA GUARD #1   Rocking chair.

LIEUTENANT PORTUONDO   Rocking chair, check.

MILITIA GUARD #1   Picture of lady with a fan.

LIEUTENANT PORTUONDO   Picture, check.

Lights start to fade down on the MILITIA GUARDS. MARIA CELIA *is in full light now holding a letter, which she folds and places in her pocket as she speaks to her husband in the distance.*

MARIA CELIA My dear husband: I'm standing on top of this roof,
wanting to leap into the sky and send you this letter.
Almost three months and two weeks now, and not a word from you.
Today a few militia guards came to search the house.
They took inventory of all our things. I don't know what this
means. This is usually done when somebody is leaving the country.
Yesterday we heard on the radio about amnesty for political
prisoners, so I'm keeping my fingers crossed.
I tell Sofie that 1991 is our lucky year. We've been allowed back home.
At least here we can walk all the way from the kitchen to the living
room, and that's a long distance compared to the size of our cell back
in prison. So many things are happening out there
in the world, my love. . . . A new way of thinking. . . . Freedom . . .
I always tell Sofie how much I love the leader Gorbachev,
any man who has a birthmark that looks
like an island on his forehead is a blessed man.
I'm thinking that from now on I should use the name
Gertrudis, my favorite poet, when writing to you.
And you should forget about sending me correspondence through France.
The state officials are confiscating my mail.
They must know about our trick.
I'm writing a new story, my love, which I'm sending you a page at a time.
It's what keeps me going. The writing. The man and the woman in my new
story. They take me out of this house. Their walks to the sea.
Only when I write do I feel free and alive again.
I miss you more and more, my love. I pin all my hopes to this TV
antenna, this metal tree which offers testimony that communication
must exist out there in the world. A big kiss and hug, Maria Celia
or from now on Gertrudis.

Allegro piano music is heard. Lights fade up on SOFIA *playing the piano, as
lights fade down on* MARIA CELIA. *She climbs down from the roof.*

Act I

Scene 1: The Man behind the Wall and the Lost Letters

MARIA CELIA *walks toward* SOFIA. *All of a sudden* SOFIA *stops playing the piano.*

MARIA CELIA Why did you stop?

SOFIA Shshhh . . .

MARIA CELIA But you were playing so beautifully . . .

SOFIA (*whispering*) I thought I heard something.

MARIA CELIA What?

SOFIA (*whispers*) Next door.

They both speak in low voices.

MARIA CELIA I didn't hear anything. You think he's home? That's probably your imagination. Play that song again.

SOFIA *presses her ear to the wall.*

SOFIA (*whispering*) No . . . Listen. Come close to the wall.

MARIA CELIA *moves close to the wall.*

MARIA CELIA I don't hear a thing.

SOFIA Shshhhh . . . I did. You hear that?

MARIA CELIA (*walks away from the wall*) Nonsense. That's the wind or a cat walking on top of the roof. There's nobody there.

SOFIA Yesterday he came around this time. I heard him.

MARIA CELIA Where was I?

SOFIA Where else? You were up on the roof writing. He sat by the doorway with a drink in his hand. He smoked and drank and listened to me for more than an hour. Music is like medicine. I touched his soul.

MARIA CELIA Bah. You're falling in love with an invisible man.

SOFIA You can still love a person and not be physical.

MARIA CELIA Then it turns into a lie. A lie of the heart. That's for young girls who fall in love with a man in a book or a movie. You're twenty-four years old, and you know very well that people like him don't like people like us.

SOFIA You like to press your ear to the wall as much as I do.

MARIA CELIA I listen when I'm bored and tired and fed up with this house. Don't roll your eyes at me. You stand next to this wall every five minutes. I don't know what could be so interesting about him.

SOFIA You really want to know? I heard him tell his friend how much he wanted to lie in bed with the two of us.

MARIA CELIA Yeap . . . A rotten, putrid mind he has!

SOFIA He must see something in us, Maria Celia.

MARIA CELIA Yes, I can see what he sees.
Two women unable to go out the door,
under house arrest. A harem next to his house.
Wake up, Sofia! Can't you see he's a dog!
You've heard what he does when he's on duty.
He sneaks a woman into his office.
He makes love to her all over his paperwork.
Can't you see the kind of man he is—what goes through his head?

SOFIA I still think it would be an adventure.
You on this side of the bed, and me on this other side.
We'll drive him wild and crazy,
to the point that he'll go to work hypnotized in a trance.
Then he'll drop dead from all the rapture,
and there on his tomb will be inscribed,
"Here I rest in peace for loving the Obispo Sisters."

MARIA CELIA I'm starting to think you have canaries inside your head.
Let's go back to work. You're too naive, sometimes.
The other night I had a dream with Mami.
I swear she looked as if she had come down from the sky.

I saw her standing at the end of a road, and I could hear her voice,
"Celita, my child . . . Sofie my hummingbird . . .
Don't let the dirty Communists brainwash you . . .
Don't forget to place a glass of water on the altar for the angels.
They get thirsty from watching over you.
Teach your sister to walk through life.
Pin a prayer to the hem of her dress."

SOFIA Did she say that? (*Smiles*) Poor Mami . . .

MARIA CELIA (*produces a small piece of paper from inside the piano*) I wrote
something on a piece of paper. I was going to pin it to your dress without
telling you, but then I thought of putting it inside the piano.

SOFIA What is it?

MARIA CELIA A prayer. Let me have the hem of your dress. (*Kneels down to
pin it to* SOFIA's *dress*)

There's a knock at the door. MARIA CELIA *goes to the entranceway and listens.*
SOFIA *stays at a distance.*

SOFIA (*in a low voice*) Who is it?

MARIA CELIA Shssh . . . I don't know . . . (*Listens for a moment, then in a loud
voice*) Who is it?

LIEUTENANT PORTUONDO Lieutenant Portuondo, open up.

MARIA CELIA *brings her arms up expressing the burden of the visit. She opens
the door.* LIEUTENANT PORTUONDO *wearing militia clothes comes in and
stands by the entranceway.*

MARIA CELIA If you're here for inspection, we had inspection two days ago.

LIEUTENANT PORTUONDO (*enters the space as if he owns it*) No. I'm not here
for inspection. I came to talk to you.

MARIA CELIA What can I do for you, Lieutenant?

LIEUTENANT PORTUONDO It looks as if you're not well disposed towards
visitors, *compañera*.

MARIA CELIA What can I do for you?

LIEUTENANT PORTUONDO This letter . . .

MARIA CELIA I wrote it.

LIEUTENANT PORTUONDO Well, I received it a few days ago . . .

MARIA CELIA I sent it to the ministry.

LIEUTENANT PORTUONDO Then we need to talk. We need to have a private
conversation.

Looks at SOFIA. *She exits. He strolls around the room.*

Your letter is more like a petition or an application.
What sort of thing are you applying for?

MARIA CELIA I'm asking you to put an end to the postal theft.
You hold up all my letters from abroad.
You open up all my correspondence, I haven't received a letter
from my husband in almost three months.

LIEUTENANT PORTUONDO (*smiles*) You're absolutely beautiful, *compañera*.
I remember the first day they brought you to the ministry.
I couldn't look at you too much.
(*Opens file*) I must say, this picture on your file doesn't do you justice.
I should try to get a photographer in here and photograph you again.

MARIA CELIA I don't like to have my picture taken, Lieutenant.
Can you do something about my mail, or not?

LIEUTENANT PORTUONDO I suppose I can do a lot about your mail.

Opens his knapsack. Pulls out two packs of letters tied up with a black ribbon.

You receive a considerable amount of correspondence. Dangerous correspondence. Someone found a weapon inside a letter the other day. I was
informed that one of our officers at the post office almost bled to death.
They found these razor blades inside an envelope. (*Produces razor blades*)

MARIA CELIA They shouldn't have gone through my mail.

LIEUTENANT PORTUONDO Is that a provocation, *compañera*?

MARIA CELIA I just want . . .

LIEUTENANT PORTUONDO Is somebody sending you razor blades so you can slice someone's throat? Or are you going to do some harm to yourself?

MARIA CELIA Those are for my legs, Lieutenant. To shave my legs.

LIEUTENANT PORTUONDO Our Soviet razors don't cut it for you?

MARIA CELIA I thought we were going to talk about my mail.

LIEUTENANT PORTUONDO We are talking about your mail. The razors.

SOFIA (*interrupting*) Would you like some water, Lieutenant?

LIEUTENANT PORTUONDO No, thank you, *compañera*.

SOFIA Maria Celia?

MARIA CELIA No, thank you.

SOFIA *exits.*

LIEUTENANT PORTUONDO This sort of thing is considered a weapon, illegal . . . Don't you know that?

MARIA CELIA I didn't send it, Lieutenant.

LIEUTENANT PORTUONDO (*pulls out a small sample package of moisturizing lotion*) I gather this is for your legs, too . . . Lotion de rose . . . Smells of roses, France. Who is this Monsieur Lamont? He writes to you often, sends you lots of things. Did you give your legs to this man?

MARIA CELIA Look, you don't have the right . . .

LIEUTENANT PORTUONDO Let me see your legs, *compañera*. (*She walks to another part of the room, disregarding him*) Yes, you have nice legs. You deserve rose lotion for those legs. I'll consent to the razors and the lotion. Back in prison you wouldn't be allowed to receive these things. Are you in love with this man?

MARIA CELIA I don't think that's important . . .

LIEUTENANT PORTUONDO Was he your lover?

MARIA CELIA No.

LIEUTENANT PORTUONDO No?

MARIA CELIA He's a friend.

LIEUTENANT PORTUONDO And all the romantic letters?

MARIA CELIA I don't know about any romantic letters.

LIEUTENANT PORTUONDO You don't know about any romantic letters.

MARIA CELIA No, I don't know. How would I know when I don't get any mail?

LIEUTENANT PORTUONDO You're pretty good at keeping a straight face when you lie. Your husband in America is slipping correspondence through France, using the name André Lamont. I have them all here.

MARIA CELIA I don't know what you're talking about.

LIEUTENANT PORTUONDO You know what I'm talking about!!!!

MARIA CELIA (*with contained anger*) Why do you keep on insisting
that I know, that I know?!
What am I supposed to know?!
What am I supposed to do when I live in this hole!

Pause.

(*Takes a hold of herself*) Please—I'm not asking for much.

LIEUTENANT PORTUONDO I can't give you any mail—not when your husband
is going to every human rights commission,
spreading bile against our system.
Not when he's trying to publish your book in France.
You must know all about it. I have all the information here,
"Les Editions de Minuit will publish in October the translation of
The Seagrape, by Maria Celia Obispo.
(*Mockingly*) Imagine, *compañera* . . . *Foi, foi* . . . *La vie shoo, shoo* . . .
Just a few months from now your book will be all over France,
Europe. Isn't that something, *compañera*?
Makes me hungry, that name—Minuit.
Reminds me of mignon, filet mignon.
It's amazing that a word like that can make your mouth water.
(*Arranges the letters*) Means *midnight* in French, doesn't it?
A lot of money, this Minuit company—your father and your husband

are going to get rich from your books.
Lots of lonely people out there in the world—empty beds . . .
I've been reading one of your books. That's my new bed companion.
Can you believe it, *compañera*?

MARIA CELIA People should read whatever they like.

LIEUTENANT PORTUONDO What makes you think I like your books?

MARIA CELIA Who cares what I think, Lieutenant? You could be one of
those people who reads books to fall asleep at night.

LIEUTENANT PORTUONDO Oh, I read for meaning, *compañera* . . .
What was that line I like so much in your story?
"There was that fugitive night in her"—
Is that the way it goes? You don't know what those words do to me.
Does that surprise you, *compañera*, that I'm reading your book?

MARIA CELIA Nothing surprises me, Lieutenant.

LIEUTENANT PORTUONDO Well, I don't see the big fuss about your books.
All the delegations say they're bourgeois propaganda, antirevolutionary,
people's blood boils with indignation, but I'm not of the same opinion.
I'm probably your number one fan.

MARIA CELIA Oh, just give it up, Lieutenant! I've gone through all the mind
games!

SOFIA *comes in with a coffee tray.*

SOFIA *Café.* I made some *café* . . . Thought you would like some,
Lieutenant.

LIEUTENANT PORTUONDO Why don't you tell your sister that I didn't come
here to do her harm?

SOFIA I hope not. (*He takes a cup*) If you kill her,
she'll come back from the dead, right, Maria Celia?
(*Smiles. Takes sides with her*) She'll pull you by the feet when you're asleep
and haunt you for the rest of your life. You don't know my sister.

LIEUTENANT PORTUONDO Yes, you're right, I don't know your sister. (*Sipping
coffee and looking at her*) But I'd sure like to get to know her.

SOFIA Maria Celia . . . The Lieutenant is talking about you. He wants to get to know you. You want *café*?

MARIA CELIA No.

SOFIA Is that the mail you have in your knapsack? If you give her the mail you'll have her on your good side.

LIEUTENANT PORTUONDO And what's her good side like?

SOFIA He wants to know about your good side, Maria Celia?

MARIA CELIA Did you start cooking the beans?

SOFIA They're cooking. They're cooking all right. (*Looks at him then at her*) There's a good side to her cooking, I can tell you that much.

LIEUTENANT PORTUONDO So she's a good cook.

SOFIA The best chicken fricassee in town.

LIEUTENANT PORTUONDO Best chicken fricassee.

SOFIA Get her a chicken. Give her the mail, and she'll make you chicken fricassee.

LIEUTENANT PORTUONDO Is it true that you're a good cook?

MARIA CELIA Am I going to get anything out of this?! Am I going to get my mail or do I have to put myself through a hunger strike?! Do I have to starve to get somebody's attention?! . . .

LIEUTENANT PORTUONDO I'm sorry, *compañera*. I can't let you read about your husband's tactics.

MARIA CELIA I don't care about his tactics. I just want to know about him. If he's dead or alive, if he's sick or in good health! If he's still my husband, for God's sake!

LIEUTENANT PORTUONDO If he's still your husband! . . . So he is your husband!

MARIA CELIA Please . . . *compañero*, if you don't mind, I'd like you to go now.

LIEUTENANT PORTUONDO No, I'm not leaving till we finish this talk.
Let me give you some advice, *compañera* . . . You should write a letter to
your husband and let him know that all those public denunciations he
made, maybe got you out of prison, but that's not going to get you out of
this country . . . Do you understand? This concerns you, too, Sofia.
(*To* MARIA CELIA) If you want to write him about this, I'll make sure the
letter gets to him.

MARIA CELIA Thank you, Lieutenant.

LIEUTENANT PORTUONDO (*strolls around the room*) When do you usually write
your stories, *compañera*?

Silence. SOFIA *looks at* MARIA CELIA *and makes her way to her.*

SOFIA She doesn't write, Lieutenant. She stopped writing.

LIEUTENANT PORTUONDO Oh, I know she writes. Her husband talks about a
story she was going to send to him. A new story. Something about a man
and a woman in a glass tower, stolen boats . . . I want to know if I could
read it.

MARIA CELIA I never finished it. I threw it away.

LIEUTENANT PORTUONDO Is it a love story?

Pause.

I'm asking you if it's a love story.

SOFIA Her stories are always about love, Lieutenant.

LIEUTENANT PORTUONDO Can I have a moment alone with your sister?

SOFIA Sure.

SOFIA *exits.*

LIEUTENANT PORTUONDO So what happened to this story?

MARIA CELIA I threw it away.

LIEUTENANT PORTUONDO What would it take for you to write it down again?

MARIA CELIA It would probably be very different now.
It always happens with stories, they change.

LIEUTENANT PORTUONDO Then you still have it in you.

MARIA CELIA Nothing really goes away, Lieutenant.

LIEUTENANT PORTUONDO What if I pay you to write it again?

MARIA CELIA You? It sounds like you're asking me to write my own death sentence. Or have you forgotten why we're still locked up in here? That would be a risk, don't you think?

LIEUTENANT PORTUONDO It seems like everything is. My asking you to accept payment. My standing here talking to you about this . . .

MARIA CELIA It's not the same. You are the lieutenant.

LIEUTENANT PORTUONDO No. We run the same risk. There will be the evidence of the payments, if you let me pay you to write it down.

MARIA CELIA There is no evidence in money. It's a bunch of papers with number signs.

LIEUTENANT PORTUONDO So how can it be done? I want to know about this story. Would you consent to tell me all about it, if I let you have all of these? (*Refers to the letters*)

MARIA CELIA That would certainly compromise you, if you let me have all the letters.

LIEUTENANT PORTUONDO You're right. But I can always read them to you.

MARIA CELIA Then you don't want any evidence either. It has to be a clean crime.

LIEUTENANT PORTUONDO Well, if you want to put it that way. I'm willing to read you the letters.

MARIA CELIA I have more to lose than you do. You know that.

LIEUTENANT PORTUONDO Why don't you think about it. You don't have to give me an answer now. Good day, *compañera*!

The LIEUTENANT *exits.*

MARIA CELIA (*in a loud voice*) Sofia, come out. Are you there?

SOFIA *comes out.*

Were you listening? Did you see all those letters?
Did you see the whole pack? Hundreds of them.

SOFIA I knew Antonio hadn't forgotten you. I knew.

Lights fade to black.

Scene 2: The Bedspreads of Desire

Daytime.
Soft grayish white lights.
It is raining outside.
The sisters are knitting.

SOFIA We're almost out of the good yarn.

MARIA CELIA What's wrong with this other yarn?

SOFIA It's tough on my hands. It's like steel wool for scouring pots. You start weaving and purling with that thing and you'll end up with minced meat for hands.

MARIA CELIA That's the only yarn we have left.

SOFIA I have to protect my hands.

MARIA CELIA Use a pair of gloves. If we don't knit there won't be any bedspreads. And if there's no bedspreads what are we going to give Cirilo to sell? Come on, pick up where you left off.

SOFIA (*wipes her forehead*) It's days like this I could play the piano the whole day.

MARIA CELIA I bet. You tell me that every day.

SOFIA I can't play it anymore. The piano is falling apart.

MARIA CELIA What about the permit you got to have it tuned?

SOFIA I sent for a piano tuner—hasn't shown up.

MARIA CELIA Give it some time.

SOFIA (*stands up, shakes her hands*) Look at my hands,
veins starting to show up from all this knitting.
That's always been my fear. On men the veins look good.
On men, yes—because it makes them look strong and virile,
like their plumbing works well and lots of blood flows through
all their parts. I hate those needles. I hate all this knitting.

MARIA CELIA I know. You tell me every time we knit.

SOFIA Oscarito had lots of veins like a Roman aqueduct. Everywhere.
I loved how they showed his strength. All the rivers from his heart.
Oh, I feel like listening to music. I wish I had a glass of rum with ice.
A man . . . A man, is what I wish I had . . . I loved doing it when it rained.
(*Stretches*)

MARIA CELIA You sound like a cat in heat.

SOFIA Take a break, for God's sake! I don't know where you get all that
energy, when all we had to eat were eggs and mangoes.

MARIA CELIA I'm tired, but I keep at it. I keep at it.

SOFIA If the lieutenant comes again you should ask him if he could get us
something to eat.

MARIA CELIA I told you I'm not going to ask him for food.

SOFIA Why not? He could make life easier for us.

MARIA CELIA No. I've been thinking of having him read me the letters
and that's all.

SOFIA Are you really going to do it?

MARIA CELIA I'm not going to give him any papers.
I'm just going to tell him the story.

SOFIA I wouldn't do it. He'll find something in it. It always happens.

MARIA CELIA What could he possibly find? It's a simple love story, for God's
sake!

SOFIA He could testify against you. You keep me out of it.

MARIA CELIA Keep you out of it, and you want me to ask him for food!

SOFIA Well, we have it bad as it is.
I don't want anything else to do with your writing.

MARIA CELIA I can't believe you!
I can't believe the things that come out of your mouth!
You might as well turn me in.
Sometimes I don't understand you.
I don't. Nobody to trust. Nobody to talk to.
Nothing but rust. Just rust, eating away everything.

SOFIA (*sits down and starts to knit*) I didn't mean it that way.

MARIA CELIA Forget I said anything.

SOFIA You know I'd do anything for you. Come on, tell me the story. At least tell me the name.

MARIA CELIA Like the Gottschalk song you play on the piano.

SOFIA Which one?

MARIA CELIA "La Savana."

SOFIA Why that name?

MARIA CELIA I don't know. One day it came to me, the whole story.

The music of Gottschalk is heard.

You were playing that song on the piano.
I'd never heard it that way before. The whole music . . .
I felt as if I had to leave my body. I went to the sea. Next minute,
I was writing about this man and this woman in the marina.
The story had gotten inside me like a sickness.
For three days I stayed up at night writing.
The woman in the story, it all came to me that day.
She goes to visit him at the marina when he's on duty.
She always tells him that she wants to know about the sea . . .
She wants to learn from him. The first night she goes to him,
she asks if he eats alone, and he tells her that he does.
She tells him it's sad to see men having dinner alone.

A person should never eat alone.
She asks him if she could cook for him,
that they could have dinner together overlooking the sea.

SOFIA Does he accept?

MARIA CELIA He's not allowed to receive visitors when he's on duty.
But she tells him that she wouldn't be a visitor,
she'd only come to bring him food.

SOFIA That'd be something I would say.
And I would show up to see him even if he said no.
I'd show up in a white dress.

MARIA CELIA She wears a white dress.

SOFIA Maybe a long blue scarf, to go with the sea, white sandals and a parasol.

MARIA CELIA It's nighttime, Sofie. Why would she have a parasol?

SOFIA That's true. You said it was nighttime. I'm sorry. You took me there with the story. (*Laughs*) —Do you realize this is going to be another summer that we won't be able to go to the sea?

MARIA CELIA Yes. I know.

SOFIA I was sitting there with him at the marina with a picnic basket. My feet dangling from the pier . . . And me occasionally dipping my toes in the water, then looking at him.

MARIA CELIA They meet on a tower, Sofie. A glass tower, and it's not a picnic.

SOFIA Go on. Don't mind me. I'm making your story into something else.

MARIA CELIA Now I forgot where I was.

SOFIA The glass tower.

MARIA CELIA Yes the glass tower surrounded by blue boats . . . Fishermen retrieving their nets from the sea. Seagulls.

SOFIA Yes, lots of seagulls.

MARIA CELIA The woman walks by the sea taking puffs from her
cigarette, leaving smoke behind like a steamship.
She climbs the stairs to the glass tower. She goes to see him,
with her purse full of bread, rice, plantains, beans, boiled
eggs, avocados, guava marmalade, napkins, forks, spoons,
salt, and pepper. A whole restaurant in her little bag.

SOFIA That should be the name of the story,
"Picnic by the Light of the Moon."
I guess you can tell him all about it.
What could be wrong with a picnic in a marina?
But don't show him any papers.

VICTOR MANUEL Sofia . . .

Both sisters look at each other.

SOFIA Someone called my name.

There's a knock at the door.

VICTOR MANUEL Sofia . . .

MARIA CELIA Who is it?

VICTOR MANUEL Victor Manuel.

MARIA CELIA Who?

VICTOR MANUEL Victor Manuel . . . I came to take a look at the piano.

Pause. The two sisters look at each other again.

SOFIA Yes . . . yes . . . Coming . . . Coming . . . —It's the piano tuner . . .
The piano tuner . . . And me looking like a mess! Do I look all right?

MARIA CELIA Open the door . . .

VICTOR MANUEL Open up . . . It's raining up a storm out here.

SOFIA *rushes to the door. She fixes her hair a little and looks down at her clothes
to see if she's presentable. She opens the door.*
VICTOR MANUEL *enters.*

VICTOR MANUEL What a storm . . . What a storm . . . It's a monsoon
out there. (*Notices* SOFIA. *Reaches out for her hand*) Polita sent me here with
this permit. She told me the piano needs tuning.

He takes out a handkerchief.

Which one is Sofia?

SOFIA Me. I'm Sofia.

VICTOR MANUEL I'm Victor Manuel.

MARIA CELIA And I'm Maria Celia, her sister.

He shakes her hand.

VICTOR MANUEL At your service, *compañera*.

SOFIA (*stares at him. Becomes nervous. Awkward pause*) The piano is right
here. We didn't know you were coming. (*Uncovers the piano*) My sister
covered it as if it was a child. (*He looks at her*) Humidity!

He plays the piano. Then plays individual keys.

VICTOR MANUEL Yes, it sounds bad. (*Key*) Yes, bad. (*Key*) Bad. (*Key*) Bad.
(*Key*) It buzzes a little. Hear that . . . (*Key*)
I'll have to check the soundboard and the ribs.

Takes out a flashlight from his pocket. Inspects underneath the piano.

When was the last time you had the piano tuned?

SOFIA I guess more than two years ago. (*Looks at* MARIA CELIA)

VICTOR MANUEL Neglect ruins a piano, *compañera*. It's in real bad shape.
When a piano is neglected, it dies. It's like a plant, a tree.
When you don't water a tree, it withers away.

Continues talking as he inspects the inside of the piano.

I always say there should be mandatory rules for the use of pianos.
If they are not being played . . . If they're not being put to good use,
they should be donated to schools, hospitals, recreational parks.
The Interior Ministry should intervene in this matter.

Take inventory of all the pianos in the city, number them all and
place them into categories, "The so-and-so family, living at such-and-such
address, makes use of their piano. The so-and-so family,
at this other address, uses the piano for family pictures and ashtrays."
That's the only way we're going get rid of the old system of using
pianos for decoration. The old way of showing wealth and social class,
through a piano in the living room.

MARIA CELIA We're not bourgeois, *compañero*, if that's what you're
implying.

VICTOR MANUEL I'm talking to myself, *compañera*. I'm talking to myself.
(*To* SOFIA *now*) There's some rust and corrosion on the metal parts.
Some of the felt has to be changed . . . Some of the wires have to
be replaced. You also have to change some of the wood in the bottom . . .
See in there . . .

SOFIA What's wrong with it?

VICTOR MANUEL It's rotting. It looks like water got inside the piano.

MARIA CELIA The dogs got in here, wrecked the whole place apart,
stole things when the house got closed up.
It's a good thing they didn't take an ax and chop it to pieces.

SOFIA Maria Celia . . . please . . . So what should we do? Can you fix it?

VICTOR MANUEL Well, I suppose I can fix some things. As far as the wood
in the bottom, that would mean dismantling some parts and having them
custom-made. That will mean sending the piano to a repair place, where
they can do that kind of work.

SOFIA Where is this place?

VICTOR MANUEL The only one I know is in Oriente.

SOFIA Well, if it needs to be sent there . . .

MARIA CELIA That's like saying the Himalayas. It would cost a fortune.
We don't have that kind of money.
—Can't you fix it somehow and make it sound pretty again?

VICTOR MANUEL Well, I can certainly try. I'm just telling you about the major problems.

MARIA CELIA You haven't told us how much you'll charge us.

VICTOR MANUEL Twenty . . .

MARIA CELIA Twenty? That's a lot of money.

VICTOR MANUEL That's how much I charge.

MARIA CELIA Ten pesos. That's how much we can afford.

VICTOR MANUEL *Compañera*, that's not enough to buy a can of sardines. How about five dollars? . . . Five if you have dollars.

MARIA CELIA We don't have dollars, and that's too much money for just pulling a couple of strings.

VICTOR MANUEL (*starts placing his tools in his bag*) Well, that takes care of that. Perhaps I should leave.
You're wasting my time . . . And time is money.
Money you won't spare. Money you don't have.

SOFIA No . . . Please. Don't leave. Wait one second.

SOFIA *exits.* **VICTOR MANUEL** *looks at* **MARIA CELIA**.

VICTOR MANUEL Where is she going? What is she going to do? I can't be wasting my time. I have other appointments. With all the celebrations for the Pan American games, everybody wants their pianos tuned. You know it's the big event this year. Parties everywhere. There's people here from all over the world. —I'm sorry. Here I am carrying on and you stuck in this house . . .

MARIA CELIA It's all right, *compañero*. It's all right . . .

VICTOR MANUEL It's a shame what happened to you and your sister.
You know, I've read some of your stories.
The one about the woman who walks into the sea.
I never thought the books were . . . You know . . .

MARIA CELIA What?

VICTOR MANUEL   I mean . . . The books . . . It's a shame you started writing other kinds of material.

MARIA CELIA   What are you trying to get at, *compañero?*

VICTOR MANUEL   I mean . . . The . . . The new material . . . Your new stories. Your views, *compañera.* How you changed your opinion about the revolution.

MARIA CELIA   Is this an interrogation, *compañero?*

VICTOR MANUEL   No, of course not. Why would you say that?

MARIA CELIA   Then why all the little questions?

VICTOR MANUEL   I'm . . . *compañera,* please, I didn't mean to pry. Polita asked me to come and tune the piano . . . She gave me this permit.

MARIA CELIA   Anybody can say that, *compañero.* Anybody can grab a doctor's bag like yours . . .

VICTOR MANUEL   Now, look! . . . Look, I can show you my identity card.

MARIA CELIA   What identity card? The government can fabricate those in a blink. How do I know you don't have a recording machine inside your doctor's bag, under your shirt?

VICTOR MANUEL   (*opens the bag, furiously*) Look . . . I don't . . . I don't . . .

Shows her the bag and drops it on the floor. He opens his shirt and shows her his belly.

Look . . . You can see . . . I have nothing under my shirt.

MARIA CELIA *doesn't look.* SOFIA *enters with a shoe box.*

VICTOR MANUEL   You want to look inside my pants? You want to see inside my pants?

Starts to unfasten his pants.

SOFIA   What's going on?

VICTOR MANUEL   Your sister wants to look inside my pants! She says I'm an informer. Now here's my identity card. So, have I wasted my time by coming here or are you going to tune the piano?

SOFIA Yes, of course. Maria Celia, please . . .

MARIA CELIA We can only afford twenty pesos. That's all we can afford.

MARIA CELIA *exits.* SOFIA *looks at* VICTOR MANUEL.

SOFIA (*kneels down and opens the shoe box*) I wanted to know if these shoes
fit you. They're new. They belonged to my father. I thought this would
make up for the rest of the money we don't have.

VICTOR MANUEL (*closes his eyes in disbelief*) Ave Maria purisima!

SOFIA Please . . . These are almost brand new.
If the shoes don't fit, you can always sell them.

VICTOR MANUEL *is trying to control himself. He brings his hand to his forehead
as if trying to make sense of the whole situation.* SOFIA *is now trying to take off
his shoes.*

SOFIA Please try them on.

VICTOR MANUEL What are you doing?

SOFIA What size do you wear? (*Gently tries to lift up his foot*) I think these
are a nine and a half. Is that your size?

VICTOR MANUEL No, thank you, *compañera*. I wear a nine. Don't touch . . .

SOFIA They'll fit you. These are nine and a half. (*Trying to take off his shoes*)

VICTOR MANUEL Please, *compañera*, don't . . . Please, lady, don't . . . Please . . .
Don't touch . . . My feet are ticklish . . . (*Tries to keep from laughing*)
Don't . . . (*Laughs*) . . . Don't touch my feet, please . . . (*Tries on the shoes*)
I can put them on by myself! . . . I never let anybody touch my feet!

SOFIA How do they fit?

VICTOR MANUEL The left one feels . . .

SOFIA Good leather.

VICTOR MANUEL Well . . . I . . . I don't . . . (*Feels the comfort of the shoes*)
They actually . . . I . . . I mean . . . I can actually use a new pair of shoes.

He's walking around the room to get a feel for the shoes.

You have nothing to worry about . . . We'll give the piano a quick fix. The rest can be solved later. If a 1956 Chevy can run with Soviet parts, I can make this piano sound like a concert grand.

Goes for the bag and opens it.
There is a knock at the door. VICTOR MANUEL *looks at* SOFIA. SOFIA *is motionless.*

LIEUTENANT PORTUONDO *(offstage)* Can't you see the puddle, jerk! The streets aren't just for cars.
(Knocks again) Maria Celia . . . *(One more knock)*

SOFIA *goes to open the door.*
LIEUTENANT PORTUONDO *comes in. He speaks rapidly as he takes off his raincoat. He holds a package.*

LIEUTENANT PORTUONDO *(straightening his clothes)* —What a storm out there! We'll be swimming like fish by the time September gets here . . .
(Opens a paper bag) I brought some food, maybe it got all wet.

The LIEUTENANT *looks up and notices.* VICTOR MANUEL. *He's surprised to see him. He acts formal.*

SOFIA He's tuning the piano.

LIEUTENANT PORTUONDO Can I see your identity card, *compañero?*

SOFIA He's got a permit. He's got a permit from one of the inspectors to tune the piano.

VICTOR MANUEL *(shows him the permit)* Just servicing the piano, *compañero.* Just here for work.

MARIA CELIA *enters the room.*

SOFIA The lieutenant is here to see you, Maria Celia.

MARIA CELIA Good afternoon, Lieutenant.

LIEUTENANT PORTUONDO Good afternoon, *compañera.*
Thank you, *compañero.* *(Gives him back the card)*

MARIA CELIA Come this way, Lieutenant.

The LIEUTENANT *and* MARIA CELIA *move to the left of the stage. The lights shift to this area.*

MARIA CELIA Did you think we hired a piano tuner without a permit from the inspectors?

LIEUTENANT PORTUONDO Just doing my job, *compañera.*
(*Giving her the bag*) I brought you some food. I know it's hard to get food nowadays.

MARIA CELIA That's kind of you, Lieutenant.

LIEUTENANT PORTUONDO Also brought you these books, thought you might like to read them. (*Gives her the books*)
Simone de Beauvoir. Have you read her?

MARIA CELIA Not this one.

LIEUTENANT PORTUONDO Good. Now you have a book to read.

MARIA CELIA And this book on perestroika?

LIEUTENANT PORTUONDO What about it?

MARIA CELIA Why are you giving me this book?

LIEUTENANT PORTUONDO Thought you might like it.

MARIA CELIA Are you testing me, Lieutenant?

LIEUTENANT PORTUONDO No. Not at all. You're too suspicious, *compañera.* Don't you like perestroika? Didn't you and all your artist friends send a letter to the government about perestroika?

MARIA CELIA I have this book.

LIEUTENANT PORTUONDO Then I'll take it back.

MARIA CELIA Wasn't it also taken off the shelves?
I had to buy it from someone off the streets—exchanged a whole bag of rice for it.

LIEUTENANT PORTUONDO That's almost a month of rice on your table.

MARIA CELIA It's food for thought, Lieutenant. What we've forgotten on this island, to feed the mind. The fact that there are revolutions within revolutions. Are you recording what I'm saying? Is this why you brought these books, for me to run my mouth, and see if I've gone through political rehabilitation?

LIEUTENANT PORTUONDO No. Not at all. On the contrary, I'm giving them to you because I thought you would like them. The one with the blue cover, this poet always writes about the sea, like you. I'll pretend I never gave them to you. I'm not a demon, *compañera*. I hope with time you'll learn to trust me. See, I trust you already. (*Pulls out a letter from his pocket*) I brought you a letter from your husband. I can read you part of it. Full letter if you decide to go ahead with the agreement. Would you like me to read you some?

MARIA CELIA If you like.

He looks at her. He opens the letter. She closes her eyes. Piano music swells, "Chason de Gitane," by Gottschalk. Lights fade down on MARIA CELIA *and the* LIEUTENANT. *Lights fade up on the other side of the stage.* VICTOR MANUEL *is playing the piano.* SOFIA *stands next to him, lost in the music. After a while the song finishes.*

SOFIA What is it about that song? What is it about music?
It just goes right to your soul.
Why isn't this kind of music played on the radio?
Why are we neglecting it?

VICTOR MANUEL Oh, I don't neglect it. It's my favorite song. I play it all the time.

SOFIA You do. But try playing it in public and people will say you're bourgeois and sentimental . . . We don't play Lecuona because he was too romantic, Gershwin because he was American, Chopin because he was European.
It's like everything old reeks of death.
But how can one talk about these things, Victor Manuel?

VICTOR MANUEL Well . . . I . . . I . . . I don't know . . . I—

SOFIA Does it make you uncomfortable to talk about it?

VICTOR MANUEL No . . . No . . . I play what I like in my house.
I play this kind of music all the time. It's what I love.
I don't know about other people, but I still play it.

SOFIA How come I never met you before?

VICTOR MANUEL Oh, I don't know, I used to work at Carrion's piano store,
before it burned down.

SOFIA Yes . . . I remember when it happened, couldn't walk through that
street, after the fire. I couldn't bear to see all those melted pianos.

VICTOR MANUEL Well, I should be running along. I really ought to be going.
It's raining less now . . .

SOFIA Please, stay with me a while longer.
It's not every day I get to talk about the music I love.
And sometimes, you never know who you can talk to.
But you . . . My sister says I'm a fool because I trust any
person who comes in here and stands in front of me . . .
Because I speak my mind . . . Because I haven't lost the habit of
saying things the way they're meant to be said . . .
When you came here I thought . . . I thought . . .

VICTOR MANUEL That I came to interrogate you . . .

SOFIA You talked about the inventory of pianos.
For a moment I thought you were going to . . .

VICTOR MANUEL Take away the piano? No. I wouldn't. I wouldn't do
that to you.

SOFIA (*touches the piano*) More than ninety years living in this house. Part
of the family. My mother played it, my grandfather. He's like an old uncle.
Probably the only one who still takes me out for a walk.
Would you come back? (SOFIA *holds his hand*)
Why don't you come back tomorrow?

VICTOR MANUEL Look, I'd . . . I'd like to . . . But I don't know . . . You and
your sister . . . This permit . . .

SOFIA You can always say you haven't finished tuning the piano.
You have a permit.

VICTOR MANUEL I mean . . . I wouldn't know . . . It's difficult . . . It's risking . . .

SOFIA I understand. (*There are tears in her eyes*)

VICTOR MANUEL Look, I would like to. I like talking to you.

Pause. Gently lifts up her chin.

Please, you're making me feel . . .

SOFIA (*more contained*) It's all right. I understand.

Silence. He gathers some of his instruments and places them inside his bag. He looks at her.

VICTOR MANUEL How about next week, I'll be less busy. The end of the games. I'll try to come.

SOFIA All right.

She kisses him.

VICTOR MANUEL Tuesday then.

He walks to the doorway. Then turns to her and waves good-bye. Lights change to MARIA CELIA *sitting on a chair. The* LIEUTENANT *stands behind her.*

MARIA CELIA Would you read me part of another letter, Lieutenant?

LIEUTENANT PORTUONDO If you want.

He looks at her. He opens another letter and begins to read.

My dear love: A few moments ago I woke up and walked to the store to buy writing paper, and I stopped by the bay. I stood there facing the water thinking of you.

MARIA CELIA Please, read slower . . .

He looks at her. MARIA CELIA *closes her eyes.*

LIEUTENANT PORTUONDO I remembered how much you like to sit by the sea-wall and write for hours. The whole blue landscape had me holding your arms, your whole body once again. How I love your skin, your smell . . .

MARIA CELIA Slower . . .

LIEUTENANT PORTUONDO How much slower do you want me to read?

MARIA CELIA Just a little slower if you're not going to read me the whole thing. (*Closes her eyes to listen*)

LIEUTENANT PORTUONDO I spent a couple of weeks in Sweden.
I wonder if you got my postcard.
I bought you a beautiful book on butterflies.
I know how much you like them. Such a long time since
I heard from you last.
I've been in absolute torture for months now,
but I don't let the dogs eat away my hopes to see you again.
I go nuts counting every day and week that goes by,
and I just want the moment to come when I can have you free.
(*No longer reading the letter, but looking at her*) I close my eyes
and try to imagine that day, when I can undress you
like the first time and discover you all over again.
Enter every secret place in your body.
I want to make love for weeks and months, make up for all the lost time.

MARIA CELIA You can stop now.

He pretends to be reading.

You can stop.

LIEUTENANT PORTUONDO Are you all right, *compañera*?

MARIA CELIA Yes.

LIEUTENANT PORTUONDO Your husband is mad about you.

MARIA CELIA He misses me.

LIEUTENANT PORTUONDO I don't blame him. I would miss you, too, if I were him. Have a good afternoon, *compañera*.

The LIEUTENANT *exits. The stage is fully lit now.*
MARIA CELIA *is sitting on the sofa.* SOFIA *runs to her.*

SOFIA Maria Celia, what did he bring us?

MARIA CELIA (*lost in thought*) He read me part of a letter. I wish you could've heard him read it to me. For a moment I thought Antonio was in the room. It was like listening to him talk.

SOFIA What did it have to say?

MARIA CELIA Oh, Sofie, you know the secret codes Antonio uses in his letters, the butterflies . . .

SOFIA Yes.

MARIA CELIA He's been to Sweden.

SOFIA Sweden?

MARIA CELIA Yes. He's trying to find us political asylum there. He said he bought me a book on butterflies and that's what it means. He's still trying to get us out . . .

SOFIA What else did the letter say?

MARIA CELIA He didn't read me the whole thing.

SOFIA Why not?

MARIA CELIA There was probably information he thought I shouldn't know about.

SOFIA I noticed all the food he brought us. Maybe he means well after all.

MARIA CELIA Maybe he does. But we still have to be careful.

SOFIA What did you think of the piano tuner?

MARIA CELIA He kept on asking me questions about my books.

SOFIA But did you notice his hands?

MARIA CELIA No. I was too concerned with his eyes, trying to look through him.

SOFIA They're soft and gentle. I saw his soul in his hands.

MARIA CELIA Oh, dear.

SOFIA What? I've invited him over, and he said he'll come next week . . .

MARIA CELIA Are you crazy! You had to get a permit to have him come in this house . . .

SOFIA So what? If somebody interrogates him,
he can say that he hasn't finished tuning the piano.

MARIA CELIA You don't know this man, and you're inviting him over.

SOFIA You have no faith in anybody.

MARIA CELIA It's hard to know who's who.

SOFIA That's no way to live! I don't want to be that way . . . You're not yourself anymore. You used to be so free and giving.

MARIA CELIA You're right. I'm not myself anymore. Sometimes I don't know how else to be.

SOFIA I think it stopped raining. Let's go upstairs to the roof to get some fresh air.

MARIA CELIA Wait. If I tell the lieutenant about my new writing, I want you to be in the room when he reads me the letters. I want you to be a witness.

SOFIA Anything you want. It can all be done quietly. We can live life quietly . . .

MARIA CELIA Maybe sometime soon we'll be free. Sooner than we think, tear down these walls and walk out of this house.

The music of Gottschalk plays.
Lights fade to black.

End of Act I.

Act II

Scene 1: Waiting for Him on Top of My Roof

Evening.
As the lights start to dim we hear music.
Lights fade up on SOFIA *sitting on a chair. She wears a simple colorful dress.*
MARIA CELIA *stands behind her combing her hair.* SOFIA *is applying lipstick and looks into a small compact mirror.* MARIA CELIA's *mind wanders to her letter writing while she combs her sister's hair.*

MARIA CELIA My dear love: I write to you in my mind, on my skin,
even when I go about doing housework.
Tonight Sofie has invited to dinner the man
who tuned the piano—not that we can afford another dish on our table,
but we'll have a visitor for a change.

SOFIA *gets up and climbs upstairs to the roof.*
She stares into the distance waiting for VICTOR MANUEL.
MARIA CELIA *walks around the room with a cloth dusting the sofa and the piano.*

There are fewer and fewer products in the markets these days.
We're running out of everything.
We use milk of magnesia for deodorant. Soon we'll be out of lipstick and
we'll have to use beet juice to color our lips. I probably sound vain,
because lipstick isn't necessary, but it's good to add a touch of red to the
face for those blue days.

SOFIA Maria Celia . . . I think I see him coming . . . Warm up the food. I
think he's coming this way . . . He's walking down the street . . . I think it's
him . . .

MARIA CELIA (*in a loud voice*) Shouldn't I wait till he's actually here? This is
the third time I've warmed up the food.

SOFIA I think it's him walking this way . . .

MARIA CELIA Are you sure this time? It's almost nine thirty now.

SOFIA It's got to be him.

MARIA CELIA Just come down, Sofie . . . Come down . . .

SOFIA Wait . . . First I want to see . . .

MARIA CELIA You've been up and down from that roof the whole night.

SOFIA He's crossing the street now . . .

MARIA CELIA Is it him?

SOFIA (*climbs down from the roof and enters the house*) You're right, he's not coming . . . It wasn't him.

MARIA CELIA Oh, Sofie, maybe something happened.
Don't get that way. Maybe he went to one of the games.
You know how men are, they are like children when it comes to sports.
Maybe he's afraid of being seen here.
Come on, cheer up . . . You and I will have dinner.
I'm going to play a record, we'll have a good time.
I want you to dance with me. Come on . . .

MARIA CELIA *goes behind the sofa and plays a fast Cuban song.*

Dance with me . . . Dance . . .

The music livens up the mood. MARIA CELIA *starts dancing with* SOFIA . . .
She gives in to the dance. They start showing off their best steps and turns. They laugh as they enjoy their dancing. There is a knock at the door. MARIA CELIA *goes to turn off the music. There is another knock.* SOFIA *fixes her hair and her clothes and goes to open the door, expecting the piano tuner.* LIEUTENANT PORTUONDO *enters dressed in a summer suit.*

LIEUTENANT PORTUONDO Listening to music?

SOFIA Yes . . . We . . . We were . . .

Pause.

LIEUTENANT PORTUONDO Celebrating the end of the Pan American games?

SOFIA / MARIA CELIA No . . .

MARIA CELIA We're . . . just . . . just listening to some records . . .

LIEUTENANT PORTUONDO You're all dressed up this evening.

MARIA CELIA (*nervously*) We are . . . Aren't we? . . . tired of the same clothes.

LIEUTENANT PORTUONDO I brought some rum, thought maybe you'd like to have a drink with me.

SOFIA No. You'll have to excuse me, Lieutenant, I'm going to bed.

MARIA CELIA Stay up awhile longer.

LIEUTENANT PORTUONDO Have a drink with us. Would you bring some glasses? It's a night for celebration. We won over seventy medals in the games. We beat the Americans in almost everything. Can you believe it?

SOFIA Our radio is broken, Lieutenant. We don't get any news. We don't know what's happening out there in the world.

LIEUTENANT PORTUONDO You should give it to me. I'll have it fixed.

MARIA CELIA *has given him the glasses. He is opening the bottle now.*

MARIA CELIA No. You don't have to, Lieutenant.

LIEUTENANT PORTUONDO I'll fix it for you. I know someone who fixes radios. (*Pours the rum*) Sweet poison, this rum.
Everywhere there are tourists drinking tonight,
burning their guts out. Can you hear the drums?
They make the island come alive.
They release things from inside people. (*Raises glass*) Salud.

MARIA CELIA *Salud. (Smells the rum, takes a sip)*

SOFIA *Salud.*

MARIA CELIA I haven't had rum in so long, forgot what it tastes like.

SOFIA Me, too.

LIEUTENANT PORTUONDO Well, drink up. I brought a whole bottle.

SOFIA It seems like the whole island is out tonight.
How come you're not out celebrating?

LIEUTENANT PORTUONDO Because I wanted to see the two of you.

SOFIA An odd place to visit.
Not even the moon comes to this house.

LIEUTENANT PORTUONDO Well, that's the moon for you. I like visiting you.

MARIA CELIA If it weren't this late I'd go out into the patio
and pull a few mint leaves from our plants.
A little mint would give the rum the finishing touch.

LIEUTENANT PORTUONDO What's the matter, you're afraid of darkness?
Tell me where the mint plant is. I'll pull a few leaves.

MARIA CELIA No. It's not good to disturb the plants at this hour.
It's an old African belief, respect for the night, the plants . . .
Our mother used to say, Never ask a tree for a fruit at night,
because the whole wilderness sleeps after sundown.

LIEUTENANT PORTUONDO You fascinate me, *compañera.*

SOFIA That was our mother, Lieutenant.

LIEUTENANT PORTUONDO Well, I think the two of you are fascinating.

SOFIA No. Not like she was.

MARIA CELIA She was a lovely woman, Lieutenant.

SOFIA Yes, she was.

MARIA CELIA Every time she entered the patio out there, all the plants
rejoiced in her presence.

SOFIA And here in this room, every afternoon she'd sit to play the piano
and the whole neighborhood would quiet down to listen to her music.

LIEUTENANT PORTUONDO So talent runs in the family, you and your mother
played the piano, and Maria Celia writes . . . How about your father?

SOFIA He was an accountant . . .

MARIA CELIA Someone had to do the numbers. Oh, we can tell you stories
about our family. Every day we discover things about mamá for the first
time, why her room was on the east side of the house, because she loved
the morning light.

SOFIA Why she used to write prayers on the soles of our shoes.

MARIA CELIA Why she had her own views about the revolution.

LIEUTENANT PORTUONDO So she was a revolutionary?

SOFIA Maybe not the kind you would like.

MARIA CELIA We've always been revolutionary, Lieutenant. The whole family.

LIEUTENANT PORTUONDO So why did you father leave the country?

SOFIA He felt he couldn't speak his mind.

LIEUTENANT PORTUONDO I see. I suppose it can be difficult sometimes.

SOFIA You suppose right enough.

LIEUTENANT PORTUONDO My old man, he left just like your father.
He got fed up one day, said, This isn't going anywhere,
got tired of waiting. He wanted to take me with him,
but I was already in the military. Sometimes I wonder
what my life would've been like if I'd left.
The poor man, ended up in some snowy town,
up there in the North. Never married again after my mother died.
He used to say he was old and didn't have anymore
heart left in him. Was a good man, my father. Hard worker . . .
Had an old Buick, used to travel the whole island selling milk
containers to farmers. I used to help him on the road. Many a time,
I saw his eyes water when an old bolero used to play on the radio,
and I'd ask him, "Why you crying Pipo?"
And he'd say, "I just saw Pucha, your mother, through the mirror."
And I'd turn around to look and there'd be no one on the back seat.
And he'd keep on telling me, "Oh, I know she's there, I can smell
her sweet powder." It used to give me the creeps.

MARIA CELIA Why?

LIEUTENANT PORTUONDO Knowing my father, he'd let go of the steering
wheel and jump on the back seat with her.

They laugh.

More rum?

MARIA CELIA Just a bit.

The LIEUTENANT *pours some rum in her cup.*

LIEUTENANT PORTUONDO You know, every time I come to this house I seem to forget the world. Something about you and your sister. You're different.

Pours some rum in SOFIA's *cup.*

SOFIA I'm sure we are, especially now.

LIEUTENANT PORTUONDO No, what I'm talking about is something in the blood.

MARIA CELIA In the blood?

LIEUTENANT PORTUONDO Yes. What is it? What is that something that is passed on, that makes us who we are? I mean intelligence . . . Grace . . . You're pure . . . You are who you are, unlike me. I don't know what I'm saying . . . Ey, what would I know! I come from the middle of nowhere. A miserable town made of mud. Houses made of palm leaves. Dirt floor. No running water. I think people die there from looking at the cows. You know, the only thing I liked about that place were the hurricanes. I loved the hurricanes. I was always waiting for the wind to blow hard enough and blow me away from there.

Drinks. Sound of voices coming from the outside, firecrackers.

MARIA CELIA What is that noise?

LIEUTENANT PORTUONDO It must be the people going home from the stadium.

SOFIA They sound happy and cheerful.

MARIA CELIA They do. (*Pause*) Did anybody see you come in here at this hour? There's always somebody keeping an eye on this house.

LIEUTENANT PORTUONDO Don't worry. People know who I am.

MARIA CELIA I'd be careful if I were you. It's not five o'clock in the afternoon.

LIEUTENANT PORTUONDO Well, I wanted to see you, and that's all that matters. I'd like to get to know the two of you. I'd like for us to talk.

MARIA CELIA Talk about what, Lieutenant?

LIEUTENANT PORTUONDO I mean talk.

MARIA CELIA We are talking, aren't we?

LIEUTENANT PORTUONDO No, I mean . . . When are you going to trust me?

MARIA CELIA Trust you how, Lieutenant?

LIEUTENANT PORTUONDO How can I make you stop seeing me as the enemy?

MARIA CELIA Being the enemy is not necessarily a bad thing.
You probably know that more than I do.
Lets you keep your resistance, your perspective in life.

LIEUTENANT PORTUONDO And what's your perspective in life?
How do you know it's any different than mine?

MARIA CELIA Oh, come on, Lieutenant.

LIEUTENANT PORTUONDO That isn't fair . . . You hardly know me.

SOFIA I'm going upstairs to the roof . . . It seems like there are people dancing in the streets. I want to watch them from up there.

LIEUTENANT PORTUONDO Have another drink with us?

SOFIA No, you'll have to excuse me. (*Exits*)

LIEUTENANT PORTUONDO (*pouring more rum in* MARIA CELIA's *glass*) A little more rum.

He refills his glass.

LIEUTENANT PORTUONDO (*continued*) Salud.

He raises his glass. She doesn't toast, but stares him in the face. He smiles and drinks. He's amused by her control.

You know, the more I get to know you, the more I understand your husband's letters.

MARIA CELIA What do you mean?

LIEUTENANT PORTUONDO This man would do anything to have you by his side. It's all here, in this letter.

MARIA CELIA Do you always carry my husband's letters with you?

LIEUTENANT PORTUONDO No. I brought you this letter tonight because I thought you'd like to know about your husband's trip to Sweden.

MARIA CELIA What about his trip?

LIEUTENANT PORTUONDO I don't know. These lines may lend themselves to more than one interpretation, and you know very well what I mean. He talks about the photos he took in Sweden. Something about them looking sad and gray. What do you think that means?

MARIA CELIA I don't know. They say those northern countries look sad and melancholy.

LIEUTENANT PORTUONDO Are you sure that doesn't mean something else? He writes about several objects he bought on his trip. They seemed to have gotten lost in the mail . . . A painting, an old book on butterflies. Could this mean that he's not having any luck getting you out of this place? Was he trying to find you asylum in Sweden?

MARIA CELIA What are you after, Lieutenant? What do you want to know?! Just tell me. I mean, I'm standing here listening to you and I'm thinking, is this a new game? . . . Is it really his letter? Or is this some kind of new trial I'm supposed to endure?

LIEUTENANT PORTUONDO Look, you can see for yourself. It's his handwriting.

He shows her the letter, then folds it and places it in his pocket. Silence. A part of her seems to have left the room. She walks to the other side of the stage. There are tears in her eyes.

MARIA CELIA You should go, Lieutenant.

LIEUTENANT PORTUONDO I'm sorry.

MARIA CELIA Just go, please.

LIEUTENANT PORTUONDO I want to try to help you, Maria Celia. Why won't you let me help you?

MARIA CELIA What can you do? We both know what that letter is saying. You know everything about my life. That was my last hope.

Her mind is somewhere else outside of this room. But she takes refuge in the absurdity of the whole thing with a faint smile.

—Well, what would Sofie and I do in Sweden. We would probably look like two out-of-season tropical palms.

LIEUTENANT PORTUONDO I don't think you should leave the country once you're released from this house.

MARIA CELIA And what would I do here, Lieutenant?

LIEUTENANT PORTUONDO You are needed here, and I don't tell you this because you're standing in front of me and I have a couple of drinks in my head . . . Look, I'm all for change, just like you . . . That manifesto . . . What you and your friends wrote about perestroika . . .

MARIA CELIA It got me in prison, Lieutenant!

LIEUTENANT PORTUONDO It just wasn't the right the time. But now . . .

MARIA CELIA Please, I prefer not to talk . . .

LIEUTENANT PORTUONDO Listen to me . . . The island is going to open up soon, just like the rest of the world . . . Things are going to change . . . —You know, tonight I came here wanting . . . You and I . . . We treat each other . . . Look, I was hoping for some kind understanding between the two of us.

MARIA CELIA I think I stopped trying to understand many things . . .

LIEUTENANT PORTUONDO And so have I. I certainly don't try to understand why I'm here in this house. Why I'm willing to read you these letters. I gave up trying to understand long ago. You know very well I'm risking my skin.

For the first time he realizes this is a political confession and also a confession of the heart.

SOFIA comes down from the roof. She stays at a distance to listen to the conversation. The LIEUTENANT *takes* MARIA CELIA's *arm.*

I'd like to help you stop waiting.

Pause. She looks at him.

MARIA CELIA I love my husband, Lieutenant.

LIEUTENANT PORTUONDO I know. And I love that about you. That's how I met you. I love everything about you . . . Your writing . . . Your mind . . . The way you think . . .

SOFIA If you're leaving, Lieutenant, you should go out the back door. The head of the neighborhood committee is sitting on her doorsteps.

LIEUTENANT PORTUONDO That's all right, *compañera*. Thank you. Would you give me the radio before I go? I'd like to fix it for you.

MARIA CELIA If you insist.

She gives him the radio.

LIEUTENANT PORTUONDO Have a good night.

MARIA CELIA Lieutenant . . .

LIEUTENANT PORTUONDO Yes . . .

MARIA CELIA Before you go I want ask you . . . Bring me a letter tomorrow and I want you to read me the whole thing. We'll go ahead with the agreement.

LIEUTENANT PORTUONDO Tomorrow then. (*Exits*)

MARIA CELIA Are you all right? You've been up and down the roof the whole night.

SOFIA I want out. That's what I want. I walked all the way past Tito's house on top of the roof. I want to go out. I can't stand it here anymore. I just want out.

The sound of drums fills the stage.
Lights fade to black.

Scene 2: Her Husband's Letter for a Story

As the lights start to fade up, the sisters come in with betel palm trees in terra-cotta containers.

SOFIA Where do you want me to put this?

MARIA CELIA By the doorway.

SOFIA What's gotten into you today?

MARIA CELIA We need some life in this house.

SOFIA It would take more than these shrubs.

MARIA CELIA (*places it by the doorway*) Does it look good here?

SOFIA No. Put it by the sofa. This one will look good by the door.

MARIA CELIA *places her tree by the sofa and exits.* SOFIA *walks to the wall and presses her ear to listen.* MARIA CELIA *comes back with another palm tree and places it by the doorway.*

SOFIA We haven't heard the man next door in more than two weeks.
Not a sound from in there.
You think something happened to him?

MARIA CELIA He's probably busy working.

SOFIA I miss listening to him. He's never been gone for so long.
Maybe he's sick in the hospital.

MARIA CELIA Ay, Sofia . . . Why would he be in the hospital?
He's strong as a horse.

SOFIA You're right, he's strong. Have you seen his arms?
He's built like a bull. (*Places the pot on the floor*)

MARIA CELIA Help me bring in the other pots.

SOFIA I suppose the lieutenant will be coming this afternoon.

MARIA CELIA I suppose he will.

SOFIA And you'll want me to sit here.

MARIA CELIA I was hoping you would.

SOFIA I was hoping, she says. I might as well be another plant in the room.

MARIA CELIA I'll bring in the other plants.

SOFIA That's fine. I'll do whatever you want me to do. Like always, until doomsday.

There is a knock at the door.

Oh, God! It's probably him.

She goes to open the door. The LIEUTENANT *comes in.*

We weren't expecting you until much later.

LIEUTENANT PORTUONDO Left work early today.

SOFIA Maria Celia is out in the patio.
This is her new plan for today, to fill the house with plants.

LIEUTENANT PORTUONDO It looks good.

SOFIA You think so? I can't even tell the difference.
Everything looks the same to me in this place.
Can I get you anything, Lieutenant?

LIEUTENANT PORTUONDO No, thank you.

SOFIA How are things out there in the *world*?

LIEUTENANT PORTUONDO It's hot. The streets are burning from this heat.

SOFIA Not any hotter than in this house.
Have you been to the movies lately?

LIEUTENANT PORTUONDO No, I haven't.

SOFIA I used to love going to the movies, especially in the summer.
It's a good place to escape the heat.

LIEUTENANT PORTUONDO Yes, it is.

SOFIA Oh, I wish you could get us a permit, Lieutenant.

LIEUTENANT PORTUONDO What kind of permit do you want?

SOFIA Something to go out of the house, even if it's just once a week.

MARIA CELIA *enters with a plant.*

MARIA CELIA (*entering*) I think this bromeliad will look nice inside the house. (*Notices him*)

SOFIA I was just about to call you . . .

MARIA CELIA Hello, Lieutenant!

LIEUTENANT PORTUONDO Hello.

SOFIA Give me the plant, I'll put it on the table. Sit here on the sofa, Lieutenant. I think I'd rather sit by the piano.

LIEUTENANT PORTUONDO (*to* SOFIA) I imagine this is like the old days, when your friends used to gather here to read stories and poems.

SOFIA No. It's not the same.

LIEUTENANT PORTUONDO I'm sure there were more people and it was livelier.

SOFIA Many more. This place was full of life before.
Now everything has a sad stare . . . Every piece of furniture has a tag like an agony. Sometimes I think I'm going to go mad in this closed-up house. I spend so much time in this damn place.

MARIA CELIA Well, perhaps we should start now, Sofie.

MARIA CELIA *turns to look at the* LIEUTENANT.

LIEUTENANT PORTUONDO (*takes out a letter and begins to read*) My beautiful Gertrudis: Your letter came yesterday and brought with it a garden of palm trees, the wind from your patio.
The little place where you sit on the roof.
Sometimes I can see you without seeing you,
as if I were there next to you. I can picture what you do in the morning, at what time you have coffee, comb your hair, at what time you wash your face and undress. (*He looks at her*)
Everyday I dream about you, my love.
I can feel your arms and legs wrapped around my body like before . . .

Your skin soft, delicate, tender, and hot . . .
Your face madly alive when I'm inside you . . .
Your voice calling out, asking me to go further . . .
To go as far as death . . . I'm holding your last letter in my hands now . . .
Tonight I'll sleep inside you, my love. Please write to me soon.
Antonio.
PS I'm including a few jasmine flowers from the tree outside
my window. They remind me of you.

MARIA CELIA   May I see the flowers?

He gives her the three little dry flowers. She smells them. He looks at her.
Silence.

SOFIA   I . . . I feel . . . I feel as if I should do something. Maybe have
something to read. So quiet all of a sudden. Maybe I could play the piano.

LIEUTENANT PORTUONDO   Yes. Play something.

SOFIA   How about "Yo te quiero siempre"? You know this song?

She begins to play the song "Yo te quiero siempre" by Lecuona. He walks toward
the piano. He leaves the letter with MARIA CELIA. *She's reading it now as*
she smells the flowers. SOFIA *immerses herself in her music. She looks at the*
LIEUTENANT *as she plays. He stares at* MARIA CELIA. SOFIA *turns her face to*
MARIA CELIA, *then back to the* LIEUTENANT. *The* LIEUTENANT *lets himself*
be taken by the music sometimes, but his eyes always return to MARIA CELIA.
Holding the flowers, MARIA CELIA *walks to the upstage area, perhaps to look at*
the light entering from a window. He turns toward her. SOFIA *closes her eyes to*
recoil herself in the music. The LIEUTENANT *walks toward* MARIA CELIA. *She is*
smelling the flowers, then hands them for him to smell.
SOFIA *closes the piano and walks out of the room.* MARIA CELIA *and the*
LIEUTENANT *turn toward* SOFIA.
MARIA CELIA *is about to go after* SOFIA . . .

LIEUTENANT PORTUONDO   Don't go . . .

MARIA CELIA *remains still, looking in the direction that her sister left the room.*
LIEUTENANT PORTUONDO *comes closer to her. He touches her shoulder. He*
kisses her neck. He turns her face. He kisses her lips, her face, and all over her

neck and shoulders. He makes his way down her body. He's down on his knees now kissing her legs, pulling up her dress. Her back arches, then bends forward to him as if succumbing to the pull of pleasure.

The two bodies have become one on the floor. The sound of nightfall drowns the whole moment into a gentle darkness. Then full darkness. The lights come up again.

MARIA CELIA *is lying on the floor with the* LIEUTENANT, *telling him the story.*

MARIA CELIA Then she moves around the room,
like the light that enters slowly from the lighthouse.
She changes the conversation.
And slowly like the high tide that creeps in the afternoon,
she brings the calm sea to the room. The whole room drowns in a blue glory. He no longer remembers the marine reports.
He can only smell the wet air of the bay.
His whole body becomes a vessel, a galleon.
His open shirt, a flying sail in the wind navigating towards her open sea.

SOFIA *enters the stage, but stays at a distance, watching.*

LIEUTENANT PORTUONDO So the woman in your story is responsible for the stolen boats. She distracts the man while she's upstairs in the tower? Does the woman love this man?

MARIA CELIA I think she does. But she probably doesn't want to know this.

LIEUTENANT PORTUONDO Is that why she's lying to him?

MARIA CELIA Perhaps he's been lying, too. Maybe he knew the boats were being stolen all along, but he pretended not to know.

LIEUTENANT PORTUONDO Why would he do that?

MARIA CELIA So she could always come back to him.

They kiss.

Are you as hungry as I am?

LIEUTENANT PORTUONDO Yes, for you. (*Kisses her neck*)

MARIA CELIA No, wait. I think there's some mangoes left in the kitchen.

LIEUTENANT PORTUONDO Messy fruit, the mango.

MARIA CELIA Messy like you.

LIEUTENANT PORTUONDO Let's eat it naked in your room.

MARIA CELIA *takes him by the hand. They exit. The sounds of the night fill the stage. The lights become darker. The scene moves deeper into the night, as time passes.* SOFIA *enters the stage cautiously, holding a bundle of men's clothes. She wears a fedora hat. She drops the bundle of clothes on top of the sofa, as she glances toward her sister's room. She listens for any sounds coming from there. She stands by the sofa and starts to disguise herself as a man. She puts on a pair of pants and shirt. She tucks her dress inside the pants.*
MARIA CELIA *enters the stage.*

MARIA CELIA Who's there? Who's there?

SOFIA (*in a low voice*) Shshhhhh . . . Don't scream . . . Don't be frightened—it's me.

MARIA CELIA Oh, my lord . . . You gave me a fright. I was . . . I thought someone . . . I thought someone had gotten in . . . What are you doing . . . What are you doing dressed like that?

SOFIA Shssh . . . Go back to bed, it's still dark.

MARIA CELIA Why are you dressed like a man? You gave me a fright.

SOFIA I'm trying on Papi's clothes.

MARIA CELIA What do you mean, you're trying on Papi's clothes?

SOFIA I couldn't sleep.

MARIA CELIA You're lying. Were you going out? Is that why you're dressed in those clothes?

SOFIA No.

MARIA CELIA Yes. You were going out. I can tell. I know you.
(*In a low voice*) Take off those clothes.

LIEUTENANT PORTUONDO (*offstage*) Maria Celia.

MARIA CELIA (*in a loud voice*) Coming . . .

SOFIA I'm not taking them off!

MARIA CELIA (*starts taking off her shirt*) Sofia, are you crazy?

SOFIA (*pulls away*) I don't care what you say. I'm going out.

MARIA CELIA What's gotten into you! Do you realize what you're doing?
(*Grabs her by the shirt*)

The LIEUTENANT *enters the room but stays at a distance, watching.*

If you get caught you're going back to prison.

SOFIA The hell with you. Let go. (MARIA CELIA *lets go of her arm*)
I'll finish dressing in back of the house.

SOFIA *takes the jacket and hat and runs offstage.*

MARIA CELIA (*in a low voice*) Sofia . . . Sofia . . .

LIEUTENANT PORTUONDO Maria Celia . . .

MARIA CELIA *stays motionless. Pause. She turns to him.*

MARIA CELIA Would you keep this between us? — Please, would you do that
for me?

He looks at her. He walks out of the room.
MARIA CELIA *remains alone on the stage.*

Lights fade to black.

Scene 3: Counting the Lost Stitches

*Downstage, the sunlight entering from a window forms a slanted rectangle of
light on the floor. The sisters take a couple of chairs and sit in the rectangle of
light. They are framed by the dying light of the sunset.* MARIA CELIA *starts knitting a blue bedspread.* SOFIA *stands behind a chair. The light from the window
will fade slowly as the gray darkness of twilight slowly claims its domain.*

SOFIA Last night I overheard a whole group of men
talking about something that happened in Moscow.
I didn't want to get too close to them.
But they were talking about some kind of revolt . . .

Something big has happened there, Maria Celia.
They were saying that the Soviet Union has broken apart.
It's over . . .

No response from MARIA CELIA.

I thought you'd like to know.

MARIA CELIA I told you I don't want to talk to you.

SOFIA Are you going to torture me the whole day?
I'm trying to tell you something, and you treat me as if I wasn't here.

MARIA CELIA And how do you expect me to treat you?

SOFIA You can at least talk to me.

MARIA CELIA Talk to you . . . Talk to you. After what you did last night, do
you expect me to talk to you?

SOFIA I'm just trying to tell you something, for God's sake!

MARIA CELIA I told you I don't want to talk to you.
It's bad enough being stuck in this house with your foolish self.

SOFIA And do you think I like being stuck in here with you?

MARIA CELIA At least I don't do anything to jeopardize you.

SOFIA Jeopardize me? You have the lieutenant stay in this house, and
that's not putting me at risk?

MARIA CELIA He could've turned you in for going out, and he didn't.
He could've taken you back . . .

SOFIA Don't try to give me a guilty conscience.
It's because of you that I spent two years in prison.
It's because of you I'm locked up in this place . . .
You and your rotten books . . . Your friends and their literary meetings . . .
That damn letter they wrote about perestroika . . .

MARIA CELIA You were the first to sign the letter.
You were the first to play music at the literary meetings,
when Oscarito read his poems. That scoundrel you were in love with.

SOFIA   Ha! I should've left with him to Spain.
Don't I wish that I had him back in my life!
Him and all the men that came my way.

MARIA CELIA   He was a lowlife, a drunk, and everybody knew about it.

SOFIA   He was a writer, like you . . .

MARIA CELIA   I suppose that's the crux of the matter. He was a bad writer.
An opportunist, who went off to Europe spouting information in all the
papers about the two of us in prison.

SOFIA   He was trying to get us amnesty.

MARIA CELIA   What amnesty? I don't see any amnesty.

SOFIA   At least he tried helping us. Not like your lieutenant,
who hasn't done anything to get us out.
Just listen to what happened out there in the world.
The world has changed, and we didn't even know about it.
Sometimes I think he wants us stuck in this place.

MARIA CELIA   Oh, you're just being resentful and jealous.
All your life begrudging me something.

SOFIA   Begrudging you what?!

MARIA CELIA   Don't talk to me now! You made me lose my place in the
knitting. See how you start mixing me up . . .

SOFIA   Why would I be jealous of you?
Maybe the lieutenant is making it harder for us to get out.

MARIA CELIA   Don't talk to me! I'm counting, goddamn it . . .

SOFIA   I'm trying to tell you something, and you . . .

MARIA CELIA   Can't you see I'm counting . . . Row three through the
loops . . .

SOFIA   Knit and purl, knit and purl . . .
I hate those stupid needles! (*Takes her needles and throws them on the floor*)

MARIA CELIA   Pick them up . . . Pick them up, I said.

SOFIA *stays motionless.*

You act like a child, rash and reckless . . .

MARIA CELIA *goes to pick up the needles.*

If there's one thing we can learn from all this knitting,
it's that you have to go back where you left off . . .
You have to pick up the lost stitches.

SOFIA I've lost a whole life of stitches in this house. A whole life.
That's what gets to me. So many days, gone . . . I could knit a whole
bedspread for this island with all the lost days.
I can't even remember where I left off living my own life,
my own place in this mess! I'll never forget that day when Papi left
this country. When he kissed us on the forehead
and told us not to fall in love, not to get married,
because he was going to send for us . . . You remember?
As if love was a car one could stop with the touch of the brakes.
I don't know about you, but for me time stopped. I felt my feet stop
growing, my bones, my breasts, as if I had frozen in time,
because I was saving myself for North America.
It just feels like all my life I've been waiting and
I haven't lived. You got to travel with your books.
You got married, when you got tired of waiting.
But me, stuck here. Stuck, piano lessons, a few students,
taking care of Mamá. Stuck . . . Stuck . . . Stuck . . .
And now stuck even more.

MARIA CELIA Sofie please . . . (*Holds her arm as if trying to console her*)

SOFIA No. Can't you see what you're doing?!
Can't you see what you're getting yourself into with that man?
He's not going to make it better for us.
I've watched him . . . He got rid of all the inspectors who used to
come to this house. He's the only one who comes here.
Can't you see it spelled out on his forehead?
Ownership! Everything about him, his eyes, the way he walks . . .
Everything about him screams out zookeeper.

MARIA CELIA That's enough, Sofia! That's enough!

Pause. SOFIA *looks at her a moment.* MARIA CELIA *is shaken by what* SOFIA *has told her.*

SOFIA I'm sorry, I had to tell you. This is what this place does.
This closed-up house, it doesn't let you see who's in front of you.
Last night I couldn't sleep . . .
I couldn't stop thinking of those men talking about Russia . . .
Their voices over and over again in my mind.
I just kept on seeing those images they were talking about . . .
Thousands of people in the squares . . . All over Moscow celebrating . . .
Statues tumbling down . . . Are you all right?

MARIA CELIA *walks to another part of the room. She seems to be somewhere else, lost.*

SOFIA Maybe something will happen here, too.

MARIA CELIA Maybe.

SOFIA One man was even talking about the new maps . . .
He was saying the world is going to seem bigger with all
the changes. Can you imagine? Someone is out there sketching new maps
of the world.

MARIA CELIA Oh, Sofie . . .

Lights fade to black.

Scene 4: After the Soviet Coup

The lights start to fade up on SOFIA *and* LIEUTENANT PORTUONDO *standing by the doorway.*

LIEUTENANT PORTUONDO Where's your sister? Did you tell her I came by earlier?

SOFIA I did.

LIEUTENANT PORTUONDO Did you tell her I wanted to talk to her?

SOFIA I did. She said that she didn't think she'd be able to get up from bed. You look a little sick, too, Lieutenant. You haven't been sleeping well?

LIEUTENANT PORTUONDO No.

SOFIA Me neither. The summer heat is agonizing, isn't it?

LIEUTENANT PORTUONDO Can I get your sister something?

SOFIA She'll be fine. You must have a lot of work, Lieutenant . . . I mean, with everything that happened in Russia, you must be busy . . .

LIEUTENANT PORTUONDO What about Russia?

SOFIA I mean . . . So much has happened out there in the world. I mean the big revolt in Russia . . . When I heard about it, I thought . . .

LIEUTENANT PORTUONDO I'd like to talk to your sister. Why don't you call her?

SOFIA I told you she's . . .

LIEUTENANT PORTUONDO Call her . . . (*In a loud voice*) Maria Celia. Go get her.

SOFIA I told you she's not feeling well.

LIEUTENANT PORTUONDO Go get her, I said. (*Calling*) Maria Celia.

SOFIA *exits.*

LIEUTENANT PORTUONDO Is she coming?

SOFIA (*entering*) I suppose so. She's up on the roof.

MARIA CELIA *enters the room.*

LIEUTENANT PORTUONDO What's the matter with you?

MARIA CELIA Sofie must've told you, I haven't been feeling well.

LIEUTENANT PORTUONDO Sick, and you were up on the roof.

SOFIA She needed some air.

MARIA CELIA I wanted to know what's happening out there in the streets.

SOFIA Yes, what's going to happen here, Lieutenant?

LIEUTENANT PORTUONDO Is it possible to have a word with you?

SOFIA *exits. He looks at* MARIA CELIA.

LIEUTENANT PORTUONDO It seems like you didn't want to see me.

MARIA CELIA Sofie told you . . .

LIEUTENANT PORTUONDO Do you need anything?

MARIA CELIA Why didn't you tell me?

LIEUTENANT PORTUONDO Tell you what?

MARIA CELIA We heard about Russia. The whole world knew except us. Why didn't you tell us?

LIEUTENANT PORTUONDO Tell you what, Maria Celia? . . .

MARIA CELIA When did it happen?

LIEUTENANT PORTUONDO I don't know . . . I guess two days ago.

MARIA CELIA Two days!

LIEUTENANT PORTUONDO It hasn't even been announced on the news.

MARIA CELIA Two days! And you're keeping the people in the dark.

LIEUTENANT PORTUONDO I didn't make that decision.

MARIA CELIA But everybody is talking about it on the streets . . .

LIEUTENANT PORTUONDO They probably heard about it on the American stations.

MARIA CELIA Please . . . I want you to bring me back the radio.

LIEUTENANT PORTUONDO All right.

MARIA CELIA What do you think is going to happen here?

LIEUTENANT PORTUONDO Nothing is going to happen. That has nothing to do with us.

MARIA CELIA Of course, it does. What does the government have to say?

LIEUTENANT PORTUONDO I don't know what anybody has to say!

MARIA CELIA Of course, you know! You must know!

LIEUTENANT PORTUONDO (*losing control*) Did you see the line of cars in front of the gasoline station?!
Did you see how it extends for blocks?
That's what people are talking about.
The dregs the Russians left behind. The whole mess . . .
(*He moves close to her*) Look, I didn't come here . . .
I've been hearing about the stinking Soviets the whole day . . .
I came here to talk to you, to be with you. (*Holds her arm*)

MARIA CELIA No. We should stop all this.

LIEUTENANT PORTUONDO Why this change all of a sudden?

MARIA CELIA It's just the way things are.

LIEUTENANT PORTUONDO Look at me . . . What are you saying? Why are you running away? What are you afraid of?

MARIA CELIA I'm afraid of what locked-up places breed.

LIEUTENANT PORTUONDO And what is that?

MARIA CELIA Please, just forget . . .

She walks to another part of the room.

LIEUTENANT PORTUONDO Forget what? What do you want me to forget?
I know you, Maria Celia . . . I know you like I know my own skin . . .

MARIA CELIA No. You're wrong. You don't know me.

LIEUTENANT PORTUONDO All I know is you were a different person the other night. Someone who said she wanted to remember who she was. Someone who gave herself to me . . .

Pause. She looks at him. She doesn't know what to say. Then she turns away. She looks into the distance, wanting this moment to disappear. She tries to gather her strength. She's decisive and serious.

MARIA CELIA Everything has been defined for us. I'm locked up in here, and you're out there, and we should keep it that way.

LIEUTENANT PORTUONDO You're afraid. You're running so fast you don't
even know where you're going. You don't even know what to do with
yourself . . .

MARIA CELIA No. I'm not fooling myself anymore.
I've been closed up in this house for a long time. Too long.
Apart from anything, it does something to your mind.
A sort of blindness, that makes you close your eyes and
see somebody else who's not there in front of you . . .

LIEUTENANT PORTUONDO And who's that? Your husband. Is that who you
see? You see your husband in me.

MARIA CELIA What you've been doing is a crime.
The same corruption that goes on out there in the streets,
in the black market, people bargaining for a meal,
for a bar of soap—except you've been bargaining with my life.

He shakes his head.
He will not be bullied by her excuses.

LIEUTENANT PORTUONDO We're beyond all that, Maria Celia.
I mean, who are you fooling? I mean, what do you take me for?

MARIA CELIA Something's going to happen in this country soon.
I know so. I can feel it coming like a storm.

LIEUTENANT PORTUONDO Nothing's going to happen here, I can tell you that
much. If anything, there's talk about fortifying the regime, so we don't fall
altogether like the Soviets.

MARIA CELIA It's what I'm holding on to, Lieutenant!

LIEUTENANT PORTUONDO You know, I'm tired of hearing about the fuckin'
Russians! Who cares what happened in Russia!
Who the fuck cares, goddamn it!

He throws an object against the floor.
Pause.

MARIA CELIA I think you should leave, Lieutenant.

LIEUTENANT PORTUONDO Oh, no . . . I'm staying right here.
I'm not going anywhere.
I'm not going anywhere.

He paces back and forth.

It's strange this thing you have over me.
The worst of it is you can't make it stop,
and I can't do anything about it either.
I've always been a clean revolutionary—as clean as can be.
Not one stain on my record.
You came into my life, and you got inside me like a war.
I don't even recognize myself. I can't even think straight anymore.
You know well that I've been throwing my life away because of you!

MARIA CELIA Do you really think this can go anywhere?

LIEUTENANT PORTUONDO Why not? Tell me, why not?

MARIA CELIA Yes, the two of us like outlaws, criminals of some kind.

LIEUTENANT PORTUONDO You know very well that if I could have, I would've
stolen you from the law, from this house, long ago.

MARIA CELIA There's another side to me.
I carry a whole past behind me . . . A whole past . . .
Something you have to face . . . I made certain decisions long ago,
which have me locked up in here.

LIEUTENANT PORTUONDO You're talking as if I didn't . . .

MARIA CELIA No! You can never put yourself in my place!
Try and spend a day in this house. A week.
A month locked up in here.

LIEUTENANT PORTUONDO I'm not giving up on you so easily.

MARIA CELIA Do you honestly think I can possibly live in this country
when I'm out of this house? Do you really think there's a place for me
here?!

LIEUTENANT PORTUONDO Calm down . . . Calm down . . . Listen to me . . .
I've been making plans for you and your sister.
I've been talking to the high officials about the two of you.

MARIA CELIA I don't expect this to make much sense to you,
but I don't want any help. The world has changed out there.
If I'm not out of this house any time soon,
I'm going on a hunger strike . . .

LIEUTENANT PORTUONDO A hunger strike . . . And what are you going to get
out of it?

MARIA CELIA I want out. I've been locked up in here for too long!

LIEUTENANT PORTUONDO And do you think a hunger strike would help?
Have you considered well what's happening out there?
I suppose you don't realize what's going on.
As we speak, brigades are being formed everywhere in the island,
to crack down any rebellion or demonstrations . . .

MARIA CELIA That's not going to stop me. I want changes, like the rest of
the world. And I'm not afraid of making any declarations!

LIEUTENANT PORTUONDO You do any kind of demonstration, and the two of
you will go back to point zero.

MARIA CELIA We are at point zero!

LIEUTENANT PORTUONDO No you're not. I warn you. You try to do your silly
strike, and you'll have a mob storming into this house to force-feed you . . .
And not with food but with every one of your books.

SOFIA *enters.*

SOFIA Get out! Get out of my house.

LIEUTENANT PORTUONDO Ask your sister if she has anything else to say.

Silence.

You want change? Then things will change!
Good day, *compañeras.*

The LIEUTENANT *looks at her a moment, then makes his way out of the room.*
He closes the door behind him. SOFIA *turns to her sister.* MARIA CELIA *crosses to*
the piano.
Lights fade to black.

Epilogue: Twining Our Lives

The piano has been taken away. The house looks more empty. SOFIA *sits on*
a chair where the piano used to be. She looks into the distance. MARIA CELIA
twines yarn as she recites a letter to her husband.

MARIA CELIA It is late at night now, and I strain my eyes to see your face.
This morning I opened the door of the wardrobe and hugged
your black suit, which hangs next to my clothes.
Here nothing has changed, my love.
If anything, the regime has reduced the distribution of food once again.
As for clothing supplies, each person can expect
a dress or a pair of pants every two years.
Sofie hasn't been doing well.
Yesterday the only joy and little amusement we had,
was taken away from us.
A couple of men came to our house to take Sofie's piano away.

SOFIA *walks to the wall. She presses her ear against the concrete partition.*

This year the guava tree in our patio has given so many fruits,
we don't know what to do with all the guavas.
And since Sofia and I are not eating, and the neighbors won't accept
anything from us, we bring the fruits into the house and put them
everywhere, because the fragrance of guava reminds us of Grandma
Carucha and Mami. The house also seems less lonely with the aroma of
guavas. It's as if an invisible woman with a sweet perfume is staying with
us, and the house feels less empty.

SOFIA *looks as if she has lost her mind.*

SOFIA Maria Celia, I think he's home. Come here.
I thought I heard him. Do you hear anything?

MARIA CELIA I don't hear a thing.

sofia Shshh . . . Come close to the wall.
You hear his footsteps? He's come back.

MARIA CELIA *goes along with what her sister is hearing, as a way of consoling her.*

MARIA CELIA Yes. I can hear him.

sofia You think he's alone?

MARIA CELIA No.

sofia Did you hear other footsteps? He's standing still.

MARIA CELIA I think he's drinking.

sofia Already.

MARIA CELIA He must drink to forget. The pangs of love, Sofie.

sofia Maria Celia, I used to play that song on the piano. You remember? He's playing that song in his house. What should I do, Maria Celia? What should I do?

MARIA CELIA Just listen, Sofie. Be still and listen.

Soft piano music is heard through the wall.
The music plays louder.
LIEUTENANT PORTUONDO *knocks on the door.*
The music swells. The sisters let themselves be taken by the music, disregarding the knocking at the door. The music continues to swell.

End of Play.

Maria Celia (Adriana Sevan, on the stairs) and Sofia (Jill Remez, at the piano) in *Two Sisters and a Piano*, South Coast Repertory, 1999. Photo: Henry DiRocco. Courtesy SCR.

Lieutenant Portuondo (Carlos Sanz) with Maria Celia (Adriana Sevan, right) and Sofia (Jill Remez, left) in *Two Sisters and a Piano*, South Coast Repertory, 1999. Photo: Henry DiRocco. Courtesy SCR.

José Esteban Muñoz

The Onus of Seeing Cuba: Nilo Cruz's *Cubanía*

Old Cubans say that if you walk to the very end of Key West you will able to see Cuba. I myself don't know any Cubans, young or old, who have actually seen the island from this point, but there is a plaque at that spot that marks it as "officially" ninety miles from the island of Cuba. Of course, a lot more separates Cuba from Key West than those piddling ninety miles. There is a haze that obscures any view, ensuring that one will indeed never see Cuba from that or another vantage point. That haze is comprised of certain ideological mists that we might understand as the United States's endless propaganda war against the island, the rage and melancholic romanticism of the Cubans outside the island, and the North American Left's precritical celebration of the revolution. Cuban exile art thus needs to respond to the onus of breaking through the distorting cloud that keeps us all from actually seeing Cuba. In this way Nilo Cruz's work is both admirable and necessary, insofar as it not only understands the onus of "seeing Cuba" but in fact tries to do something about it. Cruz's writing practice attempts to cast a picture of *cubanía*, of Cubanness as a way of being in the

The *South Atlantic Quarterly* 99:2/3, Spring/Summer 2000.

world; this picture not only helps us begin to achieve a historical materialist understanding of Cuba, but it also encourages us to access *cubanía* as a structure of feeling that supercedes national boundaries and pedagogies.

If this play, *Two Sisters and a Piano*, were to be addressed on the level of plot, such an explication would dwell on the way in which the work attempts to interrogate a difficult and pivotal moment in Cuban history. The play is set in Cuba of 1992, at the moment of perestroika. Through the lives of four characters (two sisters—one a writer and the other a musician—a lieutenant in the nation's military, and a piano tuner) a charged moment of historical transition and entrenchment is described with dense nuance. The two sisters are political prisoners who have been upgraded from penitentiary incarceration to house arrest. The house they are sent to is their now dilapidated family home, and they settle among its ruins. Maria Celia, the older sister, is forbidden her vocation as a writer. The other sister, Sofia, is allowed to play her out-of-tune piano for a time, until that, too, is taken away from her. Throughout the play she trembles with desire for the outside world and the bodies of men, while Maria Celia longs for her husband, a political activist who has escaped Cuba, denounces it from the outside, and labors to get his wife and sister-in-law out through diplomatic mechanisms. Maria Celia is desired by Lieutenant Portuondo, the military representative who is in charge of her detainment and enforces her restriction against writing. His great conflict is this assigned duty and his love of Maria Celia's writing and body. The play's other major character is Victor Manuel, the piano tuner. Maria Celia treats him with suspicion as he is desired by Sofia. His major concern is the state of the family piano.

A reading that focused primarily on plot would miss some of the important cultural work that Cruz is doing. The play is about *cubanía* as a *manera de ser* (a way of being), and it attempts to provide an affective understanding of the world. These characters, anchored in the Cuba of 1991, are witness to a moment of world historical turmoil. They face this moment with manifold desires and longings: some desire social change, while others desire sexual and psychic liberation. Still others are invested in the state and strive for the survival of the existing system. These feelings speak to the emotional life world of *cubanía*. The sisters are full of desire for another place and time, one in which their desires will be realized, a then and a there. They dream through their writing and music of a moment when longing will be fulfilled. These men stand in for a certain aspect of nation. They themselves are not without ambivalence, yet they nonetheless represent an established order, a here and a now. The women represent something that we might understand as a melancholic attachment to a lost Cuba and, at the same time, a utopian longing for a reformulated evolution that perestroika promised to some on the island. (We know now that perestroika and the end of Soviet economic aid did not bring a new golden age to Cuba, but instead made the island even more susceptible to the U.S. government's savage embargo and brought on an especially hellish "special period" of scarcity.) The sisters dream of another temporality while the men are anchored to a notion of presentness.

Throughout Cruz's oeuvre we encounter women who dream and desire different times and places. The world they represent is familiar to anyone who has lived inside or outside of a Cuban community here or there. The playwright deploys female characters as melancholics whose affective relationship to the world is a critique of its current conditions. They are personages outside of a national order whose desire exceeds the bounds of the national here and now. This strategy echoes what we can today understand as Tennessee Williams's queer ventriloquism. Through his memorable and often tortured heroines (a partial list would include Laura and Amanda Wingfield in *The Glass Menagerie*, Blanche and Stella in *A Streetcar Named Desire*, Maggie from *Cat on a Hot Tin Roof*, or *Suddenly Last Summer*'s Catherine), Williams was able to represent the affective reality of homosexual desire. While Williams was never able to (and perhaps never desired to) write what we would reductively call an "out" gay play, the affective landscape of pre-Stonewall homosexuality was certainly represented in his work through these powerful dramatic female conjurings. Maria Celia and Sofia seem like a tribute and intertextual reverberation of this particular mode of rendering emotional realities through analogy and allegory. The fact that Maria Celia and Sofia's desires are suppressed and literally under house arrest certainly speak to the revolution's problematic relationship to public displays of queer desire and ontology.

Cruz uses emotion as an instrument to see Cuba beyond a certain ideological fog. To better understand this strategy we might then compare his work to two other important Cuban American theater artists. Maria Irene Fornes is a Cuban American playwright who seems to eschew identity labels like *Latina*. This refusal or reluctance to embrace an uncritical model of Latina identity is a critical and theoretical act. The playwright is instead interested in rendering an affective landscape that speaks to the quotidian reality of Cubans, U.S. Latinos, and Latin Americans. Only a few of Fornes's plays actually feature Latino/a characters. *Conduct of Life* is staged in a generalized Latin American nation, and *Sarita* features characters who are clearly marked as Latina/o. Even though most of her plays do not directly index Latino names and lives, all of her dramatic personages represent Latina/o affective reality. Their way of being, their modes of negotiating the interpersonal and the social, stand as thick descriptions of ethnic feeling within a hegemonic order. Fornes's oeuvre stands out from the mainstream of American theater insofar as one is not able to easily assign motivation to her characters. Traditional narrative arcs of character development are all but absent in her work. This difference is often understood as the avant-garde nature of her plays. Such a reading is only half right. This particular mode of avant-gardism can be characterized as representative of specifically transcultural avant-garde. Her plays appear mysterious to North American eyes because they represent a specifically Latina/o *manera de ser*. This mystery is not accidental or some problem of translation, but strategic, measured, and interventionist. The short play *Mud*, for instance, is set in an economically impoverished U.S. locale. Mae, the play's female protagonist, finds herself trapped in a life where she is unable to actualize her emotional and intellectual potential. This boundness is similar to the chains that keep the two sisters from achieving their own liberation in *Two Sisters and a Piano*. Mae's plight is meant to be felt by anyone who is sensitized to the transnational gendering of poverty, yet it speaks to a Latina/o cognoscenti in powerful and culturally specific ways. The mysteriousness of Fornes is akin to a mysteriousness that saturates Cruz's work. His characters do not conform to the strictures of character development that dominate North American theater. The motivations of his characters are not available to North American viewers who are unable to "see" psychology and feeling outside of their own emotional confines.

It is also useful to compare the playwright's work to that of a younger Cuban American dramatist. Jorge Ignacio Cortiñas's *Maleta Mulata*, like much of Cruz's work, challenges the affective protocols that U.S. culture routinely prescribes. The play is set in a Miami household in the eighties. Family members struggle with the literal ghost of their Cuban past as well as contemporary imperatives to become American. *Maleta Mulata*, like *Two Sisters and a Piano*, offers valuable insight on what I call melancholia of *cuba-*

Four special issues at one special price!

Please enter my one-year subscription (four issues) to *SAQ* at the low subscription rate of $32.*
Subscribers outside the U.S.: Please add $16 for postage.
Canadian subscribers: Please add 7% GST to the subscription rate, in addition to the outside-U.S. postage.

☐ Enclosed is my check, made payable to Duke University Press.

☐ Please bill me (no issues will be sent until payment is received).

Please charge my ☐ VISA ☐ MasterCard ☐ American Express

Account Number   Expiration Date

Signature   Daytime Telephone

Name

Address   E-mail Address

City/State/Zip   SQ2l1

* Individual subscriptions only.
Send your order to Duke University Press, Journals Fulfillment, Box 90660, Durham, NC 27708-0660.
To place your journal order using a credit card, call toll-free 1-888-387-5765 (within the U.S. or Canada)
or (919) 687-3602 (elsewhere). www.dukepress.edu

Library request for a subscription/examination copy

Please enter our one-year subscription (four issues) to *SAQ*.
Libraries and institutions: $112 (add $16 for postage outside the U.S.;
Canadian libraries add 7% GST to the subscription rate).

Institution

Address   SQ2l1

☐ Purchase order enclosed.

☐ Please bill our agent:

☐ Please send a free examination copy to the address listed above (libraries only).

Volume 101, 2002 (4 issues)
ISSN 0038-2876

Send your order to Duke University Press, Journals Fulfillment, Box 90660, Durham, NC 27708-0660.
To place your journal order using a credit card, call toll-free 1-888-387-5765 (within the U.S. or Canada)
or (919) 687-3602 (elsewhere). www.dukepress.edu

NO POSTAGE
NECESSARY
IF MAILED
IN THE
UNITED STATES

BUSINESS REPLY MAIL

FIRST CLASS MAIL   PERMIT NO. 1000   DURHAM, NC

POSTAGE WILL BE PAID BY ADDRESSEE

Duke University Press
Journals Fulfillment
Box 90660
Durham, NC 27706-9942

NO POSTAGE
NECESSARY
IF MAILED
IN THE
UNITED STATES

BUSINESS REPLY MAIL

FIRST CLASS MAIL   PERMIT NO. 1000   DURHAM, NC

POSTAGE WILL BE PAID BY ADDRESSEE

Duke University Press
Journals Fulfillment
Box 90660
Durham, NC 27706-9942

nía. This complex affective formation, in the case of Cortiñas's excellent play, focuses on Miami-based Cubans' inability to accept the reality of a socialist present on the island. A similar melancholia characterizes Maria Celia and Sofia's struggle with the island's present. Furthermore, Cruz's play foregrounds the Cuban state's own melancholic longing for a pre-perestroika universe. In this fashion, Maria Celia's writing and Sofia's music threaten to wake Cuba up from its willful melancholic slumber, forcing the country into a post–Cold War temporality.

Cruz, like Fornes and Cortiñas, and, for that matter, a host of Cuban American cultural workers that would include and not be limited to Coco Fusco, Carmelita Tropicana, Marga Gomez, Ela Troyano, Delores Prida, Raul Ferrera Balanquet, Ernesto Pujol, Achy Obejas, Caridad Svitch, Tony LaBat, Marcos Bequer, and the late Felix Gonzalez-Torres, all negotiate the onus of seeing Cuba, which is again the almost impossible project of looking beyond this vision-obscuring haze to a rich life world of affective particularity. Cuba and Cuban America are both obscured by this haze and, at the same moment, constructed as monolithic. If we ever hope to understand Cuba, it seems especially important to really see it at this particular moment, as multinational capital encroaches on the island and the U.S. embargo shows no sign of abating. Cruz's drama functions as an elegant and penetrating optic that may well be indispensable to the task at hand.

Jody McAuliffe

Interview with Nilo Cruz

JODY MCAULIFFE *How would you describe your relationship to Cuba?*

NILO CRUZ I left Cuba when I was ten years old. That was in 1970. I left with both of my parents, leaving two sisters behind. They were older and they had gotten married. They could not leave the country because their husbands were of military age.

So your parents stuck around for a while after the revolution?

We were definitely not the upper or middle class that left in the early sixties. Actually, my father went to prison when I was two years old. He was caught leaving the country on a boat. He had attempted to go at that time in the early sixties in order to make way for us, to get to the United States as a refugee. But he got caught and became a political prisoner.

Was it his release from prison that finally prompted your exit?

My mother really wanted to leave the country. We were for the revolution at the beginning,

The *South Atlantic Quarterly* 99:2/3, Spring/Summer 2000.
Copyright © 2001 by Duke University Press.

and when the revolution started to get more leftist, you know, they had particular agendas that tended to be more Marxist, that's when my parents thought, "Oh," especially when they started to take property away from people and when everything became nationalized; they thought it was time to go.

And they went to Miami?

Yes.

And what was that like?

Well, imagine being new immigrants—not immigrants—exiles, there's a big difference. They had heard of the violence of the United States. There were a lot of racial tensions during that time in Miami. I led a very sheltered life as a boy. And then, of course, having to deal with a new language. I was starting to go to school and learn English. My mother started to work at a purse factory, and my father started to work at a shoestore.

What got you interested in theater?

I always wrote poetry when I was in my teens. Theater, you know, it's funny because it sort of fell in my lap. I had a couple of friends who were taking theater classes, and I visited the class once and really loved the professor. My professor used to teach theater with a book of Krishnamurti in one hand and a Stanislavsky book in the other hand. This was at a community college in downtown Miami. Besides being an actor and a professor, she was also a poet. I really felt at home there. It was almost like a calling. I started to take classes with her. Instead of bringing scenes to class, I would write my own scenes. And then a lot of the students wanted to be in my scenes. She felt that I was not an actor. She said, "I think you're a director or a playwright." Much later on I met Irene Fornes. She came to Florida and conducted a workshop. During that time I was working in cargo at the airport. She said, "I do these workshops at Intar in New York, and at the moment I have one place in the workshop, so if you're interested you can come up to New York with me." But I had to make a decision right away, so I quit my work. It was a matter of calling them on Friday or Saturday and then getting on an airplane on Sunday. And from then on my life changed.

What was it about the workshop that was most influential?

I had made a tremendous connection to her work when I read *Mud*.

Great play.

Yeah, and *Conduct of Life*. I just thought what she was doing was amazing. And also because she's Cuban; here was a Cuban woman who was really writing for the American theater. And I thought, if she can do it, I can certainly try and do the same.

Something that I would certainly say about your work and hers as well is that because English is a second language you achieve a very sharp, pungent, intense poetic language.

Yes, that's true. I think that's what attracted me to her work. There's something about language and poetry and lyricism that we both share.

One of the things about Two Sisters and a Piano *that I like very much is the way that you use storytelling. It becomes a vehicle for several things: one, it transports the characters, and they transcend their place. It also becomes the engine of the erotic connection between Maria Celia and the lieutenant.*

I'm glad you picked up on that.

There's a tradition of having letters dramatized, but I think they have a real force in the play. Both the letters and her story.

This is the late eighties in Cuba. Castro called it "a special period" because the Russians were pulling out and the economy was in shambles. The Cuban people use a phrase: *no es fácil.* Which translates to "it isn't easy." Here are these women living under harsh conditions: they're under house arrest, they lack liberty. But it's through the work that they do — one of them escapes the house via the piano and the other one with her storytelling. And the lieutenant also escapes his immediate reality through the letters. And the way these two women live their lives in this —

Cell, it's essentially a cell —

Yeah, absolutely. I think that political loss is when you stop being yourself, when you stop being an individual —

Yes, and the lieutenant, as the military fascistic figure, is the one who has really lost himself —

While these women haven't. They're still keeping traditions. They're still holding on to an old world, very particular to the way people live on this island.

The smell of guavas, the way they fill the house with all those fruits—that's a perfect image of them remembering the past and staying closer to nature.

Absolutely. It's funny because I didn't want to write a play about the oppression of jails. I wanted to do the opposite. What do you do when you're in jail? How does the human spirit transcend all of this?

Even the lieutenant comes full circle in the end. They're in their house on hunger strikes, and he still is desperate to get in there. They're the most plugged into life. And he is dying next door.

There's a quote from Marguerite Duras that political loss is joining a party. You adhere to a certain mentality, and even though you're fighting for certain values, they're not all your values as an individual. There's a certain loss when you join the Communist Party because it has limitations. I think even at one point Duras was sort of leftist, and then she resigned from the whole thing and wanted to be more like an individual. That's something that I really wanted to touch on in this play, even though I think some people expected the play to be completely different, but I just chose as a writer to concentrate on this.

And you reveal some deep ironies, thereby, and you don't do a kind of knee-jerk . . . well, as you say, what people expect—they expect to see these women suffering.

Yeah, I do the opposite.

They're not suffering, it's he who's suffering.

Absolutely. Finally it makes them so strong. They're living under these harsh realities. They make something out of nothing. Going back to that phrase— it isn't easy but we still . . .

Yeah, but we endure.

We endure. And it's these two sisters who are doing the enduring. It's also the metaphor of the island, that it has endured for forty years.

Under a lot of stress.

Under a lot of stress from both sides. From the Soviet Union, certainly from the United States, and living under basically a dictatorship in many ways. I mean, there are no votes.

I always thought this was true about the Soviet Union. It essentially was just a military dictatorship, with a label of so-called communism.

I remember being in Cuba when I was a little boy. You know, Jody, I could not wear the color green for the longest time because it just reminded me of oppression and militancy, militancy more than anything

It's a uniform. [Pause.] The other thing I thought of in connection with your play was Arabian Nights.

Yes, this wonderful notion that Maria Celia has to tell these stories in order to live. You know I find that *Arabian Nights* is probably the most political because it was Scheherazade who stopped the killing of all the women, of all the brides. A woman was killed every night, and she stopped that through art. I am so glad you picked up on that.

I think it's a wonderful balance of those elements of piano music, dialogue, and her storytelling and letters. They have an equal weight in the space. I really appreciate the flexibilty of location within scene. The way that these different sounds take people to different places, transport them. That's a wonderful effect that the play has. I think that's what is quintessentially theatrical about the play. It's ephemeral. It's almost like a memory, an image.

That's why I was concerned. I wrote a little note for designers at the beginning of the play, not to be so concerned about the oppression.

Right, that it needs to be open.

Then you can go to other places. I always thought that once these women start talking about the sea that the sea starts coming into the house.

The place itself is a poem. Their house is not what it is. It's a cell. It's the sea. It's the roof. And all of those places are extremely strong images, and they're associated with sound.

It's so funny that you talk about sound so often, you know this started as a radio play.

When you went from the radio version, which I guess was a shorter version —

It was a much shorter version — twenty-nine pages, and the lieutenant was not in it at all.

So that was the big change.

I think that even theater can benefit from it a lot more. When you move an actor on stage it is clunky in some ways, because you have to move a body, while in film you cut, you edit, and you can go from one scene to the other. But there's something about sound which I loved doing the radio piece. Immediately through sound you can go to another place in a very subtle way. If you put the sound first you can travel faster and the image can then follow it.

Plus we have deep associations with sound; for example, in the play some of the music is so politically charged.

Yes.

It's not permitted, so the fact that they're playing it is this dangerous thing and that sort of thing would probably really register with a Cuban audience, and it's in the play so we understand it. Plus the music draws a very specific emotional response that in that context is forbidden.

It's very European, actually, the music, and it also breaks the stereotype, because we have this notion of what Cuban music is like — very danceable, very rhythmic — but there is classical music in Cuba, too, certainly something we inherit from Spain.

I know you did your graduate degree at Brown, and I wonder what, if any, influence Paula Vogel had on your development as a writer?

Paula was very influential, I think more as far as structure is concerned. Brown allowed me to experiment more with structure. It also gave me two years to be in a safe environment. They gave me the room and the license to go ahead and just exorcise my playwriting demons.

That's what you're supposed to be doing.

Right, and she was so supportive that there was no right and there was no wrong. And you can see that with her structures: watching slides from a trip the actors never take in *Baltimore Waltz*, and lessons on driving in *How I Learned to Drive*.

I know you've directed a good bit of your own work and the work of others and worked with directors. What's the big difference for you?

With *Two Sisters*, it took me about two years to write it. I felt I needed to work with a director because I needed an outside perspective. It was really good to have a dialogue as far as how the play was moving. I prefer to work with the director for the premiere and then after that for me to direct it even though it's hard to forget how it was done. I tend to direct less now. Directors add another dimension to the play. They bring another level to it.

How much writing do you do in production, and how has the developmental process served you?

I do a lot of rewriting in production. I did some for the McCarter — I changed a whole scene. When "Two Sisters" was done at South Coast Repertory, I took scenes from the second act and brought things to the first act. It's when you get to do the real work, because you have the canvas in front of you and you can see what's working and what's not working. It's essential for a writer to open up to the writing process during rehearsals.

How does the American theater look from your perspective, and, as a function of that, what's your experience in the regional versus New York theater?

I'm glad you're asking me that question, because I find that I'm trying to do something, I find that my work tends to be a little more magical and a little more theatrical—

You mean than what you see?

I find there's a certain realism that takes place in North American theater, and there is realism in my work, but my work is also asking for lyricism. And I find that that seems to be lacking in North American theater. I don't shy away from creating lyrical language for the stage. I also think, who are we kidding, we're doing art, we're doing theater; if we're going to do naturalistic dialogue we might as well just go to the grocery store and listen to people talk

Or do TV.

But even TV, I was hoping that it would be more of an art form but obviously it isn't. Every time I look at a painting, even though the painting might look completely realistic you always realize that it's a painting, and I think it's the same with theater. When we go into a space we realize that this is not happening in the time of life per se, that this is a performance, this is theater. We might as well take artistic license and work with the art form, I mean the early plays—they were written in verse, and the language is always heightened, and I'm interested in that.

Do you find that people involved in productions of your work are able to achieve this lyricism?

It's difficult sometimes.

Is it the artists or is it the audiences?

There is a big difference in Latin American theater. Latin American theater tends to be a lot more metaphoric, it's more physical, it's definitely more theatrical, you have room to boast with dramatic acting choices. I noticed that theater in England is done from the neck up, that really people don't use a lot of their bodies, it's not a corporeal theater, and I find that if you really look at New York—we kind of worship English theater.

I know it's very Anglophile.

I think that influences the writers also.

It's a postcolonial legacy.

It is, I know. Even some North American writers that think they're not doing the kitchen sink play, and then they do this other thing where they talk to the audience, and they think that's not kitchen sink . . .

But it's not dramatic, it's narrative.

I have a big concern with the word *sentimental*; just because you deal with emotions in your work it doesn't mean that you're sentimental.

No.

I find that theater tends to be intellectual instead of dealing with the emotional life of characters.

I went to school in Russia and just speaking about the connection between Russia and Cuba—several years ago some Russian students from the Moscow Art Theater School came to the North Carolina School of the Arts to perform, and what was unbelievably startling was the physicality of the work. Their vocal work was not so good, but that's more a British thing.

The British are very good at that.

But the physical work was so beautiful and intense. Ironically, it's the thing that attracted the people in the Group Theater to Stanislavsky, but then what deteriorated into the Method—some of them lost the physicality and became preoccupied with emotional memory. They became less and less histrionic in the best sense of that word and more and more kitchen-sinky. We missed the best part. It's kind of a neat connection between Russia and Cuba.

What happens is that a lot of actors haven't had the training. They play gangsters in films; their vocabulary is very limited.

No poetry.

No poetry at all. I love Lorca. Lorca deals with lyricism in his plays, but there's a lot of room for physicality.

Because there's so much tension between their bodies and what they say, and the repressed sensuality is almost painful. When you see those plays done well, they have a visceral impact. Your play has that force.

I did a translation of *Bernarda Alba*—talk about sexual repression. I'm actually doing a translation of *Dona Reseda, the Spinster*. I'm interested in that kind of theater. I'm hoping that I'll find a place in North America to do that kind of work.

I hope so, too.

It seems that I'm better able to do that work in regional theater than in New York.

New York can be restrictive.

I'm not interested in just doing "downtown work." There's a formality to my work that you were talking about, if you look at the scenes, the way they're structured, they have something of the well-made play kind of quality to them, but they also bleed into something else.

You want to reach a broader audience.

I find that I do reach a larger audience when I do regional theater.

Like at South Coast, for example.

Certainly.

You get a very different crowd than you would get downtown.

What's the alternative in New York? You have Broadway, and then you have the Public, which is sort of in between both those places. And Lincoln Center is like Broadway.

It's a huge institution.

I feel like you can still experiment in regional theater.

I'm glad you've found that to be true.

Interviewer's Note

Other plays by Nilo Cruz include *A Park in Our House, Night Train to Bolina, Drinking the Sea, Dancing on Her Knees, Betty and Gaugin, Graffiti,* and *Hortensia and the Museum of Dreams.*

Erin Cressida Wilson. Photo: Dixie Sheridan.

Erin Cressida Wilson

The Trail of Her Inner Thigh

The Trail of Her Inner Thigh received its world premiere at Campo Santo at Intersection for the Arts, in San Francisco, on June 4, 1999, with the following cast—Sean San Jose (Kasper), Lisa Steindler (Patricia), Rachelle Mendez (Jolene), Fe Bongolan (Maria), and Selana Allen (Kymmie, Bunny, Stephanie); and creative contributors— Rhodessa Jones (Director), Margo Hall (Codirector), James Faerron and Donyale Werle (Sets), Marsha Long (Lighting), and Marcus Shelby (Music).

The *South Atlantic Quarterly* 99:2/3, Spring/Summer 2000.

Characters

One man and the women in his life . . .

KASPER, *Male. Thirty. Latino. Jolene's father.*
PATRICIA, *Female. Forties. Hippie. Trashy. Jolene's mother. Proud of the fact that she could seduce a fifteen-year-old boy. Sad that she is now over forty.*
JOLENE, *Female. Teens. The daughter of Patricia and Kasper.*
MARIA, *Female. Forty-five. Latina. Kasper's mother.*

The following three outside women are played by the same actress:

KYMMIE, *Female. Twenties–thirties. Sexy, adorable, funny, smart, fucked-up, voice like a fly, turns into a goddess.*
BUNNY, *Female. Teens. Jolene's friend.*
STEPHANIE, *Female. Thirties. Needs to get her hair done.*

LOCATIONS:
San Francisco, California.
Outside Phoenix, Arizona.
Las Vegas, Nevada.
Hurricane, Utah.

Simple set that can represent several locations. Should be nonliteral. Only a few props.

Prologue

Present Time: Wandering and Chasing Each Other

Music—sexy, a flash of tattoos.
KASPER *in the foreground praying—with the four women in his life behind him. Their backs are to the audience, they wear short retro black hotpants.*
KASPER *runs his finger along the tattoos on his body . . . women's names. As he names them, the corresponding woman grinds. A dance of asses. In the shadows. No faces. Flash of tattoos on his body . . .*

KASPER   Maria . . . Jolene . . . Patricia . . . Kymmie . . .

KYMMIE *does the biggest grind of all, as the music swells and* JOLENE *moves away from the women and into her own space—a girl at pay phone.*
KASPER *speaks;* JOLENE *translates underneath.*

KASPER (*in the clear*) *Estoy buscando, estaba buscando, estuvi buscando.*

JOLENE (*in the clear*) I am looking. I have been looking. I looked.

KASPER *Cuando voy a encontrar lo, lo que es . . . es que me falta, mi familia.*

JOLENE (*simultaneous with* KASPER's *next lines*) When am I going to find my family? . . . my other self.

KASPER *Que esta adentro de mi, adentro de mi corazon quien vive? La mujer que hizo el hombre de mi, el hombre que cree en las mujeres. Mi otro yo, que no.*

JOLENE (*simultaneous with* KASPER's *next lines*) Please. Bless me with a kiss from the little angel of my dreams.

KASPER *El otro lado de mi, Mama. Por favor me bendiga con un beso de mi angela bella. . .*

KASPER (*continued, in the clear*) *La angelita de mis suenos.*

KASPER *and* JOLENE *look at each other across the other women.*
Blackout.

Introduction

San Francisco: 1978

Spot fires onto KASPER's *face. He speaks to the audience.* MARIA *speaks from her sickbed.*

KASPER San Francisco. 1978. He was fifteen years old.

MARIA *Jovencito.*

KASPER Named . . .

KASPER/MARIA Kasper.

KASPER Taking the 24 Divisadero from the Marina to the Mission, she spotted him.

PATRICIA Because he was beautiful.

KASPER She sat next to him, talked to him.

PATRICIA And the next day fucked him in her apartment. Straddled him, sucked him off, and gave him a line of blow.

KASPER But it was speed—stepped-on bad—and he vomited in her toilet and sat back high as a kite.

PATRICIA She tricked him.

KASPER Since all the other lines had been coke. But he didn't mind, he was in heaven . . .

PATRICIA She was thirty-one years old . . . It took her only two and a half months to get pregnant, at which point she decided she was leaving town. And she did.

KASPER He went back to *pinche* high school, slammed speed in the parking lot, fired up glass pipes under the bleachers, and nine months later received a telegram from Arizona. The *baby* was born.

Spot on JOLENE's *freckled face.*

KASPER Her name was . . .

JOLENE Jolene Wilkinson.

KASPER He buried the telegram in his mattress and became a speed freak.

JOLENE (*whispered*) Blackout.

Blackout.
Lights up on PATRICIA *and* KASPER *on a city bus.*

JOLENE Lights up on Patricia and Kasper when he was fifteen. San Francisco: 1978. *Before the first kiss.* This is how they first met—on a Muni bus.

PATRICIA What are you reading?

KASPER Geometry, nothing.

PATRICIA Oh . . . you're reading geometry?

KASPER I like nonfiction.

PATRICIA Yeah?

KASPER Yeah.

PATRICIA Does this bus turn left on Twenty-sixth?

KASPER Yes.

PATRICIA You live in . . . ?

KASPER What?

PATRICIA Where? You live?

KASPER What? I'm gonna tell you where I live?

PATRICIA What street?

KASPER Why?

PATRICIA Trying to see it. See where you live. I could give you a lift sometime. Instead of the bus. My bus is better.

KASPER Your bus. Like flower power bus?

PATRICIA Yeah.

KASPER Oh. Like bed in the back flower power bus?

PATRICIA Uh-huh.

KASPER Oh . . . yeah . . . I live at Valencia and Twenty-fourth.

PATRICIA You live in Noe Valley.

KASPER I like to think of it as the Mission.

PATRICIA And the geometry?

KASPER Where are *you* getting off?

They fall together. Kiss really hard. On the floor. He holds her neck down and she straddles him.
Blackout.
He goes down on her.
Blackout.
He's at her feet . . . washing her feet. She puts her fingers through his hair. During their love-making, JOLENE stands above and speaks to the audience.

JOLENE She was thirty-one years old. Named Patricia. My Mama. He was fifteen years old.

MARIA (*horrified at their love-making*) *Jovencito. Mi hijo.*

JOLENE It took her only two and a half months to get pregnant (she would have done anything), at which point she packed it all up and . . .

PATRICIA/JOLENE Left town.

JOLENE He came to her VW bus one day after school.

KASPER Flowers or some shit, between his teeth . . .

JOLENE He came to her VW bus, and all that was left was . . .

KASPER An empty parking space.

JOLENE He went back to . . .

KASPER *Pinche* high school. Got fucked up *torcido* . . .

KASPER *ties his arm tight, shoots up.*

JOLENE Got fucked-up loaded at recess. And nine months later received a telegram from Arizona. The *baby* was born. Her name was Jolene Wilkinson.

MARIA *Tu, angelita.*

KASPER He buried the telegram in his mattress and became a speed freak.

KASPER *throws the needle down.*
Blackout.

Part 1

San Francisco: 1993
Fixing the Broken Thing

MARIA *and* **KASPER** *stand at the front door.*

KASPER Fifteen years later I pack everything up. I'm thirty years old now.

MARIA Still a *jovencito* face.

KASPER Mama. *Ya.*

MARIA *Vete.*

KASPER I'm going!

MARIA I tell him, "Go, find the woman, find your daughter, to be a man, so I can go and leave you whole."

KASPER Don't die while I'm gone.

MARIA And then he places his lips on the indentation . . .

KASPER The bowl.

MARIA That holds my cross.

KASPER Mama, I'll find my daughter.
I'll move to Arizona and get the first job I can, working at a gas station.

Lights focus on the thighs of JOLENE. *She's sliding her legs down, twisting her bare feet around each other.*

KASPER I mention my trippy name of *Kasper* to every customer, until one day a young thing in hotpants seats herself across the street from the gas station, stares. And even from across the street, I can see she's got a spray of freckles across the bridge of her nose. I get somehow, you know, aroused or some shit, seeing those freckles, seeing her now-retro hot-pants. I walk into the bathroom, don't jerk off, just think of refrigerators, refrigerators, refrigerators. Until I lose this hard-on. I've heard that men get this way when they see their children born.
She's still sitting there when I leave work that night. I don't look at her because I'm gonna pretend that she found me instead of my calling her. This babychild from a fifteen-year-old telegram.
Back at the *rascuache* highway motel, I comb Tres Flores through my hair with my fingers. And dream that I drink the spray of dots across her nose and blow them out again, across her shoulder. Because she is mine.

Crossfade to BUNNY.

BUNNY It's raining and it's hot. So hot the walls burn your hand when you touch them.

JOLENE In a motel.

BUNNY It's outside-a Phoenix.

JOLENE Waiting for my best friend.

BUNNY It's Bunny!

BUNNY/JOLENE *Hey!!* We hang in the motel rooms, because we know the cleaning lady—

BUNNY It's Jolene's mother.

JOLENE Mama.

PATRICIA Patricia. An old hippie, used to be a junky.
"Jolene, your father was a junky, too."
I've told her. But Jolene, she's straight.

JOLENE And not from being in any damn "program."
Got milky white skin on my thighs, and any time I'm lonely, I put my hand on my thigh and break into tears. I pretend it's my father's hand touching my Mama's thigh.

PATRICIA/JOLENE/MARIA This fifteen-year-old boy named "Kasper."

JOLENE I gets a job cleaning rooms when Mama sets up a beauty parlor.

BUNNY Girl, you know your Mama got you that job. Frontin' like you found it.

JOLENE So. Anyway.

BUNNY (singsong) You're feelin' crunchy, because you're moldy, because I faced you, I got the job at Baskin Robbins, and you don't have it.

JOLENE So what. I got a better uniform.

BUNNY Oh, you know I make the pink and brown stripes work. I come off fly.

JOLENE Not with that *corny*-apple hat they make you wear.

BUNNY Well, okay. But I still look better in my uniform than you look in your apron and shit.

JOLENE No way. Men love girls in maid outfits. I mean they really love it.

BUNNY For reals?

JOLENE That's right, honey.

BUNNY Woo!

JOLENE So I get this job—maid uniform and all—to help out. Then one day Bunny visits me in one of the rooms.

BUNNY I heard that someone named Kasper is working at the gas station, and you know that's a weird-as-shit name. You think that's your . . .

Lights up on KASPER *pumping gas.* JOLENE *from across the street . . .*

JOLENE From across the street he looks sexy—like Johnny Depp or some shit.

BUNNY Duh!

JOLENE Bet he's strong. I pull a Marlboro Light out of my silver miniature backpack. Light the smokes. I pull at the callus on my baby toe as I take a long drag from the cigarette.
I'm looking at him and also thinking that at home I've got a collection of used soap from the motel rooms, that I'm going to boil down, put into molds. To make a starfish and a shell. There will be a large selection in a tray in the big house that I will live in with my man named Kasper.

Lights shift, JOLENE *suddenly runs up to* KASPER.

MARIA And then she's standing there in front of him.

JOLENE Can I use your bathroom?

KASPER Yeah . . . yeah, uh-huh.

Door to bathroom slams.

JOLENE Ten minutes later I walk out of the john with berry-stained lips, stand at the end of this old red Corvair that he's pumping, I look at him and won't speak.

KASPER What?

JOLENE And I don't have any idea why I do this but I make up—I'm three months pregnant, I feel sick, I need to sit down inside.

KASPER I'll get you a Coke.
And I reach into my pocket for the coins that fall into the machine extra loud, and I'm shaking, but I hand it to her. Don't even slide along her fingers. Don't touch her. She takes a sip.

JOLENE It feels almost like tears, not so much from the thought of seeing my father but from the secret I've got. That he doesn't know that that's who he is.

KASPER I just stand there and shuffle receipts.

JOLENE I look at his nose in profile, listen to his breath. And smoke. His fingers are yellowed from filterless cigarettes . . . like mine.

She spreads her fingers across her thighs to see how they are yellowed like his.

KASPER *Hijo de la gran puta* . . . I've got an erection again. I hate *mi pinche vida*. It pisses me off no fucking end, so I take two hundred dollars out of the cash register, walk out from behind the counter.
Here.
And put the money in her hand and walk out.

JOLENE What?

KASPER What?

JOLENE What the fuck's the cash for?

KASPER You.

JOLENE Like I'm a hooker.

KASPER Hell, no.

JOLENE What then.

KASPER You're pregnant?

JOLENE No.

KASPER You were lying?

JOLENE Yes.

KASPER Why?

JOLENE Can't help it.

KASPER A pickup honks outside, and I leave the room. Thank God.

JOLENE I draw the outline of his nose with the end of my finger onto my bottom lip.

KASPER I walk back inside, the pickup's still outside.
Fuck.

JOLENE Fuck what.
Sip the coke. Suddenly, I think he knows—
Do you know Bunny?

KASPER Who?
Like I'm mad-doggin' her, but I can't look at her, and I get some change out of the cash register.

JOLENE My friend.

KASPER Look, lady, I don't know who you are.
In a voice that sounds like a wack John Wayne. It's such an ill thing I said. I decide I got to get outside. Think of something quick. So I grab a travel mug and a scratch-off bingo card, go out and give it to the pickup guy. *Chingao!* I memorize her face into my eyes, and decide I never want to see her again. I walk away into the desert, like some fucking Indian macho guy that I am not, that somewhere in the back of my head I think I am.

The glare of the midday sun in the eyes of the audience. Pause.

JOLENE Three hours later I'm there alone, eating beef jerky and pumping gas. I keep looking down the empty road for him. Then Bunny comes by.

BUNNY Holy shit!! What's up?!

JOLENE I draw with my shoe in the dirt the name *Kasper* and the silhouette of his nose. I realize there will be no soap dish and think about becoming a private detective. As I look up—

KASPER I'm coming back.

JOLENE Fuck!!
I brush the dirt with my foot, erasing his name.

KASPER Thanks for taking over. Here's fifteen dollars—that's five dollars an hour. OK. You can leave now.

JOLENE Won't leave though.
I know how to change tires and—(*talking without sound*)

KASPER In my mind I'm getting the fuck out of this town. I'm seeing her hand as a baby that I never saw, as a star with all the fingers pointed out.

JOLENE I'm seeing the soaps that I will make.

KASPER I shove the bills in her hand.

JOLENE My throat tightens. I've seen it on TV movies of the week. Fathers shoving money into daughters' hands.
You . . . you're . . . not . . . leaving?

KASPER I'll see you tomorrow.

JOLENE You're not leaving.

KASPER I'll be there.

JOLENE Where?

KASPER Her hair place.

JOLENE Whose?

KASPER Patricia's.

JOLENE Whose?!

KASPER OK?

JOLENE What time?

KASPER Four—no, four fifteen.

JOLENE Where are you from?

KASPER San Francisco.

JOLENE What's your name?

KASPER Kasper.

JOLENE Kasper what?

KASPER And yours?

JOLENE Jolene Wilkinson.

KASPER I decide, it's time to kill Patricia.

Change focus to the wall onto a framed pair of scissors and a lock of hair.
PATRICIA *puts on false eyelashes.*

PATRICIA Patricia's now pushing fifty. Still young enough, working now in my own hair salon, on a corner, with plants, and an old velvet couch in the middle of the room. And all the right magazines.

KASPER *enters the store.*

KASPER Can I get a trim?

PATRICIA Fifteen dollars for men.

KASPER . . . Without a hint of recognition. I sit in the barber chair and watch her fingers twist around my hair and then watch both of our faces in the mirror — *Memorias que viven.*

PATRICIA I'm cracking jokes and asking
when's the last time you got a cut. You long in this podunk town?
I look up at him in the mirror. Him. No. Look down at his brown neck, *his* neck, the scar, back up at his face, those eyes . . . Walk all the way to the other side of the store and press the little blue button for ice cold water into a Dixie cup. Drink it. Drink another. Drink another. God. Look at the door, think about leaving.

KASPER *Por fin.*
I like it kinda shorter on the sides!

PATRICIA Right.

KASPER And not too much off the top. I like a regular cut.

PATRICIA Right.
Sometimes when I'm very nervous, I suddenly sweat and perspiration

drips down my freckles, my arms, then my forearms, and actually off the tips of my fingers. It smells like skunk and some men have told me it's a turn-on, "musky babe."

KASPER (*to himself*) Say something. C'mon.

PATRICIA (*to herself*) I'm no longer sexy to you, am I? But I don't say it.

KASPER (*to himself*) What are you thinking? C'mon.

PATRICIA I realize that at one time in my life I was simply an animal, that all I wanted was to look into the eyes of a child, play washing machine in the pool with my baby, and to breast-feed. Yeah, I knew what I was doing. But I would have done anything. And I did. But I say nothing to Kasper and just start cutting his hair again and cut a curl off, put it in my apron, having the thought that I'll put it in a locket and give it to Jolene one day. I'll do the motherly thing . . . And then I realize Jolene must know he's in town. Shee-it. And that's when . . .

KASPER A customer walks in.

STEPHANIE Hello, Patty!

PATRICIA Hey there, Miss Steph. Have a seat.
I am not taking my eyes off Kasper and then, don't know why, but I smile. Would you, uh, please like to step outside.

KASPER *Ya?* Aren't you gonna finish cutting my hairs?

JOLENE Jolene walks in the door.

PATRICIA Motherfucker. I want to haul off and hit Jolene, but instead I pull the dark curl out of my apron and throw it in Kasper's face—making absolutely no impact at all . . . cause for some reason I want to ask him over and over again, please I thought you would never . . . those kisses under Eucalyptus, at Land's End, . . . your skin . . . like cocoa butter . . . like cocoa butter.

JOLENE What's the matter, Mama?

KASPER I take the curl from my lap and hold it out to Jolene, who walks over and slides her hand under my fingers.

JOLENE They're rough just like I thought they'd be, callused like my little toe.

PATRICIA Don't give her that curl!
Like an idiot.

KASPER *Y porque,* you were keeping it for her anyways, *que no?*

PATRICIA What?! What?!! What's with the Mexican?!

KASPER Shit, that temper.

PATRICIA What do you want?

KASPER What—you gonna put that curl in a locket. Keep me in a clasp like a memory she can hold onto to know her father.

PATRICIA Her what, her what, her what?

KASPER Oh, free love and all that, write up a telegram, send it off. It's the seventies, after all, people don't mind having their sperm stolen from them to hop around the planet in the form of beautiful girls that they can't never see.

PATRICIA I was a fem libber.

KASPER Yeah.

Silence. Then it's broken by STEPHANIE, *who refers to* KASPER.

STEPHANIE Hey, Patty, excuse me—we've never met, why my my, who's this.

PATRICIA My four-fucking-fifteen.
I turn around and walk out of my own store, pacing outside, smoking a cigarette, and looking through into the window. Jolene's writing on the mirror with the can of paint that I bought to write specials on the mirror. Jolene's writing . . .

KASPER/JOLENE *Kasper*

PATRICIA And then the strange words . . .

KASPER *Pah Tempe.*

PATRICIA Kasper pulls a Polaroid camera out of his pocket.

KASPER I take a picture of Jolene and me in the mirror.

STEPHANIE Hello . . . ? Your customer, who's waiting,
I come storming out of the hair salon.
I need my perm, hon.

PATRICIA Fuck your perm.

STEPHANIE Whoa—wait—would, you, uh—repeat yourself?

PATRICIA Fuck your perm.

STEPHANIE And I start to laugh for no reason because the word *fuck* makes
me so nervous.
And I pull my purse back behind my head like a three-year-old, really fast,
as a way to laugh with Patty and pretend she didn't really say "fuck," but
my purse, for some reason, *hits* the glass of her storefront and it shatters.
Falling. It shatters in sheets.

JOLENE As he takes his last picture.

PATRICIA The glass falling everywhere.

KASPER In sheets.

JOLENE It's crazy. Like an earthquake or a tornado—but it's Kasper.

PATRICIA And he's taken a picture of my little girl.

JOLENE I'm looking up at him, Kasper—the secret he told me, then the
look of my Mama, and how I got the secret of Pah Tempe, and I know the
stuff to do. He walks out of the store.

KASPER Right past her without looking.

JOLENE The look of my Mama.

PATRICIA Oh, he's getting off on this. My fucking store.

JOLENE Shattered.

PATRICIA I walk right back into my broken glass store. See the camera
sitting on the counter, and I pick up the picture. Of my baby girl, of her

"father." And I remember the shell. That I had always thought of Jolene as a beautiful shell that I had sculpted with the teeth and the gentle knives of my womb. That Jolene had been "immaculately conceived." And in a childish way I had called him my friendly ghost because he was like an angel. Fifteen years old, giving me a baby in my womb. He had left the snapshot and in that way killed me. Together—this boy and me—we had walked down the streets in the Mission and put coins in all the parking meters. Made love in the stacks of the library at Mac High. I had worn the same skirt for two and a half months, gently lifting it and placing him inside me as I straddled him in public and moved until we both came talking to one another, underneath the palm trees of Dolores Street. It is at this moment that I decide to invite him to dinner. Call up the gas station from the wall phone. Leave a message that tonight—six—no, six-thirty. Dinner. We live at 733 Sycamore.

———

MARIA A satellite.

KASPER She is my satellite.

KASPER/MARIA *Mi estrella.*

PATRICIA She is my shell.

JOLENE He is my dream.

KASPER But none of us are people.

PATRICIA No shit, we don't even know how to have dinner.
But I've got a red checkered picnic tablecloth in a drawer somewhere that I pull out, heat up a preroasted chicken, a jug of Chianti, potato chips, a pack of smokes, flowers on the table.

PATRICIA *and* JOLENE *wait at the kitchen table, but nobody shows up.*

JOLENE When Kasper *doesn't* show up.

PATRICIA I look at Jolene.

JOLENE But I won't look back.

PATRICIA Instead she goes to her room.

JOLENE *storms into her room, leaving her mother alone.*

JOLENE Take out a map of the United States, pin the curl to the top. He will be my mystery. I will be his private detective. I will close my eyes at night and my eyelashes will lick his cheeks and he will know that—

KASPER She is mine.

JOLENE Flying through the night.

KASPER Satellite love.

JOLENE *turns to the audience to introduce part 2 with a whole new energy.*

JOLENE Las Vegas: 1993: *sex.*

Part 2

Las Vegas: 1993
Sex

KASPER *shoots to Las Vegas on the bus.*

KASPER *Me voy! A la Onda!* Crossing over the Nevada border, passing a flashing neon cowboy, the sexy thighs on the broad two seats back. Put my hand in my pocket and feel the *ferria*—few hundred bucks—*pero* I feel the *fuego,* and I want to tongue some girl down, as I jump off the bus in Vegas. Then I think, fuck it, *eh,* what I want is, it's not so much a fuck, *no soy suavecito,* I just want to get *mis manos* on some girl's stockings—and rip the crotch out. *Simon,* I'm trippin'. So I go into a casino shop, pocket a pair of hose. The darkest I can get. Midnight blue.
Go to the roof. Look west, east, north, south. *Como un Indio.* It is a good day to die. Standing on tar, I open the package. Put the stockings on my *pito,* hard.
Bust a nut and admire it. *Chinga la pinga!*
Throw the stockings down in a corner, in a puddle, with some *chicle.*
Ay que cochino a la chingada! I stick my hand in my pocket and feel the crumpled note from the gas station, from her call. With the address and time of dinner. Dinner! Thanks a whole hell of a lot. *Yo la tengo!*
And then in my pocket, feel the six keys in my palm. They are sharp, then round and smooth enough to hold the tip of a finger. I pulled these keys

out of a couple of manual typewriters, with a wrench—before I left San Francisco.

These six keys hold the letters that make up the name *Jolene*. And this is how I write, this is how I right the wrong, make her right this time, in my palm. This is how I make my own girl to hold. *Jolene*, shining through my fingers.

Holding the letters, getting my nut off has made me strong—I'm-a find a broad by morning.

Sliding female pleasure. Spotlight on KYMMIE.

KASPER   *Orale!* And I spot her.

KYMMIE   Standing, chewing, fucking with my tight-ass stockings, pretending to be waiting to buy more poker chips.

KASPER   She's got the right kind of dark bruise lipstick that I like, but I don't know what to say to her.

KYMMIE   Shit, I peep this dude from deep, give him a look, you know, for real.

KASPER   *Hijole,* she really is a *puta de la calle. Chale!*

KYMMIE   Now I really work him with a fierce-ass look. Mmm-hmmm. 'S alright, he lookin' kinda alright. And he take me up to his room where . . .

KASPER   I shove the typewriter letters up her *panocha.*

KYMMIE   Daaamn! And then you go' bust another nut. Like that.

KASPER   *Y me llevo mi chaqueta.*

KYMMIE   And walks out. Now I heard of some Ben Wah balls—but Blood, you on some other level of the freak game with this shit. Oh, hell no. It really is go' be like that. Trick.

KASPER   Then I call Jolene from a pay phone—and hang up.

JOLENE   I know it's my daddy and star 69. But it doesn't work.

KASPER   Cause it's long distance.

KYMMIE The prostitute. The ho, whatever you call it. You sureasfuck don't know the difference—so don't even trip off it. Got a wad of bills in one hand now, and with the other I'm pulling out letters. Damn. He's a freak. "J to the L to the N to the O." Now I'm good with anagrams and graffiti tags but can't come up with nothing. I'm filing for divorce from my pimp in my mind. Fuck a pimp, it's so seventies.
Opening the filing cabinet in my head, and putting the letters in a folder titled "Reasons I'm Quitting the Biz." But I don't got no cabinet, so. But really tho', I keep these stanky little letters like a gift. I stick the letters in my cheap-ass purse and walk out the door. The funky-ass mark is standing at the end of the hall next to the elevator, pressing *up*, then pressing *down*. Like that's gonna make the elevator come faster. Then he turns to look at me, and I think I see him crying.

Spot on JOLENE.

JOLENE On my bed I bring my feet together, sole to sole, and open them like a book. It is my secret Bible that lives in my feet that I consult. And the Bible feet say . . . "Go! Go to him." So I grab the map, the curl, and the directions and jump down the side of my Mama's house. Because I'm ready. To follow Kasper.

Bright light. PATRICIA *stands alone in the awful yellow morning sunlight, waiting for the phone to ring, and it does.*

KASPER I'm ready to talk.

PATRICIA You're too fucking late! She's left to find you. And by the end of the week I intend to have her face on every milk carton in the state—and Mexico.

KASPER Keep a copy for me.

PATRICIA And he hangs up.

KASPER I hangs up.

PATRICIA That morning when Jolene didn't come down for toast and cof-fee, I yell up. Go up.
The bed is empty with an open window. Downstairs again, I read the note on the fridge. Like a Dear John letter except it's to her own Mama. It's held

up by a magnet with a daisy on it. I should have thrown that damn magnet away fifteen years ago. Then I'm thinking something that I know is stupid. That Jolene must have left because of the seventies magnet. Things like that make a daughter leave her mother for her only father.

I'm gonna suck on some ice cubes like when something hurts. I put a cube into my mouth. Water down my chin and I'm saying, out loud to my own empty kitchen, "Jolene, I'm not a topless cocktail waitress no more. I'm not a motel maid no more. I'm a hair stylist. I'm a fucking hair stylist for Christ's sakes. What more do you want?"

Blackout. And JOLENE *singing in the dark, on a bus to Vegas.*

JOLENE "Stay with him if you can, but be prepared to bleed. You're in my blood like holy wine, you taste so bitter baby, bitter and so sweet. Oh, I . . . could drink . . . a case . . . of you . . ."
Mmm-hmmm . . . I know where to go because he whispered in my ear, the place.

KASPER Pah Tempe . . .

On the side of the highway, KYMMIE *follows* KASPER. *She lifts up the back of his shirt and looks at his tattoo.*

KYMMIE The mark is hitchhiking on the side of the highway. I followed him from the bullshit-ass hotel casino.
I'm lifting the back of his shirt, see in red letters *Maria* around a tacky-ass heart. My gum pops, and I say high as fuck,
"Maria." Oooh. Shit.

Lights come up on KASPER's *mother*—MARIA. *In her sickbed.*

KASPER *Don't say her name.*

KYMMIE Maria? Your girl?

KASPER *Oye*—just don't say her name.

KYMMIE Oooh. So she ain't your girl, no more. What, she kicked you to the curb. Fine motherfucker like you. She ass out now, well shit, you pretty ass out your damn self.

KASPER She's not some *heina*.

KYMMIE Say wha, say wha, say whaaaaaa?

KASPER She's—not my girl.

KYMMIE Ahh, shit! It's your Mama, huh. Ta-dow! I hit it, huh.
Oooh, how sweet.

KASPER Even her voice sounds like a fly.

KYMMIE My name is Kymmie. Put *that* name on your arm—it's with a *y*.

KASPER I wonder if what I did with those letters counts as a misdemeanor.
Took the typewriter keys and placed them letter by letter. The name of my
hija inside this ho. I'm sorry I did that dumb shit.

KYMMIE What would your Mama be saying about your ass now. Mister
"got to be the freak of the week."

KASPER *Mira, soy menso.* I am sorry. *Soy baboso, no soy suave.*

KYMMIE Ooooh. You speaking all that damn Spanish.

KASPER I haven't even been with nobody in a long-ass time. I'm on a
mission, and I put you in it. And I don't know why. Something about you.

KYMMIE Oh, I'm in it now? In it to win it . . . with "Maria."

KASPER *Don't say her name!*

KYMMIE I mean, he just buggin', like it was some crazy-ass *in-vocation* . . .

KASPER Then, that soft vibration on my hip.

KYMMIE He pulls the beeper off his belt loop.

KASPER And Mama's number paints itself across my palm.

KYMMIE Hey, are you a writer or some shit?

KASPER I hit the side of the beeper with my thumb, I know the routine,
when she beeps she's either fallen on the floor, about to die, or she can't
figure out how to rewind *West Side Story.* I walk to a pay phone up the
highway.

KYMMIE I'm right behind you slick, I'm with you now. I don't care what
you is. If your ass is a reporter. I don't give a shit. I just like your style.

KASPER My style? No one's ever dug my shit.

KYMMIE I need some more money.

KASPER *Eso.* My style or my money?

KYMMIE Both.

KASPER I gotta call my mother.

KYMMIE Nah, but you know what I mean . . .

KASPER *Por favor*, pick up.

KYMMIE You the best dada.

KASPER Look . . . "Kymmie"?

KYMMIE Yeah, that's right, say my name, baby.

KASPER I got this tattoo the day my mother got sick.

KYMMIE Your mama?

KASPER Yes!

KYMMIE Oh, child, I'm sorry, there ain't nothing nice about that.

MARIA *picks up the phone; she is putting on make-up, trying to put herself together to travel.*

MARIA *Querido.*

KASPER *Mama.*

MARIA I'm sweating.

KASPER Suck on some ice.

MARIA I'm dying.

KASPER Turn on the TV.

MARIA All that's working is K-Q-E-fucking-D. And it's blurred.

KASPER I'll be back in two days.

MARIA I'm getting up, I'm coming!

KASPER No—I'm bringing her with me.

MARIA Did you find her?

KASPER Yes.

MARIA Does she look like you?

KASPER Nah.

MARIA Did you take her?

KASPER I want to be alone with her.

MARIA *La muerte* is coming fast to me, so what's the stall with you and your *hijita*.

KASPER OK, *Mama*, I'm hanging up now.

MARIA They asked me, just yesterday, down at the clinic, what you gonna miss the most about life.

KASPER *Mama!*

MARIA Did I tell you all that's working on the TV is *pinche* public broadcasting. And it's blurred anyway.

KASPER Yes, *Mama*, you told me already.

MARIA Animal shows and *gabachos* talking around a table like they're just, oh—having a conversation one day out of the blue.
The doctor says have I arranged the "details for when I die." *Mis velas, mi altar*, the small fires, what the fuck does that mean to Dr. Stanford, M.D.— and the swans, that mate for life, but *not* the birds of paradise.

KASPER What?! I'm hanging up right now.

MARIA Only these few animals need their *padres* to live to be complete, mate for life. All the others—alpha males, they all go off on their own.

KASPER Right!

MARIA Anyway, now you want to know what I'm watching on TV—all the fathers leave the packs, and families behind. But not you. Not my son.

KASPER Now!

MARIA   And here I am talking back to the TV and now to you. Shit. *Por la fucking chingada!* I used to be a sexy woman.

KASPER   You're still sexy. *Sí, ya nos vamos Mama.*

MARIA   *Ay, Cabron, Cristo!*

KASPER   Stop swearing!? Why are you swearing?

MARIA   *Mijito!*

KASPER   *Mama!*

KYMMIE   Baby is—oh, shit—I'm suddenly flashin'. Bump a little of that shit to calm my ass down.

KASPER   I love you.

MARIA   *Te adoro.*
He hangs up.

KASPER   I hangs up.

KYMMIE   He hangs up.

Dial tone.

═══

JOLENE   Stepping my toe off the bus in Vegas. I just painted my toes pink. Remembering what he said, I walk straight across town to the highway to stick my thumb out.

PATRICIA   Breaking every single dish in the house. Just trimmed my bangs to half an inch and putting on feather earrings. I've got the map of the greater Southwest, the Post-It with the words *Pah Tempe* written on it, and I'm stepping into my Dodge. Turning on the ignition.

MARIA   Turning in the sheets that are tangled between my legs as I reach for the cancer at the base of my brain and turn to the photo of Kasper and me at Christmas. *Disculpe me, disculpe me,* You want to know what I'm gonna miss the most about life, I say, I'm gonna miss not seeing my little baby, holding *la hija de mi hijo. Sí,* Kasper, I wanna hold your baby.

KYMMIE *and* KASPER *by the side of the road. He puts his hand out.*

KASPER Give those to me.

KYMMIE You want my gum? The popping bugs you, right?

KASPER The letters.

KYMMIE In your hand?

KASPER Yes, I'll take them back now.

KYMMIE You, uh, gave me those letter things. Now, the gum I'll put in your hand.

KASPER *Olvidalo.* Keep them.

He starts to walk away.

KYMMIE Well, shit, wait—wait, hold up, Pops!!!

KASPER *Que mas . . .*

KYMMIE Hey, baby! Can you feature this . . . Me, an Indian?

KASPER Huh? Look—I'm sorry I picked you up and then treated you like that, I know no hooker or nobody needs that—it's my shit.

KYMMIE Listen up, I'm-a tell you—they can call me nasty, freaky, or whatever—sexist—shoot, what ya'll know about it. I'm-a break it down like this—for real. My moms called women "broads," and she didn't mean nothing off it—broads, ladies, women, same motherfucking thang to me. Cause they can go on with they "la-la" sexist power . . . Madonna Miss Diana Coffy Brown—*whatever*!
They just divas, don't you know—but I'm me.

KASPER OK.

KYMMIE Uh-huh. Now, just listen: My sister Margie had a baby girl right before we was gonna take her to a Zapp concert for her sixteenth birthday. And that's when I was like—"OK, I am *not* goin' out like that, I'm doing my life a little different." Cause in my family, in my neighborhood, that's all it was, talking yang yang.

KASPER Yeah, well, that's why I only stay at my mom's.

KYMMIE Huh. Well, I guess you could get down like that, but in my house—it wasn't happening. My sister was supposed to *move out* as soon as she got back from the hospital with her baby girl.

KASPER Nah.

KYMMIE Oh, yeah. I ain't bullshittin' about this. My mom's boyfriend, Ed, just jammed me up, said, "Your ass got to go, too"—I mean, nigga, what!?!—I was only fifteen. And then Moms rush me out to her Chevelle, just starts driving around in a big-ass circle (I thought she was gonna wrap that motherfucka). And ran it on me: "Kymmie, girl, I'm-a give you this here blue card—this your ticket out." I was like, "Huh? Blue card for what, Moms, lunch at school?" She stopped the car—I mean dead stop. This blue card, it's like a green card, only it's better cause it's blue—it's for Indians. Moms said, "Girl, you are Indian now—you ain't got to be black no more . . . your father, that nigga was Indian—some part was, enough of his ass was, so Kymmie, girl, I'm giving you this blue card—so you go get your ass a special scholarship and you go to a special school." But I was like, "Hunh-unh. I ain't about to be up on no reservation goin' to school."

KASPER You said that to your mother?

KYMMIE She said, "You take this shit, cause Ed Dog—hunh-unh—he ain't having no more youngsters up round here—so you get."

KASPER No way—he really made you leave?

KYMMIE She pulled me real close on her chest. I crushed her Newports she pulled me so damn tight. The last thing Moms told me: "Yeah, they can say they little shit about you, but you just tell them, "Baby, I'm Indian," and they can't touch that right there." And shit, I be damned if she didn't open the door of the Chevelle . . . so yeah, I stepped my Jellies out—and uh huh, here I is, Baby Boo . . .

KASPER I can see right through her lipstick and can see the pink of her lips.

KYMMIE A big-ass semi stops right away. This dude gets real serious and pulls me in like he's gonna kiss me—but just says real direct-like—

KASPER Don't follow me.

KYMMIE No no, uh unh. You likes to be followed.

KASPER I let go of her, jump in the truck and slam the door.

KYMMIE I fall to the ground. Ain't this about a bitch. I drop the letters on the ground, moving them around in the dirt.

JOLENE I walk up to this girl and these letters, and notice they *J O L . . . ENE*! Spell my name.

KYMMIE Baby looks up.

JOLENE I know like that—this woman is crazy. And decide to keep walking.

KYMMIE Hey! Hey, man! Hold the fuck up! Girlfriend, you the type don't like motherfuckin' women or some shit.

JOLENE Turn around. I know I got a handful. I know the signs from seeing my methadone mother.

KYMMIE But just as quickly a car pulls up to this Queen Kymmie. And the guys all make noises—dumbass white boy noises. Well, hey—money is held out.

JOLENE For some reason I say, I'll see you.

KYMMIE Hey—hey, girl—don't say *Maria*.

JOLENE What?

KYMMIE Don't say *Maria*—that dude will straight throw some dirt in your face, you do that.
I jump my ass in the backseat of the car.

JOLENE I touch those letters on the ground with my toe and pick up the *J* from my name and put it in my pocket. With my heel I draw the triangle. And then spell my name, so I could see myself. With him.

A car screeches to a halt in front of JOLENE. *Blackout. Silence.*

Part 3

Hurricane, Utah: 1993
Animal

The hot sulfur springs.
KASPER *speaks from the dark.*

KASPER Pah Tempe is a river, an old Native American hot springs in Southern Utah, where an eighth of a mile or so is made of warm water bouncing over rocks. Red cliffs fly up from its shores.
I sink my feet inside the mud. I look up for the screaming rock. I hear a woman and out of the corner of my eye I see a light-green bathing suit.

JOLENE *appears in her bathing suit.*

JOLENE What religion are you?

KASPER Please—
I won't even begin with *por favor* here.
Don't talk about being a Mormon.

JOLENE Have you visited the Temple?

KASPER Don't add me to your list of converts. Please—
I turn around and it is—

JOLENE Jolene.
I smile so thick and proud of the trick that I played.

KASPER I'm scared that she actually came and can only say, What?

JOLENE He puts his hand out in the water and grabs my hand. I'm light-headed. It makes me think of the Phil Spector albums Mama always played. "He hit me and it felt like a kiss . . ." My legs sink into the sand.

She screams.

JOLENE *(continued)* Is it quicksand!?

KASPER No.

JOLENE I point to the screaming rock.

KASPER Together we walk up the river in the moonlight.

JOLENE   As I watch him move from dark to light.

KASPER   She's holding my hand.

JOLENE   Who's Maria?

KASPER   She touches the red tattoo with her finger.

JOLENE   Are you Mexican?

KASPER   She's my mother.

JOLENE   Then in my mind I say "grandmother."

KASPER   Yes.

JOLENE   I feel my blood run hot. Roots growing from the bottom of my feet.

KASPER   My mother is dying.

JOLENE   I almost slip on a rock.

KASPER   In San Francisco.

JOLENE   Oh.

KASPER   Are you OK?

JOLENE   Yes.

KASPER   Do you want to come?

JOLENE   Hell, yeah.

KASPER   San Francisco or your grandmother?

JOLENE   San Francisco. Both. Her.

KASPER   I always wanted a sister.

JOLENE   I'm not your sister.

KASPER   What are you?

JOLENE   What am I?

KASPER   Tell me.

JOLENE You know.

KASPER I want you to tell me who you are.

JOLENE I'm your daughter.

=====

JOLENE I push away and do a somersault in the water.

KASPER Her hair flops up and back, spreading water.

JOLENE Across his face. And suddenly he looks at me.

KASPER I loved you. Even though I wasn't there. I loved you.

JOLENE A thousand butterflies are released from my stomach and are flying up to my heart.

KASPER Jolene.

JOLENE An invisible hook catches my tongue.

KASPER Then I feel like I've done something wrong—*maldito*—pull myself out of the water, wrap a towel around my shoulders. It's really too small a towel for swimming. It's more like a small bathmat—fucking cheap-ass hotel/motel. Now I look at it carefully, I realize it is a bathmat. I loved you.

JOLENE More butterflies.

KASPER The light.

JOLENE Shining in my eyes.

KASPER I can't believe what's below me. This creature, wet, with a nose, two eyes, and a mouth. Two hands that work. Her teeth, perfect. —Where are your baby teeth?

JOLENE What?
Like, "You're weird."

KASPER I want to see them.

JOLENE Why?

KASPER I used to think about what are the first words you are saying.

JOLENE My first words?

KASPER What were they?

JOLENE Mama.

The awkward moment of the realization that JOLENE's *first word was* mama *is suddenly broken by a meteor that flies across the sky.*

KASPER A meteor . . .

JOLENE Flies across the sky!

KASPER —*vola por el cielo.*

JOLENE I scream!

KASPER I put my hand over her mouth.

JOLENE I want to bite his fingers. But close my eyes instead.

KASPER *Me huele su piel y su sangre.*

JOLENE My throat gets really really really tight. He dives back in the water.

≡≡≡

JOLENE Kasper.

KASPER Jolene.
Whispering with wet sulfur lips. We've floated downstream.

JOLENE We float from the water to the beach, and we keep on going like this.

KASPER Chapters of her life flowing from her lips. The words fill in the censorships, the lace of . . .

KASPER/(JOLENE) My psyche./ (His psyche.)

JOLENE I'm seeing the shells, seeing the starfish.

KASPER Closer and closer.

JOLENE *lifts* KASPER's *shirt and sees the tattoo.*

JOLENE What's this?

KASPER I cut myself.

JOLENE Who is the tattoo lady?

KASPER My mom.

JOLENE Who's that one there? I want to see it . . . "Jolene!" Oh! How did you know my . . .

KASPER From a telegram.

She gently touches the tattoo on his skin that is her name. She looks further down.

JOLENE And this scar?

KASPER Appendicitis.

JOLENE And that scar?

KASPER I got it behind a bar in the Castro.

JOLENE Will you bring me to the Castro?!

KASPER Nuh-unh. I've got a scar on my tongue, too.

JOLENE How'd you get that?

KASPER Your mom was messing around with her needle under my tongue and slipped.

JOLENE No shit.

KASPER What is this?

He points to a mole on her upper back.

JOLENE An angel kiss.

He scoops her up out of the water and walks down the river. He puts her on top of his shoulders.

JOLENE And from up there I could see.

KASPER In the way distance.

JOLENE On a screen, way ways away, so you couldn't even tell who was the leading lady and man. A drive-in movie.

KASPER/JOLENE A meteor . . .

JOLENE . . . flies across the sky!

KASPER . . . *vola por el cielo.*

JOLENE I scream!

KASPER I put my hand over her mouth.

JOLENE I want to bite his fingers. But close my eyes instead.

KASPER *Me huele su piel y su sangre.*

JOLENE Where will I sleep?

KASPER But she's fallen asleep already, and I lay a towel over her beached body. Walk out of the gates of Pah Tempe and pour my body into the bed of a stranger's truck. On my back, across my eyes, between seeing the stars above me, I'm seeing the Virgin. *La Virgen Mujer* is holding me, and I've fallen naked and gray across her lap as I fall asleep in a world without walls.

≡≡≡

PATRICIA *wears a bathing suit and a cap. Sits on the edge of a motel bed holding all her stuff.*

JOLENE Night.

PATRICIA Elastic thoughts.

JOLENE Dreams stretch.

PATRICIA My car breaks down in St. George. Being fixed, and they say it will take the night. Me, alone, in a motel with a pool that splashes. Only one hour from Hurricane. From "Pah Tempe." I want to walk outside and go swimming, show my curves like the old days, but afraid of stupid things like rape. I'm trying to be my younger self, but can't drop it ever since I had her. Instead of sex, my mind goes to the Muppets, Mr. Green Jeans, Tickle-me Elmo, I am a mother, finally.

PATRICIA *grabs her bag and heads toward Pah Tempe.*

KYMMIE And suddenly I'm standing right above Kasper's sleeping body in the back of the truck.
Dada. Wake up, dada. Your mama's here.

KASPER *wakes with a gasp.*

JOLENE I wake up early and decide to go back into the hot river. But this time I notice a brown woman who reminds me of a movie star.

MARIA I'm moving my arms in the water. I love the water.

JOLENE I swim up to her with a big smile.
Good morning.

MARIA Why, good morning.
Knowing exactly who she is.

JOLENE What are you doing here? What brings you to Utah?

MARIA Oh, I just like it here at Pah Tempe, it takes me time to relax.

JOLENE I never been here before. How'd you find this place?

MARIA My son told me about it.

JOLENE My father brought me.

MARIA Where is he?

JOLENE Walking around, I guess.

MARIA He still can't sleep?

JOLENE No.
I look up at the screaming rock and then turn to—
Are you Maria?

MARIA How did you know?

JOLENE Kasper's got power.

MARIA Oh yeah, what kind?

JOLENE And I leap into the water, and her arms, thin, take me into her chest. And I come up for air. And then the hair that smells like—

MARIA *Flores y coco.*

KYMMIE *and* KASPER, *both naked, make love in the hot water of the springs in the morning light.*

KYMMIE Up on the rocks, Kasper and me—we are *feelin'* it. It's like a high school crush.
I lace my fingers through his and blow in his mouth like the wind. Dada. How you like it, baby?

KASPER *Dulce . . . Diosa.*

KYMMIE And it all so sweet for a special second. We're not just gettin' down, we're floatin' on . . .

KASPER But I can feel my mother slipping away.

KYMMIE My finger running down his cheek.

The following lines can slowly start to overlap.

KASPER *Eres de este mundo?*

MARIA (*to* JOLENE, *teaching her*) Are you from this world?

JOLENE (*learning Spanish from* MARIA) *Eres de este mundo.*

KASPER *Puedo empujar por ti y te atengo a tu corazon?*

MARIA Can I push inside of you and hold on to your heart?

JOLENE *Puedo empujar por ti y te atengo a tu corazon?*

KASPER *Por favor.*

MARIA Please.

JOLENE *Por favor.*

KASPER *Me bendiga con un beso . . .*

MARIA Bless me with a kiss.

JOLENE *Me bendiga con un beso . . .*

KASPER *Con un beso de mi angela bella.*

MARIA A kiss from the little angel . . .

JOLENE *Con un beso de mi angela bella.*

KASPER *La angelita de mis suenos.*

MARIA The little angel of my dreams.

JOLENE *La angelita de mis suenos.*

JOLENE *kisses* MARIA *once on the face.* KYMMIE *kisses* KASPER *sweetly on the mouth.* MARIA *kisses* JOLENE *back on her face and giggles, and* JOLENE *kisses another part of* MARIA's *face until they are kissing each other's face all over and then giggling so loud that* KASPER *can hear them and stands up to come to them. He watches them laughing and kissing.*

KASPER I run to the bank of the river and see—Oh, God . . . and I fall into her hair. Feel a slice of Jolene and smell . . .

JOLENE/MARIA *Flores y coco!*

JOLENE There's one perfect breath of flowers before I see, far far away, like a tiny tornado . . . my mama's Dodge! And I grab my grandmother and run back into the river. There she whispers to me that some creatures flower right before they die, and I look into her eyes, her pupils dilate and drink up the world and me, so that her stories wash my flesh. Her flesh. My flesh.

KASPER I watch them in the water like the snapshot that I always wanted to take. A family. Dinner. A tablecloth.

JOLENE And that's when I see that girl from the highway again. But this time she is quiet.

MARIA The sky opens up.

KASPER *La sirena. Existas?*

KYMMIE Yes.

KASPER *Eres de este mundo?*

KYMMIE Yes.

MARIA *Jovencito!*

KASPER *Mama!*

MARIA *dies in* JOLENE's *arms.* JOLENE *screams.*

KASPER Mama!!

KYMMIE And he lifts his mother and carries her to the top of the bridge. As I dive into the water, the flowers swim down the river.

KASPER *Mi mama, mi madre.*
I would like to throw her over the edge. I bend to kiss the spot, the bowl that holds my lips. Where her cross falls.

JOLENE And he rips the crucifix off her neck, then pushes it into my palms. Almost violent.

KYMMIE I see them, the family, a red cloud of dust rising, and she is coming.

PATRICIA I'm down the road, raging forward to dig my teeth into the back of Jolene's neck.

JOLENE Mama! Look what she gave me!

KASPER Visions of funeral parlors, open caskets. I pray to be in the same town as her.

JOLENE I run back to Kasper, fall to the ground.

PATRICIA And storm up to him with accusations of kidnapping in my eyes!

KASPER I kick the dirt.
Shit, I was fifteen . . . you fucking, fucking, fucking . . . !

PATRICIA You fucking what?! What?!

KASPER She didn't make my mother live. My daughter did not take death away. I'm going to walk away. I'm going to walk away. I need to be the one to walk away.

JOLENE What do you mean!?

KASPER I'm leaving first this time. This is me, and this is what I do now.

JOLENE What do you mean!

JOLENE *runs up and throws her face into* KASPER's *chest. He lets her stay there for one instant and then pushes her away and holds her face in his hands.*

KASPER Two eyes. A nose and a mouth.
I take her hand again.
Drop her hand. *Jovencita.*
And turn away from the women.

KASPER *walks into the desert.*

KYMMIE He walks into the desert.

As KASPER *walks away* JOLENE *runs after him, and* PATRICIA *holds her back.*

JOLENE He walks into the desert. And I'm left looking back and forth, like a scared animal. I can see myself at pay phones for the rest of my life. Whispering.
"I am your daughter! I have more chapters. You didn't hear them all. Turn my page!"

KYMMIE But he keeps walking away. The walk away.

JOLENE I will fuck the next guy I meet and get pregnant!

KASPER *Caminando por la tierra.* She was fifteen years old, named Jolene. I will remember the freckled frame. In the steaming water and in the pool. The angel's kiss and how she touched her name across my skin.
I place my palm into the sand. Leave the print of my disembodied self. Who needs a father anyway?

KASPER *runs away into the desert.* JOLENE *runs and dives into the ground where he has touched the earth.*

JOLENE I inhale the dirt!

PATRICIA I spit on my hand and wipe the dirt off her face and make her clean.

JOLENE Then Mama just rips the crucifix from out of my hand and throws it!

PATRICIA Throws it.

JOLENE Throws it into the hot river. As it runs away.

PATRICIA And push my girl into my car. Lock the door and drive away in the dust.

PATRICIA *throws* JOLENE *into her "car"—which is made of two chairs—locks the door, pulls her daughter's head onto her shoulder, puts her hand on the invisible steering wheel, and stays this way through to the end of the play. Driving off in a fury.*

KYMMIE And I am left with the mother. "Maria." In my arms. I am saying her name. "Maria." And walk into the river. *Flores de coco* in the heat of the water. The crucifix running down and away and away.

KASPER, *alone in the desert, walking slowly toward us.*

KASPER Blood on the earth. My blood. *El sangre en el rio. Las memorias que viven, siempre viven.* The shattered. The shattered. The shattered. On this land. The promise and the beauty of the moment before the first kiss, the promise of the dinner, the tablecloth, the wine, the bread, the tribe, but we walk, I walk, because we are animals with no more funeral rites, with no way to bury the dead, with no glue to hold us to the ground, to make us . . . anything but me, I.

He walks in a large and endless circle.

KASPER (*continued*) *Estoy buscando, estaba buscando, estuvi buscando.* I am searching.

KASPER *continues his circle as the lights slowly fade on* PATRICIA *driving away with her daughter, and* KASPER *disappears into the blackness with his back to the women.*

End of Play.

Patricia (Lisa Steindler) and Kasper (Sean San Jose) in *The Trail of Her Inner Thigh*, Campo Santo, 1999. Photo: Tom Ontiveros.

Kasper (Sean San Jose) in
The Trail of Her Inner Thigh,
Campo Santo, 1999. Photo:
Tom Ontiveros.

Kasper (Sean San Jose) and
Maria (Fe Bongolan) in *The
Trail of Her Inner Thigh*,
Campo Santo, 1999. Photo:
Tom Ontiveros.

William Davies King

Everyman in His New Drama: Erin Cressida
Wilson's *The Trail of Her Inner Thigh*

Every man in his drama has a story to tell, of
every woman, and every woman in these stories
falls under age-old categories—mother, wife,
daughter, whore—and she usually speaks well-
worn lines that confirm that the man's drama is
not dramatic. It's his story. What these women
say proves to be an expression of that man, his
fantasies and realizations, and so they are aspects
of him, his good deeds, temptation, knowledge,
faith, and so on, standing in judgment before
God, who is also him, or rather He. There is no
drama to that drama because there is no other
voice. It's an epic, no matter how it lays out on
the page. The epic tradition keeps the other voice
in quotation marks; the drama puts it in play.

Arthur Miller's *After the Fall*, the most distin-
guished example of masculine "epic" nondrama,
is one of the more repellant plays of this century
because it so fervently wants to be a modern
morality play, an "Everyman," at that moment
when the liberal ego stood on the brink of realizing that it could not comprehend morality.
Critics reviled Miller's play for its "exploitation"
of the recently dead Marilyn Monroe, but it is
really the exploitation of Arthur Miller himself,

The *South Atlantic Quarterly* 99:2/3, Spring/Summer 2000.
Copyright © 2001 by Duke University Press.

in his character Quentin, that turned their stomachs. Here is a play that builds the world from the writhing, guilty ego of the author, and it is no wonder that nothing happens in that world, nothing basically changes, because Miller's character is unto himself. The passage of time simply confirms that the author is still alive and in your face. The women in that play exist by virtue of the man's experience, and they complete the picture of a world in which his life holds meaning, but they have no ground to stand on and so remain always abstract.

Wallace Shawn, in his recent play *The Designated Mourner*, has brilliantly updated and reanimated Miller's portrayal of the male liberal conscience, in a form that remains fundamentally as undramatic as Miller's. Shawn's Achilles makes bold to tell that a certain amount of time in any hero's tent is devoted to private pleasures, especially when the field of battle seems so distant and absurd. The epic hero of this nondrama answers the cry of conscience with a carefree "fuck it," and the women of his play, like the other men, finally just stop talking. Where are the Bacchae when you really need them?

Erin Cressida Wilson, in *The Trail of Her Inner Thigh*, has managed to come to terms with the nondramatic, talk-it-out story form and make it play. It is a realtor's miracle that she has found a way to house fully realized female characters in this fixer-upper, the male monodrama. The main characters in her piece include one man, Kasper, and four women—his mother, his wife (or mate, anyway), his daughter, and a whore. A glance at the list of characters seems to say it all. It's the well-worn configuration, the time-honored array, and Kasper has the classic problems sorting out familial and sexual relations among these women. The whole thing is his story: He tells us of a guy who got used as a teenager by an older woman to make her pregnant. She took off, and now, many years later, under strange compulsion, he goes on his odyssey to find the child of his loins before his own mother goes to her grave. He's the one who's always on stage, always introducing characters by his own perceptions of them. If Kasper didn't spot them, they wouldn't appear. But in this case it's *her* inner thigh on which the experience is traced. The amniotic fluids of his own birth have trickled down those surfaces, and he has returned there with desire and sperm. The play takes him again to those humid tissues—always with the *desire* to know himself in the warmth of another. Womanly flesh has enfolded this man's life, but in that age-old way that leaves him dry and hot, seeking some more deeply satisfying experience of the feminine.

"I want to be a person like somebody else was once," says Peter Handke's Kaspar in his 1967 play of the same name, derived from the history of Kaspar Hauser, the unfortunate German foundling, supposedly kept as a child in a prison hole in the early nineteenth century. Kaspar's appearance before the world attested to the innate humanity of man—or not, depending on whose account you accept, and Handke reimagines his story of meaning's struggle to detach itself from meaninglessness. This story is just as likely *not* the source of the name of Wilson's character, but that sense of a man attempting to find and know in the present the thing that was lost and forgotten in the past fits this play well. What is a man? was a question often asked in the name of humanism—or despair—as in that telling modern play *Woyzeck*. The recent answer, in the name of something other than humanism, has been, Not a woman. Once upon a time, the concept of Everyman seemed to apply, but in modern translation the term becomes *each man, each woman*, and further expansions of the phrase are standard—*American, working-class, heterosexual, of color*, and so on. Wilson explores several of these modifications of humanism in a way that does not lose sight of those Everyman themes—knowledge, faith, love, and so on.

Kaspar, who is as good a "father" for Wilson's Kasper (a Latino Californian) as anyone I can imagine, encounters the wasteland of the modern world as a grand occasion for incoherence, the human comedy with a tragic undertone. (The word *Kasper* in German means clown.) Wilson's Kasper, too, is on an epic quest to be somebody, like Everyman, like Kaspar, like Woyzeck, but his journey takes him to the mysterious core of womanhood, as indicated by the words he speaks in Spanish at the beginning of the prologue—roughly, "I am searching. I was searching. I searched. When I look at what I found, it is that thing I'm missing, my family. Who is it who lives in me, in my heart? The woman who made a man of me, the man who believes in women. My other I, no? The other side of me, Mama. Please bless me with a kiss of the beautiful angel, my angel of dreams." Through this speech the lights feature Jolene, "a little girl with straw-bleached hair," actually in her teens, just old enough to appear in the opening tableau as one of the women in Kasper's psychic configuration (like Bacchae or backup singers— mother, whore, etc.), "asses dancing." She's jailbait, and she's his daughter.

In other words, this play begins like a drama that will honor which way this man's dick points and his sentiments soar. It's all *his* psychic configuration, messed up by the woman who used and abandoned him, by years of living as a speed freak, by a frantic search for the thing that might complete him, and by the depleted world of California in the 1990s.

But in fact these women have their stories to tell as well, and in the telling Kasper becomes "he" and they remain "I." The daughter is just discovering the inarticulate longings of her body and the odd relation of a lover's and a father's place in her heart. Patricia, her mother, has become a beautician, a middle-aged woman, and a protector of her young, and she discovers that in all these respects she stands now at one remove from being the object of desire. Kasper's mother, Maria, needs to come directly into the heart of her son since she cannot occupy her body much longer, but his heart is something he must seek in these others. Their experiences hold them in a tight configuration, as they pursue a series of interlaced journeys. The play puts the audience in a position to observe the astral alignment of these bodies, the physics by which they exert emotional force on each other:

> MARIA [the mother] A satellite.
> KASPER   She is my satellite.
> KASPER/MARIA   *Mi estrella.*
> PATRICIA [the former lover, mother of Jolene] She is my shell.
> JOLENE [the daughter] He is my dream.
> KASPER   But none of us are people.

If they are not people, it is not for lack of trying. Their problem is that they are spectral to each other—potentially dangerous but ultimately more like angels or friendly ghosts. Their separate journeys will accelerate under each other's gravity as they approach, and ultimately they will bear directly on each other's lives in all the ways that men and women possibly can. Such redemption as they can find, after the fall, comes precisely in the possibility that they can be dramatically connected, not merely subsumed in each other's story. Wilson has an immense lyrical capacity to convey the sensuality and emotional cross-currents of the scenes in which these potent characters collide. There is a fine new music there. At the end, they are all still searching for a way to become, as Kaspar puts it, "anything but me, I," and the wonderful thing is that in this play there are moments when that occurs for everyone, though not for Everyman.

Jody McAuliffe

Interview with Erin Cressida Wilson

JODY MCAULIFFE *How did* The Trail of Her Inner Thigh *start for you?*

ERIN CRESSIDA WILSON I wrote it as an attempt to write fiction or a short story or novella in response to the state of theater in America, the lack of funding. And while I was writing it, it started to metamorphose into a play, and I have now done that with another play as well. I find that what may be a nice way for me to go is to start with narrative. This play has a stronger narrative than other plays of mine maybe because I started with a narrative before the play.

In the sense of story—with a beginning, a middle, and an end.

That's right. It came out of when I was fifteen. I had a friend who was fifteen who was seduced on a train by a thirty-year-old woman. Had sex with her for about a month and took lots of drugs. Then she disappeared and sent him a telegram that they had a child. And this so horrified me and fascinated me for the last almost twenty years that I was always trying to do something with that story.

The *South Atlantic Quarterly* 99:2/3, Spring/Summer 2000.
Copyright © 2001 by Duke University Press.

It struck me that if I were he I would go investigate, and so it came directly out of that fantasy of what he would do, and it also comes about with my being about that age—thirty—and my understanding her point of view in getting the sperm for the baby that she wanted on her own. So I felt I could get inside both people. And I also wrote it for a specific actor, Sean San Jose; and therefore when I had the actor, I was able to see how to make the character because Sean's thirty years old, but he seems very childish and like a man. So he could be the fifteen-year-old and the thirty-year-old who goes to look for the child. And he's perhaps retarded developmentally because of this episode.

Can you talk about the various stages in development of the play?

I've started in the last many years generally to wait—to keep my plays to myself for perhaps a couple of years, which I did with this one. Because I know if I'd gone and had a reading of this play, which speaks its narrative, and I was unsure of this and someone said, "Oh, I don't know if that's going to work," it would have cut me off. It would have really been damaging, and I've learned that lesson. So I kept it to myself, and between me and the actor who dramaturged it from the beginning on a daily basis over E-mail, and worked with you on it. When I felt okay about it there was a series of readings that I did not even attend in San Francisco at Campo Santo. And just from the feedback on that I started to get ready. This play had two workshops at Steppenwolf. They have this pretty great thing where they bring in the playwright for a series of workshops. And I prefer that it was in a city where I knew nobody and where it was okay to fail.

One of the unique things about the script is the idiom and something that I think is true about all your plays—that they make graphic certain inner workings of consciousness, which also means or includes that they use heightened or poetic language that is very physical.

Every time I get poetic I try to undercut it with very grounded, almost crude language and then undercut that.

So that the language has a dynamic with itself.

This is not the case with this play, because it has a plot, but I think that can be a plot, that can be a forward drive.

There's a tension, some kind of conflict in the language.

And hopefully a constant breaking of expectations. Once you think it's going to be mushy, it becomes very stark or very violent or very sexual. It becomes too sexual, and then it becomes funny.

You're actively pushing tones against each other.

What do you mean by the idiom?

The language itself. It's very vivid. The language that they speak, the different characters in different places, in different walks of life.

And yet I find that when I do this with actors, it's pretty normal.

I don't mean idiom in the sense of strange or remote. It feels very gut-level real.

I think that's the surprising thing that I've found with actors.

Kymmie, just as an example, has a very striking language.

It's almost another language that comes in. It's simultaneously much more grounded than any language in the play, which I think is a great relief.

She's sort of the real person in the middle of all this stuff that's going on.

She's the outsider.

Exactly.

She also speaks with a dialect that is possibly incomprehensible to some of the audience.

Well, it's like the Spanish. You have the Spanish and then you have Kymmie-speak. Each character has his own language. And the fact that the grandmother is teaching Jolene Spanish, and the repetitions in the script, this learning of language, and the names—the letters in Jolene's name; this is all a part of how these people traffic with each other.

Yes.

So there was the workshop at Steppenwolf.

And then I did it at the Taper, which was very useful.

The play changed?

In very small ways. It was mainly about learning how to play it more than rewriting.

You learning how to play it?

How big it is played.

What I was struck by in this draft was how the various languages of the characters have been sharpened.

Certainly Kymmie was expanded drastically.

To great effect. She's a kind of anchor in the world—just like the audience.

Yes.

Was there much change from the production at Campo Santo to the one at New York Stage and Film?

Yeah. I mean Sean was still in it. Script-wise I learned what was extraneous, honed it a bit so that it rushed more quickly and more succinctly to the end. What happens at the end happened a little better at New York Stage and Film. Suddenly in the last three pages, and even more in the last monologue, the whole thing seems to rush together and that causes emotion. It's very, very—

Cathartic.

On a mythic level, everybody relates to abandonment, to fatherlessness, to wanting a father, to wanting a family, to not having a family. I think that's really driven home particularly in the last line. We have no way to bury the dead, with no glue to hold us to the ground to make us anything but me, I, and then I'm searching. It's nothing new at all, and that's why I think it works—the utter aloneness and particularly the aloneness of being in America with no history and no religious ties, and divorces—

Unglued—

We're all unglued, we're all on the E-mail, we're all just floating around by ourselves.

I was reminded when I reread the script about how we'd talked about Gary Cooper in Morocco walking into the desert alone and Marlene Dietrich following him.

There were two things that happened in the play that reminded me of that movie. The thing that happens in Marlene Dietrich's house, before she leaves to go into the desert is her pearl necklace breaks and the pearls go on the floor and you just watch them go. And the moment when Patricia takes the necklace and throws it into the sand, and when Kasper walks into the desert; it was so much like walking into oblivion.

The way that Bill Foeller directed that ending was so out of control, it was so stunning. There was music, first of all. It was going to be Keith Jarrett, but it was a little too sappy, so it was something a little stronger, it was rock, electric guitar. So he had Sean do the slow walk while they're in the car—the mother and the daughter—and the lights just go very slowly, and Sean just vanishes, and the two women are left alone in the car. It was so heartbreaking.

It reminded me of all those movies about the desert, like The Sheltering Sky. *The desert just sucks people up, and there's something deeply romantic about it.*

I definitely think of *Paris, Texas.* When he walks away in that movie, he walks back into the desert. As a woman, I don't have any sympathy for him. I think you're an asshole, you're a child. So I sort of wanted to write a play that empathized with the father who is used and left.

But who walks away?

The way he claims his manhood is by getting them back and leaving them. I tried to write it in such a way that you would empathize with that need to go away and with the women being left. You see that women leave men with their children, which is not a very nice thing to do.

That's what Nora does in Doll House.

Yes.

How did you get interested in playwriting?

I was in college and had been a photographer for years and a dancer, and I came to a wall: I couldn't express what I wanted to express. I took a play-writing class and found I could express myself.

I know you were very interested in writing fiction. Even that notion opened up new avenues for you in playwriting.

I think it hooked me more into storytelling.

Which is a big element of playwriting.

And I think it was one of those things that nothing was happening career-wise, and now I have all these commissions and I have these things to fall back on. It was a nice gestation period, a nice downtime in which I could gather myself together. Of course, I had no idea I was doing that. But I found great comfort in just writing. I'm hopelessly lost in fantasy.

Is there any way that you start that is common among your plays?

It always comes from some kind of image or small story that stays with me for years, like the story of my father on a ship in World War Two; that sticks with me long enough that it starts to grow into a story.

Is it usually an image, which reminds me of what you said about photography — is it usually something personal or not necessarily so?

It's usually not something from my own life, but something that hits me personally, and then generally when I'm ready to write it, I usually write it in three to four days, the first draft. And then the subsequent drafts take a couple of years. But it does suddenly come together.

I wonder if you could describe your research process.

Mainly I read a lot of nonfiction about the subject matter. For *The Secret Ink War* I read a lot of Paul Fussell about war. I've done things like read letters or diaries; I don't do that any more. I'm constantly observing and constantly taking notes; I have a notebook everywhere. Reading a lot of books, typing up all the notes, circling what interests me, and then forgetting it. To me it's very much like research or notes for an actor. If you don't forget it, you'll just spit out the facts. But you have to just trust that it'll seep in and pop up in its own way.

You've been an actress for a long time. How has your acting influenced your writing?

If I weren't an actor I might know why. I think that I understand what it's like to stand on a stage and have to say some lines. And move around and have lights on you, what you can do with a set, what's possible and what's not possible. In fact, one of the things I know from working in theater and not just being a writer is that almost anything is possible. A lot of people stick their play in one room and that's the play. And I know from being on stage that that's just not the case at all. You can do practically anything you want.

Trail *moves all over the place and simultaneously.*

And it's no problem at all, just please don't ever make a modular set.

Why?

Oh, it's just so literal and horrible. The whole point is that they could be any-where. They could stand in the same spot and you can change the lights and sound and the whole play could work. Anyway, modular sets kind of really disturb me.

What do you look for in a director?

If they're good directors. I watch their work, if it works. It's certainly about if they can speak well, or sell themselves well. Since my work has a very strong voice of its own, I don't think it needs to be deconstructed further. Except in *The Bay of Naples* with you, or even *Cross-Dressing in the Depression* with Marcus Stern. But *Hurricane*, it would not be good to do that with that play. So what I look for is something very basic: Can the director make the actors play the scene? It's so simple.

Are there artists whose work you admire, and can you cite any artistic influences?

First thing I ever saw were puppet shows, then Peter Brook's *A Midsummer Night's Dream*, then the national tour of *Hair*, both of which were immensely influential on me. My father taught Shakespeare on film, so I saw all the Shakespeare on film—scary, scary films. I saw *Last Tango in Paris*. I saw *The Mother and the Whore*. *Swept Away*. Some of the first things I ever read on my own were short stories by Alberto Moravia. So obviously I was reading highly sexed and rather intense, violent imagery. One of my first favorite painters was George Grosz, very severe work.

Very sexed and very violent. Also political.

And I loved the expressionists. And in terms of playwrights—Kroetz and Peter Handke, Shepard, Williams, Albee.

That's a good crowd.

J.B. by MacLeish was an enormous influence on me. It was the first play that I ever read in my life that I liked.

When did you read it?

In ninth grade. It was poetic. It was repetitive. And also I like Baudelaire, Apollinaire, and Rimbaud's *The Drunken Boat*. So those were childhood influences. My parents never talked down to me—I might as well have been a Ph.D. at San Francisco State. There are good things and bad things about that. I saw very adult things. *Laugh-In* was a big influence, *The Brady Bunch*, *All in the Family*. Pina Bausch.

Pina Bausch is also highly sexed.

I think that this play for me is at the core just about abandonment. And I think that that's what's in the gut about it.

Interviewer's Note

Other works by Erin Cressida Wilson include *Hurricane*; *Cross-Dressing in the Depression*; *The Secret Ink War*; *The Bay of Naples*; *Dakota's Belly, Wyoming*; *Secretary*; and *The Erotica Project*.

Marlane Meyer. Photo: Ruth Marten.

Marlane Meyer

The Mystery of Attraction

The Mystery of Attraction was originally commissioned and developed by A.S.K. Theater Projects. A.S.K. presented the first reading in 1997 directed by Lisa Peterson. In 1998 the play received a staged reading at London's Royal Court Theatre, directed by Max Stafford-Clarke. And in 1999 South Coast Repertory presented a workshop production in its Pacific Playwrights Festival directed by Jody McAuliffe.

The *South Atlantic Quarterly* 99:2/3, Spring/Summer 2000.

Characters

RAY, *a lawyer in his midforties*
WARREN, *Ray's brother, a policeman, late thirties*
DENISE, *Ray's wife*
ROGER, *a businessman in his fifties*
LARRY, *a businessman in his early forties*
VICKY, *a beautiful young girl in her late teens*

The time is the present.

Eleven o'clock at night. A sparsely furnished living room; couch, two chairs, coffee table, lamps. An exterior door can be seen down right. Two interior doors can be seen at either side of the stage. A bottle and an ice bucket are on the table down center. The entire upstage wall is glass doors, behind which can be seen a beautiful tropical garden. It is lit for night viewing. VICKY *stands staring out the window.* RAY *and* ROGER *stand downstage, left and right, at either side, watching her.*

ROGER She's like a daughter to me, but she's not my daughter, she's my fourth wife's daughter. I raised her after the wife was killed in an avalanche. She is nothing like the mother, the mother was a monster. But the girl is sweet, docile. For years such an idyllic relationship exists between us that I'm on the verge of taking her as my bride when suddenly she is always in trouble. Escalating calamity as she matures. Disappearing every other weekend, lowlifes shaking me down, shoplifting, drug abuse, and a string of accidental homicides.

RAY *looks at* ROGER.

ROGER She says accidental and I believe her.

RAY Who did she kill?

ROGER Let's talk about who she killed this time.

RAY Okay.

ROGER Let me first say this. I've spent a lot of money keeping her out of jail. But does she appreciate it? No. She sees life as an experiment. A series of adventures. So this time, she confesses. She wanted to see, from the inside, how the justice system works. So, she confessed. The cops have the knife. Her prints are on the knife.

RAY   Who did she kill?

ROGER   I think she's doing it to spite me. That's right, isn't it?

VICKY *ignores him.*

ROGER   She's in a rebellious phase . . . Who did she kill? This guy named Vince, ex-fighter, stuntman, loser, doper . . . They came to the house in Palos Verdes one time, and when they left so did the silver. I'm talking sterling, at least twenty thousand dollars worth of sterling, and you know what they did with it? They sold it at a swap meet out of the trunk of their car. A dollar a spoon, a dollar a fork. For sterling. What are you gonna do with a kid like that?

RAY   How about lock her up?

ROGER   For stealing silverware?

RAY   For murder. I'm saying that maybe it's right that your daughter do time. Time is not the worst thing that can happen to a person who is testing the limits of morality.

ROGER   For one thing, I no longer think of her as my daughter, I think of her as my fiancée, and the second thing is the penal system is a whore-house. Guards sexually abuse the females under their protection on a regular basis. Don't you read the newspaper?

RAY   No.

ROGER   You don't read a paper.

RAY   Why should I? The news is always bad. Even when it's good, it's bullshit. It's supposed to make people feel better but it doesn't because the world is a chaos and everyone cooperates to keep it that way so they have something to blame for the shitty way their life works. I don't need a newspaper to tell me that evil flourishes, all I have to do is wake up, stay here, and people like you come to see me.

ROGER   My object in coming here is to see that she keeps from slipping through the cracks.

RAY   I understand that.

ROGER   But also that she gets the help she needs.

RAY Okay.

ROGER Because I don't want you to think for a moment there won't be retribution, just not at the hands of the state.

RAY The law should be the same for everyone.

ROGER But it's not.

RAY I think the best thing you can do is to let discipline be administered. Bad dog.

ROGER That's not why I'm here. *Counselor.* That's not what's happening here. Discipline the *dog.* She is not a dog, she's a delicious gumdrop. She kills zeroids. Nobody ever wonders what happened to them. Nobody ever publishes an article questioning what happened to all the John Does. Okay, granted, she might have problems with socialization, but she's my responsibility and I love her and I have to do everything I can for her.

RAY I'm giving you my best advice.

ROGER I think you're tryin' to shake me down.

RAY Not at all.

ROGER Because I have a lot of money.

RAY I said when you called I didn't know if I could help you or not.

ROGER Look. The situation is that when she goes to trial I want her to get off. Can this be done?

RAY This is America, and there are two types of justice, one for the rich and one for the poor. Which are you?

ROGER What do you think?

RAY Then it can be done.

ROGER Are you the man to do it?

RAY No, I am not.

ROGER I know you have connections in the system.

RAY I don't know what you're talking about.

ROGER   I happen to know you need money.

RAY   Anybody who looks at my shoe leather knows that.

ROGER   I also know you have a problem.

RAY   A man without a problem is not a man.

ROGER   You are in trouble with the animals, and the animals are about to open you up and take a piece out.

RAY   But nobody knows which piece.

ROGER   I do.

RAY   (*shaken, he laughs*) You know which piece? Really . . . you know which piece they're taking?

ROGER   Do you have children?

RAY   Supposedly, I have a daughter in Phoenix I've never seen.

ROGER   Well, at least you'll have the one child then.

RAY   (*he lets it sink in*) So you're saying they're going to . . . (*Beat*) They wouldn't do that.

ROGER   Oh, really . . . ?

RAY   It's a shitty little twenty-grand note!

ROGER   Getting bigger every day you don't pay.

RAY   Look, let's . . . you go, please . . . I don't want to be rude but, this is . . . goodnight.

ROGER   Ray, may I call you Ray? Ray, you seem more concerned about doing the right thing than saving your own dick.

RAY   Roger, may I call you Roger? Roger, I believe there is a balance and order in the world that we will all have to reclaim for ourselves one day, and Roger, if that is indeed your name? Today is my day. Goodnight.

ROGER *takes out his checkbook and tears off a check, which he leaves on the coffee table.*

ROGER   I'm leaving you a check for the amount of your debt.

RAY   I wish you wouldn't.

ROGER   And then some. If you cash it, and I'm assuming you will, then you'll handle our problem. If you don't . . . Well, I can only assume you're not as bright as you seem. (*Exiting*) Victoria, come.

VICKY *moves toward* RAY, *watches him, she's about to speak when* . . .

ROGER   (*offstage*) Vicky, get your ass out here!

VICKY *watches* RAY *a beat, then exits.* RAY *locks up for the night. He looks at the check. He can't bring himself to tear it up. He turns off the interior lights. He moves to the garden window, looks out, turns off the lights outside. After a moment, he turns the lights back on. His brother,* WARREN, *can be seen in the garden. He opens the door.*

WARREN   Hi.

RAY   How long have you been out there?

WARREN   I saw you had company so I waited out here.

RAY   Come in.

WARREN   What time is Denise home?

RAY   It's her late night.

WARREN *enters. An awkward moment.*

RAY   You want a drink?

WARREN   If you're having one.

RAY   I was going to bed.

WARREN   Uh, if you want to go to bed we'll just make it a short one.

RAY *pours a drink.*

RAY   I thought you were off the sauce.

WARREN   I am, I'm quit, just, you know, now and then.

RAY   Me, too.

WARREN   So. Who's this guy?

RAY He's a client, was going to be, maybe, but . . . not my kinda thing.

WARREN What's he doing here at the house in the middle of the night?

RAY Well . . . (*Beat*) I had to let go of my office, and I was busy all day doing fuck all . . .

WARREN You let go of the office?

RAY Don't tell Denise.

WARREN Okay.

RAY (*changing the subject*) So. What's up, Bro?!

WARREN Nothing, you know . . . I just dropped by. Haven't been by in a while, in the neighborhood and saw your lights.

RAY In the neighborhood. You live in Marina Del Rey and I live in Carson.

WARREN Ray, do you think there's something wrong with me?

RAY Yes.

WARREN Really?

RAY Yes.

WARREN Because I don't remember there always being something wrong with me, but *now* there is. You know? Before I was married I didn't think about myself the way I do now. I think about myself all the time now. And I think there's something wrong.

RAY Why don't you go home and talk it over with Sharky?

WARREN She started all this, and now she doesn't want to listen to me anymore. She tells me to put a lid on it.

RAY What, are you two fighting?

WARREN If my heart is breaking open and the words are coming out all I want is to be held . . . to be held and reassured, not told that I'm a mama's boy or that I have a Peter Pan complex or I'm a sick motherfucker, she has some mouth.

RAY Yup.

WARREN And what's wrong with having a Peter Pan complex anyway? Who doesn't want to sail away to never-never land and have Wendy take care of the details?

RAY It's the Wendies of the world who write those books.

WARREN The point is, I don't want to be fixed.

RAY Then you shouldn't be married.

WARREN I never thought there was anything wrong with me, and now I don't trust myself anymore. I find myself lying to retain my privacy, I don't like to lie.

RAY It's not a perfect world, but there are trade-offs.

WARREN Like what?

RAY How about cooking?

WARREN I do all the cooking.

RAY What about the shopping?

WARREN Since I cook I do the shopping.

RAY Cleaning up?

WARREN I do that, too, since I'm home more . . . (*irritated*) now.

RAY What about paying the bills and dealing with the auto insurance and giving advice about rashes and cuts and splinters and calling in sick for you and making hot tea, et cetera.

WARREN She never does any of that for me, and you left out sex.

RAY I don't like to think about you and Sharky having sex.

WARREN We don't have sex anymore, Ray, why is that?

RAY Jesus, Warren, I don't know.

WARREN Have you ever hit your wife?

RAY No. I am not a caveman. I have cultivated myself, cultivated my responses. I'm a civilizing influence, and to be that you must be civilized.

WARREN Uh-huh . . .

RAY Stuff like wife-beating only happens at night. You shouldn't stay up so late.

WARREN Staying up late is the problem?

RAY For some.

WARREN Don't you think that at this point in time men and women should be able to talk to each other? But we can't because women don't listen.

RAY No, they are listening. They are listening for a way to present their agenda.

WARREN Which is to fix what's wrong with you.

RAY That's not all women. Some women, well, they have a life.

WARREN A life of the mind.

RAY Sometimes, yes.

WARREN We're not attracted to those women.

RAY Yes, we are.

WARREN No, we're old now . . . and we can be honest. That type of woman scares us.

RAY I've dated women lawyers that were . . .

WARREN Very smart and you dated them a few times and you took them to bed but it didn't last because you couldn't relax.

RAY What, are you in my head?

WARREN Tell me I'm wrong.

RAY The chemistry was off. This was right after the divorce and I was having a hard time relaxing with anyone.

WARREN Oh, bullshit.

RAY I think we both pick bright women.

WARREN But we don't think they're brighter than we are until it's too late. We think we have the upper hand, they let it happen, they let us believe in our superiority, and then wham . . . one day you're going through the mail and you find the Mensa newsletter.

RAY What are you talking about, Sharky's been a member of Mensa for years, she never goes to the meetings.

WARREN I never knew that.

RAY What difference does it make?

WARREN It's huge. Knowing she's got these . . . IQ points makes me feel like I have to answer all her questions. And when I do, she analyzes everything I say. But more than that, she analyzes everything I *don't* say, I mean, who cares what it means when you're late *again*.

RAY So you were late again?

WARREN (*pouring them both drinks*) I don't have to be anybody's boy on time!

RAY You know you should call.

WARREN Ray, when God invented woman he did not say I am making you an equal, he said I am making you a helpmate. But like most men Adam's not listening because Eve's wearing not a stitch so he's in a fugue state most of the time thinking about all the ways he wants to do it to her. So when she says, "Hey, daddy, reach me that fruit," he says without thinking, "Sure, baby, whatever you want." And for all eternity we're not only totally hung up on food, we can never seem to get enough sex. But I ask you, what woulda happened if Adam had just said, "Bitch, get that fuckin' fruit outta your head," and decked her, boom! You think we'd be in the mess we're in now? No way. We'd be living in a place that looks a lot like . . . (*He looks at the garden and says with feeling*) Well, a whole hell of a lot like your backyard, Ray. I think it's one of the most beautiful spots on earth.

RAY Thank you.

WARREN I mean it.

RAY Look, for one thing, that is not a real story, Adam and Eve.

WARREN How do you know?

RAY It's a fable that attempts to explain the genesis of human suffering.

WARREN Women are the genesis, Raymond!

RAY You consider the times, Warren, men were trying to stamp out the goddess culture that was six thousand years old, it's pure politics.

WARREN I don't always trust how you talk, it's not masculine.

RAY One person cannot be the sole cause of human suffering.

WARREN Unless they are a woman.

RAY You've stopped reading, and you're watching too much TV.

WARREN No.

RAY Yes, you are, because you're talking like an idiot.

WARREN Have you, Ray, son of God, ever hit your wife?

RAY I told you . . . (*Beat*) Okay, what do you mean by hit?

WARREN Punch, slap, kick, push, trip, pinch, pull, squeeze. Shake.

RAY Okay, I might have pushed her to keep her from hurting herself one time.

WARREN To keep her from getting hurt you hit her.

RAY She was coming at me with a knife, and I pushed her away, not hard, just a little shove, but we were gassed and I guess she lost her balance and fell into this glass table and that was kind of a mess . . . stitches and bleeding and all kinds of dirty looks from nurses at the emergency room wondering if she wanted to call the cops, which she did not, of course, since she was, unbeknownst to me at the time, running that credit card scam that eventually got her popped for grand larceny.

WARREN (*incredulous*) This happened with Denise?

RAY No! Not Denise, I wasn't talking about Denise, I was talking about Sharky.

WARREN Ray, you haven't been married to Sharky in years.

RAY Seven years, Warren. Seven years and four months.

WARREN I meant the current Mrs. Potato Head.

RAY No. I never hit Denise. After Sharky I told myself, never again.

WARREN What are you saying?

RAY Sharky drove me nuts, you know that. We used to chase each other around trying to kill each other.

WARREN You're not in love with Denise like that?

RAY Correct.

WARREN (*amazed*) You're not?

RAY Don't sound so surprised, it's not like I don't have feelings for Denise . . . but it's more like she's my friend. The sex is friendly sex . . . accommodating . . . but not impossible to imagine stopping entirely at some point and not missing, and in fact, it's actually been quite awhile now that I think of it. I mean, we sleep in separate rooms, she's there, I'm here.

WARREN Separate rooms.

RAY She complained about my snoring, so I moved.

WARREN What about in the beginning? The initial attraction, the courtship, the heavy petting, the public sex . . . ?

RAY Her body is not . . . I don't know, she's not my type. Can I say that . . . ?

WARREN She's stacked.

RAY Yeah, but I never liked that big boob thing.

WARREN I love that.

RAY And she has a smell about her that's . . . I don't know what it is, some kind of skin oil, musk. Look, I don't want to say anything against her, she's one of the finest people I've ever met and I'm glad, no, I'm grateful she's my wife . . . really. I mean, when Sharky took off . . .

WARREN She didn't take off, you turned her out.

RAY I asked her to leave when she told me she was in love with you, Warren!

WARREN But I had nothing to do with it!

RAY Why are we talking about this?

WARREN Except for listening to her . . . that's all I did, she talked, I listened.

RAY Well, that was a mistake, okay!

WARREN See, you are mad!

RAY No, I mean, listening to women is how you seduce women, is to listen and pretend to be interested in what is not too interesting, you know that!

WARREN I was interested because she talked about you.

RAY Well, you shouldn't have listened.

WARREN You're my brother, I thought I was helping.

RAY Oh, Warren!

WARREN Sure, okay, I always had . . . you know . . .

RAY A *big fat fucking thing* for her!

WARREN Right.

RAY All I'm saying is that it was stupid. It was stupid of you and that's all. Okay?

WARREN Oh shit, why do we always . . .

RAY You bring it up because you feel bad, that's why! Look, it's over. You've been married a long time and . . .

WARREN But you hate me . . . you hold a grudge.

RAY What was I saying before we started talking like this?

WARREN You were telling me how you met Denise.

RAY Okay. She was working at this bar, by the office . . . why was I telling you this stupid story?

WARREN I love this story!

RAY Okay, so it's late afternoon and I'm downtown at the Red Room and it's one of those days I'm getting drunk as shit and she's working there and she tells me she has a thing for me . . .

WARREN That's not how she said it.

RAY You want to tell this story?

WARREN She said she had a crush on you.

RAY Oh, right, right, she told me she had a crush on me.

WARREN (*smiles*) That's cute.

RAY I didn't really feel the same way but I was so out of it and I felt like there was this hole in my life I had to constantly maneuver around to keep from falling into. You know how people lose people and start over, but I couldn't see my way into that until Denise showed up at my apartment that night with a casserole. She was wearing a baby doll nightgown under her coat, and she just sort of moved in, you know? Girl moved in. Took over.

WARREN Baby doll nightgown.

RAY Actually it embarrassed me at the time.

WARREN I know.

RAY Because you could see her . . . everything through it, and it shocked me, actually . . . made me draw back, and I had a hard time, uh . . .

WARREN Performing.

RAY I had to get used to her . . . body, was different, smelled different.

WARREN Baby doll nightgown.

RAY She served dinner in that outfit. Moving around the kitchen, serving dinner with her everything just . . . you know, seeing everything, Sharky'd never do that.

WARREN   No, I know, she's a prude.

RAY   She has a lot of class, Warren. She always carried herself just so. You know? Very particular . . . her clothes, just right.

WARREN   Till she lost her figure.

RAY   She let herself go.

WARREN   That's a bit of an understatement.

RAY   She's still the same person. Look, women get heavy when they're happy.

WARREN   And when they're miserable.

RAY   I always thought she was happy.

WARREN   You did not.

RAY   No, I know.

WARREN   Let's talk about Denise.

RAY   Denise is more of a . . .

WARREN   Down-home girl . . . like the song by the Stones. Remember that?

RAY   I don't like the images of women the Stones have used in a lot of their music. And if you'll notice, not one of them has a good marriage.

WARREN   God, you know . . . ! An action like that, casserole, baby doll, that would change my life! You know, someone would care about *my* needs for a change, I'd be a different man.

RAY   Warren?

WARREN   I never had somebody love me like that! I mean, that's what I envied about you and Sharky is how much Sharky loved you!

RAY   How can you say that to me?!

WARREN   Sharky doesn't love me like that! She never has.

RAY   Look, I'm over this, I am, absolutely, that was then and this is now and I'm happily married to Denise and it's fine, it really is, I'm content!

WARREN Even when it's bad it's better than dating.

RAY I dated a lot after the split. That was horrible. Picking up some poor woman, going out to dinner, getting stinking drunk and having to call her a cab so I could continue to drink on into the night till I blacked out. I had dates like that with women in the building where I worked, I see them now, we don't speak. They avert their eyes when they see me.

WARREN I answered an ad in the newspaper.

RAY An ad?

WARREN For a date.

RAY What, a personal ad? When?

WARREN Just recently.

RAY You did?

WARREN But she scared me. I went and looked her over and got scared . . . she looked hungry, like she was gonna eat me. Big teeth. Big eyes. Red dress. Ray, have you ever dated a woman in a red dress?

RAY Could you see her hands?

WARREN (*remembering*) Yes. Yes. They were big.

RAY Maybe it was a man?

WARREN Oh shit, I never thought about that . . . wow. Hmmm. That's weird. A man. I've never had sex with a man. I mean not in a dating situation . . . just, you know, on the job . . . workin' vice, but hey, couldn't be worse than no sex . . . right?

RAY Are you dating strangers when you're married?

WARREN Dating, no. Answering an ad, yes. I did that.

RAY That's creepy.

WARREN Right, considering I broke up your marriage, right?

RAY I don't like to think of it like that, Warren! I just don't . . . don't really like to think of it like that, I don't think of it like that, it's not like that, it's, it's something that happened a long time ago to people that no longer exist and nobody can know how these things occur, except sometimes in retrospect, but really, I don't want to know, you know? I just prefer to think it's history and it's nobody's fault.

WARREN It's my fault.

RAY Shut up!

WARREN *No*, it is, and I felt bad, *but* then you met Denise and I thought, whoa. Jackpot. You know, with the figure and the baby doll . . . but you don't love her!

RAY Warren . . . Denise is great. She is the best.

WARREN But you don't love her.

RAY No, no, it's just, she has a few annoying habits that . . . look, it's not a problem, I mean, after six years you get used to the way people are, I mean, you endure. Like everything in the house is perfect, not a speck of dust. But look at this place, it's furnished like a cheap motel. And the house stinks, she can't cook a meal without burning something, and she won't open a window, so everything I own . . . Smell my shirt.

He puts his arm under WARREN's *nose.*

WARREN I can't smell anything.

RAY It reeks of cigarette smoke, burnt food, this perfume she wears, and the woman herself! I can't stand to come home sometimes, Warren. The thought of it makes me physically ill. That's why I made the garden, a place to go, a refuge of sorts if you don't have one. If you've lost your place in nature by losing the love of your life, you make a habitat where you fantasize day in and day out that maybe someday your Jane will return to your Tarzan.

WARREN Oh, God, Ray.

RAY It's a joke, Warren, lighten up . . . I'm teasing.

WARREN No, you're not.

RAY (*weak laugh*) No, I know.

WARREN Shit.

RAY Odor is 90 percent of sex, you ever hear that?

WARREN Just from you.

RAY When I met Sharky she was a dancer at the Kahala Hilton and we were right up front and she dances by me and the smell of her body was like a sweeter version of my own musk . . . I took a deep breath of that and the orchids and the plumeria and I was a lost man.

WARREN I was sitting right there.

RAY I felt like the floor was sliding out from under me and I turned and told you I was going to marry her.

WARREN You were ready to fall in love. And don't forget, the magic of the islands . . . I bet if you went back to the Kahala Hilton today, you'd fall in love all over again.

RAY No, because I took Denise there on our honeymoon and it wasn't the same. It was overrun with show business people and the hotel had put in this aquarium with a dolphin that swam back and forth in this shallow trough where kids or anybody could reach in and touch him and people kept touching him and the animal seemed half-mad from all the touching. God! And Denise being fair burned easily and spent all day indoors complaining about how much I was drinking. Maybe we'd been together too long to expect a sense of celebration about our marriage, or maybe it was me, but I can trace the decline of my life from that trip, the sense of futility, the dolphin trapped in that tank. I got sick off a piece of fish I paid twenty-seven dollars for. Bad fish, in Hawaii, what are the chances of that?

Pause. Then RAY *pours more drinks.*

So. What did you two fight about?

WARREN When?

RAY Tonight.

WARREN Oh. You know. Stupid shit.

RAY Uh-huh.

WARREN (*sadly*) Yeah.

RAY What was it?

WARREN Coming home early, she came home early.

RAY Home early is the problem?

WARREN I don't always like being around other people. You know?
Just the sound of people moving around the house, scraping chairs, the
refrigerator opening and closing a million times, I guess I was just in that
kind of mood.

RAY Well, shit, Warren, she lives there.

WARREN Well, shit, Ray, if you're gonna be on her side.

RAY I'm just saying that she is living there, she is paying half of everything, right?

WARREN More than half since I got demoted and I work regular hours, no
overtime.

RAY It was not a demotion, the evidence room is a very big responsibility.

WARREN I was a detective, Ray, I was in line for a promotion.

RAY What difference does it make . . . you'll still get your pension.

WARREN I don't look at retirement the same way you do. I liked my job. I
was a good cop, that's all I ever wanted to be.

RAY But you blew it.

WARREN What would you do if you were disappointed in love?

RAY I was.

WARREN Rub it in.

RAY Why didn't you get a divorce?

WARREN I couldn't do that to you! Break up your home and then just bail.
I had an obligation to stick it out.

RAY You did it for me?

WARREN Yes, of course for you, but man, I was so miserable . . . that's when I started using. Just a little to take the edge off. Then it got in my way at work, and now I'm not the same man. I mean, I am changing in ways I don't like because, frankly, I don't have the job to put my . . .

RAY Rage . . .

WARREN Yes, into, so my mind wanders and finds itself in places sane men don't go.

RAY Look, the material point is, Sharky helps with the bills, she has the right to come home when she likes.

WARREN I know, but what about my rights, I had things I needed to do . . . I *asked her*, what are you gonna do today? And she says, I'll be gone all day. And then cool as a breeze she blows back in early, surprises the hell out of me and then she gets mad and I get mad because I think, frankly, she was checkin' up on me to make sure everything was . . . you know . . .

RAY You were being good.

WARREN If I *wanted* to get high I don't even know where I'd go anymore.

RAY You'd go to the evidence room.

WARREN The evidence room? Where I work? That would be *real* smart.

RAY So what were you doing when she got mad?

WARREN Well, you know, whatnot.

RAY What's whatnot?

WARREN This and that, this and that.

RAY Warren?

WARREN Well, art projects. Okay?

RAY Art projects?

WARREN Yes, and she came in on me while I was doing them and started screaming and . . .

RAY What were you doing that would make her scream?

WARREN I told you, art projects.

RAY What do you mean by art projects?

WARREN Why do you say it like that, I went to college.

RAY Just tell me what that means.

WARREN I take photographs.

RAY I *never* knew that.

WARREN Now you do, big deal . . .

RAY When did you start doing this?

WARREN I don't know . . . awhile ago.

RAY So Sharky was screaming at you for taking art photos.

WARREN She got hysterical and was gonna call the cops.

RAY The cops?

WARREN Hysterical, you know how she gets.

RAY What were you taking a picture of exactly?

WARREN Nothing.

RAY Warren?

WARREN What difference does it make? It was an artistic statement.

RAY I want to know what she saw that made her scream?

WARREN It was a still life.

RAY Like . . . fruit, flowers, dead birds?

WARREN My neighbor's daughter. She wants to be a model, and so I took some pictures of her as a favor to help her get started.

RAY Pictures of your neighbor's daughter.

WARREN Polaroids. That's how you do it, before you waste the film you take a few Polaroids. Because for one thing I don't actually have a good camera yet, but these Polaroids are not cheap, the film's like ten bucks.

RAY   How old is the girl, Warren?

WARREN   I don't know.

RAY   Yes you do too.

WARREN   Fourteen.

RAY   Shit!

WARREN   I was trying to help her out, help her get started. Where do you think Marilyn Monroe would be if that calendar guy hadn't taken her picture?

RAY   What was she wearing?

WARREN   Have you ever seen the painting of Venus on the half shell?

RAY   Warren . . . ?

WARREN   What?

RAY   She was naked?

WARREN   Naked with a very *long* wig!

RAY   And where did you take these pictures?

WARREN   In my studio.

RAY   You mean the basement?

WARREN   If you don't stop sounding like a wife you're gonna have to fuck me and take care of me when I'm old.

RAY   That may happen anyway. So, you're taking nude photos of a fourteen-year-old girl in your basement, Warren, and Sharky came in on you and you're mad at *her*?

WARREN   Art is a process, you know . . . it's personal, she didn't understand, she just got mad . . .

RAY   Can you blame her?

WARREN   I was doing a favor for a friend.

RAY   Warren, I'm looking right at you, I can see you, I can see inside you, I can see you had a thing for this girl.

WARREN   She's like a ripe fruit.

RAY   She's fourteen.

WARREN   This kid is very mature for her age, she has womanly ways.

RAY   Warren, she's a baby.

WARREN   You don't know these girls nowadays, man, they grow up fast what with MTV and all kinds of sexy talk in the school yard and these movies, all kinds of movies about sex and longing and the unfulfilled promise of love, and they can't say *no*, they don't have language, the schools don't encourage debate so you can do what you like as long as *you* keep talking and it doesn't hurt them and you know they all want to be models so they can be wanted by millions of lonely men humping their mattresses in the middle of the night, jerking off to these images in their heads while their wives make up stories about how *they* can't have sex tonight. Bleeding, gas, imaginary pains, and if *you* complain it's always about what's wrong with *you*, I'm selfish because I wake her up when the bed starts shaking because I have to relieve myself manually, and she is disgusted and starts screaming and it makes you want to kill these goddamn women when they lose their love for you and all they want to do is use you for a paycheck and complain to their friends about what kind of animal in heat you've turned out to be and how it's all gotten worse as you've gotten older and uglier and all the time they're keeping this precious thing you need so deep inside themselves, so hidden, they keep it deep inside where you need to be, but they won't let you back in there, they can't let you in because of something that happened, you don't know what it is, it's a mystery, they won't talk to you about it and you ask them what's wrong and they say nothing, nothing, nothing and meanwhile you're dying of loneliness because it's lonely out here.

RAY   Take it easy.

WARREN   It's a lonely fuckin' planet, Ray, and everybody is just walking around like it's all okay and it's not, it's not . . . it's fucked up.

RAY   (*beat*) So how's it stand with Sharky?

WARREN Pretty raw.

RAY Right.

WARREN It's not . . . it's not good, Ray.

RAY Why didn't you say something?

WARREN A man who loves women is no stranger to suffering. What am I supposed to say? *Ouch?*

RAY I don't know, but they say talking helps.

WARREN Women say it 'cause they like to talk you into things, but you wouldn't know that because you're not married.

RAY Yes, I am.

WARREN No. Not really. I found that out tonight. You're not. Not like I am, I'm married, even now, there is a shred of something akin to passion that runs like a golden thread through the tapestry of my hatred.

RAY You should get a divorce, Warren.

WARREN Easy for you to say.

RAY I'm telling you as a brother who loves you, you are too miserable. Your misery is eating you up and spitting out an entirely different person.

WARREN Don't you miss being married . . . ?

RAY I am married!

WARREN The arguing, the sex, the food, the bathroom smells, the inconvenience of emotion . . . ?

RAY Warren, there are other ways to be married . . .

WARREN What do you think the five senses are for?

RAY To keep you from bumping into things.

WARREN They are to hear, to see, to touch, to smell, and to taste the flesh of another human being!

RAY There is something wrong with you.

WARREN These senses locate you, Ray, they put you in the world, they place you on the earth, in all it's glory and horror, right here! Feeling, inhaling, and touching yourself alive in this flesh and blood lifetime . . .

RAY You didn't eat today, did you?

WARREN Animal in the dirt, rolling in the dirt . . . ! Groveling at the feet of the goddess!

RAY You're supposed to eat four times a day.

WARREN You can't even hear what I'm saying, you think it's my blood sugar, but I'm throwing you a lifeline!

RAY (*exiting*) I'm opening a tin of sardines.

WARREN (*screaming*) You sick motherfucker, you think it's chemistry talking, but it's more than that, you cocksucking asshole!

RAY (*offstage*) Quit screaming . . .

WARREN I am talking about what makes it real with another human being is sex and emotion and intimacy, Ray, intimacy, is what we need, knowledge of the other, deep heartfelt knowledge of yourself, of another person, of several people . . . you ever go to a swap party, Ray?

RAY It's not my thing.

RAY *comes back with a tin of sardines, crackers, and a glass of orange juice. He hands the juice to* WARREN, *who drinks it.* RAY *opens the tin and fixes* WARREN *a cracker with fish on it.*

WARREN (*calming*) Sex is what the senses are for . . . if you don't have that, what have you got?

RAY Well, for one thing, control. Okay? I'm not like you, I'm not out of control . . . that's what I couldn't stand about being married to Sharky . . . that feeling of being out of control, after a while, it's too much . . . and look at you, you're outta control . . .

WARREN But that's what marriage is for, it's to keep us from getting lost in our animal, letting our animal run us around this lonely fucking planet, Ray. Women are supposed to be the watchdogs and the saviors. I know that now. Now that I am cast adrift in this wasteland. Sharky saved you but she couldn't save me.

LARRY *appears in the garden.* RAY *stands,* WARREN *turns.*

RAY Oh, shit.

WARREN Who is it?

The men watch as LARRY *lets himself in the sliding glass door.*

LARRY Hi, Ray. What're you doin'? Havin' a party? A boy party?

RAY This is my brother, Warren.

LARRY Warren, Larry . . . glad to meet you. So you're Ray's brother. (*Beat, looks around, to* RAY) That's nice. To have a brother. How you doin', Ray?

RAY I'm good.

LARRY That's not what I hear. I hear you suck.

WARREN (*to* RAY) Should I leave . . . ?

RAY No.

LARRY No, stay here. You stay where you are. (*To* RAY) Don't you love that, the respect of men for other men's privacy, that is so important, women never understand that, do they? They are too curious. Not that I'm not a curious person. But mostly about real things. Three dimensional objects as opposed to feelings. I don't really have feelings, but I do have hobbies.

WARREN I have a hobby.

LARRY What is your hobby.

WARREN Photography. Artistic photography.

LARRY I study anatomy. It's a most useful science in my line of work. To know exactly how to separate a joint, pop, where to apply the pressure, crack, where to make an incision (*sound*). The mess you can avoid with a little education.

WARREN (*with intention*) Ray loved school, he's a lawyer, I hated school, I'm a cop.

LARRY Not anymore. Now you're a clerk.

WARREN (*to* RAY) How does he know that?

RAY I don't know.

LARRY It's because I'm in the know. I bet I know more about you two than each of you knows about each other.

WARREN That would surprise me.

LARRY Why?

WARREN Because I am a student of human nature and my brother is one of my favorite subjects.

LARRY Because you love him.

WARREN I guess that's right.

LARRY Emotional attraction. I don't feel that. In here, where feelings are supposed to live, there is a void. Calm and cold.

LARRY *pulls a collarbone out of his pocket.*

Ever see one of these?

WARREN It's a bone.

LARRY It's the clavicle or collarbone of a sixty-four-year-old used car salesman in Vegas, washed up on his luck. The trick is to take the bone while the guy is alive. They scream like babies these old men, you wouldn't believe it. Then they pass out and wake up, this area around the chest is all caved in . . . it's just impossible to imagine the pain, and you can't move without screaming in agony, and then they put this prosthetic piece in there that never sits right. There's a clicking sound every time you take a breath just so you never forget what a loser you are.

LARRY *moves to the door.*

However. This is not your fate. Clavicle. No, sir. Our mutual acquaintances have instructed me to prepare a very special treat for you. So. I'll be seein' you, Ray. Not now, but soon. By the light of the moon. (*Howls*)

LARRY *exits.*

WARREN Eeeeyuck. (*Grimacing*) Who is that guy?

RAY Who do you think he is, he's a collector, he collects bones . . . you've never heard of Bone Daddy?

WARREN Bone Daddy . . . *the* Bone Daddy?

RAY Exactly.

WARREN How did you meet him?

RAY How do you think? I made a bad loan.

WARREN Ray . . . from maniacs you borrowed money?

RAY I met him through my bookie.

WARREN What bookie?

RAY My bookie!

WARREN You have a bookie?

RAY It's just for football games, fights.

WARREN You bet on fights and football games with a bookie?

RAY And the dogs.

WARREN You bet the dog races with a bookie?

RAY Why do you say it like that, it's no big deal.

WARREN How much are you in for?

RAY Twenty.

WARREN Oh man! Have you told Denise?

RAY Of course not.

WARREN She's got savings.

RAY I know that.

WARREN Maybe if you tell her about Bone Daddy?

RAY Are you nuts? If I get the money from Denise I'll never hear the end of it. If I tell her why I need it I'll become a prisoner, I'll never be able to go anywhere or make a phone call. (*Mocking voice*) Where you goin'? Who ya' callin'? Your bookie?

WARREN   How were you planning on handling it?

RAY   I was planning on ignoring the problem and hoping it would go away.

RAY *pours more drinks.*

WARREN   Yeah . . . that works just often enough to make it a viable option for guys like us.

RAY   What do you mean, guys like us?

WARREN   Guys like us on the outside of the action.

RAY   I don't know if I'd put it that way, Warren.

WARREN   Oh, but that's how it is. We took a wrong turn, and we end up here, sitting here, talking about the past, about what's happening now, each fresh disaster, pretending they don't have a thing in the world to do with each other.

RAY   They don't.

WARREN   Sure they do, because you and me, brother, we got off the train.

RAY   What train?

WARREN   *The* train.

RAY   What is that?

WARREN   It's the path you were born to follow but you got off because you couldn't see into the tunnel, because you had no faith that there was a light up ahead, and in the darkness you panicked and jumped off and started running and you've been running ever since.

RAY   Okay, look, I *can* . . . get . . . the money . . . from Denise, I didn't want to do it but I *can* do it.

WARREN   You should never have split with Sharky.

RAY   (*beat, incredulous*) Warren?

WARREN   You made a mistake.

RAY She left me for you! *She* left *me*!

WARREN She would have come back eventually. They always do.

RAY You're a sick man, Warren, you're disturbed.

WARREN A woman loves like that once a lifetime . . . she told me that herself. You shoulda followed your heart. If you had you wouldn't be in trouble with these maniacs. You gamble because you got off the train.

RAY Look, I used to go to Vegas and win, asshole.

WARREN When you were married to Sharky.

RAY I'm gonna have to kill you now . . . !

RAY *starts for* WARREN, WARREN *ducks him, outmaneuvers him.*

WARREN Well, it's true.

RAY If you come here and let me get a grip on your neck, I swear it'll be quick.

WARREN You had phenomenal luck.

RAY *lunges at* WARREN, WARREN *ducks,* RAY *trips, gets up, keeps coming . . .*

RAY One good twist.

WARREN Don't you remember?

RAY Come here, I said!

WARREN Wait, what's that . . . ?

The sound of a key in the lock, DENISE *comes in.*

WARREN Hi, Denise. Look, Ray, Denise is home.

RAY Hi.

DENISE (*to* RAY) What's he doing here?

WARREN Okay, well . . . guess I'll be going along now . . . Ray? Bye. Bye, Denise.

WARREN *slides out the garden door.* RAY *and* DENISE *watch each other for a long beat.*

DENISE What's the matter with you?

RAY When?

DENISE Now.

RAY I'm fine.

DENISE You look weird.

RAY No. I'm fine, I'm just . . . well . . . okay, sit down.

DENISE No.

RAY I need to talk to you.

DENISE Can't it wait, it's close to midnight.

RAY I'd prefer to discuss this with you now, otherwise, I won't be able to sleep.

DENISE What about my sleep? What if what you're going to discuss with me is going to sicken me and cause me to be unable to sleep.

RAY Has that ever happened . . . ?

DENISE Yes.

RAY When?

DENISE The time you slept with my sister and you were drunk and decided full disclosure was . . .

RAY Okay, fine, we'll talk in the morning. Jesus!

DENISE What, you fuck somebody?

RAY God . . . No!

DENISE You sure, because you look very similar . . .

RAY No, it's nothing like that.

DENISE Oh, well, now I'm all curiosity. Let's talk.

RAY It's not that big a deal. Well, actually I guess it is. I'm in some trouble, financial trouble.

DENISE   Shit. (*Beat*) How much?

RAY   About . . . thirty thousand dollars.

DENISE   Jesus, fuck you . . . what happened?

RAY   I been playing cards.

DENISE   And you lost thirty thousand dollars?

RAY   I had a bad year.

DENISE   How could you keep a secret like this?

RAY   I didn't want to worry you.

DENISE   (*beat*) You go to that card joint like once a week. Right?

RAY   More than that.

DENISE   Talk to me.

RAY   Other times, I go other times.

DENISE   When?

RAY   I can't remember.

DENISE   Like when I work?

RAY   I guess.

DENISE   And when else, like when my mom was sick and I had to go stay with her?

RAY   You know from that incident with your sister that I don't do that well when I'm left alone too much, Denise. You know that. I eat out every night, greasy food, indigestion, can't sleep, TV sucks, and I don't want to screw up again so I go out and . . .

DENISE   Just tell me about gambling.

RAY   I'm telling you how it happens.

DENISE   Like when you say you're going to see so-and-so and you come home late and make an excuse, are you really sitting someplace gambling?

RAY   I don't know.

DENISE Tell me if you lied in order to gamble.

RAY *I don't remember, I went a lot, that's all!*

DENISE Don't scream at me.

RAY Sorry. Okay. Anyway. I now have this collector, from whom I borrowed money to pay my bookie, and he's talking very seriously about repayment. Or else.

DENISE When you say he's talking seriously what does that mean?

RAY That he's serious . . . it's a business with him.

DENISE And this translates to what?

RAY You know. Bad stuff.

DENISE I don't know what you're talking about and you won't be explicit and it makes me think you're lying again . . .

RAY I'm not lying! Okay? Christ!

DENISE Then what does it mean when you say he's serious?

RAY That he'll, like, hurt me.

DENISE How?

RAY He takes bones from people's bodies, okay?

DENISE Do the police know about this guy?

RAY I don't know!

DENISE Cause that is illegal. I'm no expert, but that sounds like it might be illegal.

RAY (*ironic*) Really?

DENISE Yes. So is loan-sharking. Being an officer of the court I'm surprised you don't know that. You can call the police, Ray, you could call your brother.

RAY Oh, God . . . Denise?! No. Okay? That's not what's going to happen here, alright . . . this guy is like . . . he's like a force of nature, nobody deals with him because he's what he is . . . he's outside the law . . . there's a law for people like you and me but not for me anymore because I've gone outside the law, okay? Now I'm on the outside of the law, something that most people won't even admit exists, and I'm out here with a psychopath named Bone Daddy.

DENISE *(beat)* Bone Daddy.

RAY Yes.

DENISE You want me to take my savings out of the bank and give it to a man named Bone Daddy?

RAY I know it sounds nutty.

DENISE The secret world of men and their games, that's all this is, scary talk about monsters . . . you boys, when will you grow up?!

RAY Denise, this is not a joke! I gotta get some goddamn money! Now, I know you got money when your mom died, and I need that money.

DENISE That money is for our old age.

RAY I won't have an old age if you don't help me out.

DENISE It's not just my mom's money, it's mine. I worked for that money at jobs I don't particularly like, and now I'm supposed to just give that money up because you like to gamble. You don't get it, thirty grand will clean me out, I won't have anything left. I'll have worked and worked and have nothing to show for it.

RAY And what would you have otherwise . . . a condo in Florida? You hate Florida!

DENISE I know that, but that's not the point, is it? The point is to have a dream. Something that gets you through the day. That gets you through the yes, ma'am, and no, sir, and can I get you another drink and the car breaks down and you're tired all the time and you don't have sex anymore . . .

RAY What about my dream?

DENISE This is why we haven't been making love, isn't it?

RAY What are you talking about?

DENISE You're losing your juice in these joints?

RAY (*distasteful*) Denise . . . ?

DENISE That's why you can't get it up!

RAY I hate that kind of talk. You're a beautiful woman but sometimes you open your mouth and it just . . . it shatters the illusion.

DENISE Oh, I suppose you want me to act very genteel and feminine and all fluttering concern and consolation, that's not me, money means something to me because I have a work ethic, I come from a blue-collar family, a working-class family, I didn't grow up in Rolling fucking Hills, I didn't go to a prep school . . .

RAY Oh, no, can't we please not do this lecture, I have heard this lecture, I have heard it, I don't need to hear it now, I really don't . . . !

DENISE *No!* We can't! We can't do anything you want.

RAY Look, I'm gonna go back to work for the city, and I'll have regular money again. My private practice would be okay if I could get it started, but I can't so . . .

DENISE Why don't you try going to the office once in a while?

RAY Oh, God, screw off . . . I do go . . .

DENISE You're never there.

RAY How do you know, are you spying on me?

DENISE I drive by sometimes to see if you want to have lunch before I go to work and you're never there, and then I call you up and it's always the machine. What are you, screening?

RAY Sometimes I'm at the courthouse trying to get clients.

DENISE Ray?

RAY What?

DENISE You're not at the courthouse.

RAY If I say I am, then I am.

DENISE No, you're not, you're gambling.

RAY Not every day, I didn't go every day, some days I went to the courthouse, some days I was there trying to get clients.

DENISE Ray?

RAY I was!

DENISE Look. I know you didn't try and get clients at the courthouse. That's not you.

RAY You don't trust me.

DENISE How can I trust you when you lie?

RAY Of course I lie, if I told you the truth I'd have no freedom.

DENISE Freedom for what? For gambling?

He wants to hit her, he growls in frustration.

RAY Do you understand that I was gambling so *we* could have a better life, something *you* want . . .

DENISE I want?

RAY Yes!

DENISE Everyone wants a better life.

RAY I don't want it.

DENISE You don't want a better life?

RAY I don't even know what that is!

DENISE How can you say that?

RAY Because if you really stop and think about it, what is a better life? It's stuff. It's cars and houses and vacations and insurance premiums and working yourself into an early grave for a big empty pile of shit.

DENISE Cars, houses, and vacations are regular life, not a better life.

RAY So what's a better life?

DENISE Time and money. If you have a better life you have time and money.

RAY I was still following your lead.

DENISE My lead?

RAY Yes! Because you have unrealistic expectations of success!

DENISE I do? I'm a waitress!

RAY You have unrealistic expectations of *my* success, *mine*!

DENISE Well, okay . . . I did expect that you'd do better than you have.

RAY *See?*

DENISE But so did you.

RAY At first I did, but then I didn't! How could I? I was working as a public defender. Okay! I might have thought I was going to build some kind of reputation for myself. Bringing rich man's justice to the poor. But I was overwhelmed the first week. My clients were either stupid, evil, greedy, or weak, usually all four. My caseload was enormous. The paperwork, the plea bargains, the last-minute deals, the investigating, the postponements, the bail jumpers, the very bad people calling me at home, calling me by my first name. Drug dealers, child molesters, gangsters. Hi, Ray, did we get us a good judge, Ray? I think I fixed those witnesses, Ray. I got a cut that won't heal, Ray. I think my old lady wants to fuck you, Ray.

DENISE But that's why you went out on your own, you were sick of your job, and you wanted a change so you made a change.

RAY For us!

DENISE No, that was a decision you made for yourself.

RAY I was doing it for us.

DENISE No.

RAY Yes, the job was making me nuts, and I thought if I started my own practice I'd be easier to live with, that is something I did for us, we discussed it!

DENISE You told me you were quitting after you'd already quit. You told me on our honeymoon that you'd resigned.

RAY Okay, but even my mistakes I make for the sake of our life together.

DENISE Our life together.

RAY Denise, you have to think of marriage like a business. We each put something into the business, and we take out whatever we need, new shoes and uniform for you, a new desk and chair for me, a car for you, gambling for me . . . if you got sick, who'd pay the car payment? The partners. So, who's responsible for my debts?

DENISE You are because you put *your* money . . .

RAY *My* money is *our* money . . .

DENISE . . . without asking me, into gambling.

RAY Oh, now I need your consent.

DENISE If you're treating it like a joint venture.

RAY Okay, see! *This* is what I hate about talking to you!

DENISE You've been gambling and hoping to win so that you could continue to gamble, it had nothing to do with me.

RAY I didn't want you to know how bad things were.

DENISE You think I didn't know?

RAY You didn't know that I was having problems with work.

DENISE Of course, I did . . . I'm paying the bills.

RAY Oh, great, another version of "I told you so."

DENISE Well, it was stupid to go out on your own.

RAY *See?*

DENISE I said so at the time . . . that's not you, you're not a leader, you're a sheep.

RAY *Oh, God! Denise???* (*A moment*) This is . . . damnit, this is, you know . . . I just . . . this is what's wrong with the whole bloody system of marriage.

DENISE What? All I said is you're not an ambulance chaser.

RAY That's not what you said!!!

DENISE What did I say?

RAY You said I was a goddamn sheep!

DENISE That was just my way of saying you're not an alpha wolf.

RAY But don't you see that your having this idea about me, about my abilities, is part of the problem?

DENISE Why are you always trying to put it off on somebody else?

RAY It's a no-confidence vote!

DENISE If you were in your right mind you'd know what I was talking about.

RAY No, I wouldn't.

DENISE Yes, you would.

RAY You're my mate!

DENISE Your mate? Like Tarzan and Jane . . . ?

RAY Yes. It's a primal relationship, and your approval has everything to do with my success.

DENISE We're not talking about success, we're talking about getting by. Barely making it.

RAY In the beginning when I first went out on my own and I was getting a few cases, not a lot, it would have been nice for you to encourage me . . .

DENISE I did.

RAY Instead of tearing me down . . .

DENISE I didn't.

RAY   And making jokes.

DENISE   What jokes?

RAY   Like the one about that Mrs. What's-her-name with the bad nosejob being able to play it like an ocarina.

DENISE   You didn't even know what an ocarina was.

RAY   What is it?

DENISE   A sweet potato pipe, made out of terra cotta, it's like a flute . . . (*She laughs*)

RAY   I don't know what's so funny about it?

DENISE   She had three nostrils, it was funny.

RAY   It wasn't funny to her.

DENISE   That's the last joke I ever made with you because you don't get my jokes, you don't understand my sense of humor.

RAY   What about the fat lady that slipped on the lettuce?

DENISE   I don't remember saying anything about her.

RAY   You said that kind of litigation clogs the courts, and the taxpayers are footing the bill. Footing the bill was a joke.

DENISE   No, it wasn't.

RAY   I didn't see the humor.

DENISE   I wasn't making a joke.

RAY   I laughed to be polite.

DENISE   You didn't need to.

RAY   I was trying to be a good sport.

DENISE   That's because you're full of shit.

RAY   I was keeping the peace. That's what a good husband does, he keeps the peace. He lets many things go by, he doesn't take issue.

DENISE He lies, in other words.

RAY It's not lying, it's keeping the peace.

DENISE You're not being honest, you're not being forthcoming.

RAY What's wrong with having private thoughts?

DENISE Because that's not intimacy, that's not an intimate relationship. I know I'm not the world's greatest cook or decorator, and maybe I forget to open a window, but all you have to do is say something, that's all, I'm not going to get mad. Living together is a hard adjustment even for people who . . . people who really love each other, but that's not us, is it?

RAY Well, we may not be as close as we should be.

DENISE Yeah, but that's important because you want to trade on an intimate relationship that doesn't exist.

RAY Trade, what are you saying, we're married.

DENISE If we were married, really married, you couldn't have lied to me.

RAY I didn't lie.

DENISE You weren't honest.

RAY You're not honest.

DENISE How am I not honest?

RAY You don't report all your tips?

DENISE Do you know why you're doing this?

RAY Well, if we're being honest, let's be honest.

DENISE Because you're in a hole, and since I'm the only one who seems dumb enough for you to con, you've come to me. You've come to me with all this crap about how I left you alone, I'm not supportive . . .

RAY I think we should look at some of these other issues and see how they contribute to the breakdown in communication.

DENISE If you were so concerned why didn't you say something before?

RAY I don't like to make waves, but if I'm already at sea . . .

DENISE Oh, so this is funny?

RAY No.

DENISE That was a joke, you're making a joke.

RAY Okay, forget it. You don't want to help me, fine! We're strangers who live together, that's all. We don't need each other, we can't rely on each other . . . *shit*! This is just . . . (*punching the air*) fuckin' unbelievable!

DENISE (*a long beat*) So if I give you the money you're just gonna pay these guys and that's the end of it?

RAY (*beat, calming*) That's one possibility. But here's what I was thinking. I could pay off as little as I could, as little as I can get away with, and then invest the rest and use the interest to retire the loan.

DENISE Invest the rest.

RAY Yes. Because it's stupid not to ride the market, it's a bull market and you're keeping it in a savings account and it's stupid, it's a stupid thing to do with money.

DENISE I'm stupid about money.

RAY Maybe not stupid, just ignorant.

DENISE Right.

RAY Okay, I know this sounds like a bad idea because what do I know about investing, but I was talkin' to Tank and he was telling me about this investment club that he and Freddy were gonna put together with this bartender that used to work as a broker at Smith Barney and . . .

DENISE Tank was the one that got you into that pyramid scheme.

RAY We've all grown up a lot since then.

DENISE It's just more gambling, you unlucky son of a bitch.

RAY (*beat*) Wait. Don't call me that. Don't . . . take it back.

DENISE No.

RAY You take it back, or I swear to God . . .

DENISE What are you gonna do, hit me?

RAY No, see, if you say stuff like "I'm unlucky," it'll wreck my luck, that's the first law of gambling, you watch what you say.

DENISE You're about to lose a piece of your skeleton over nonpayment of gambling debts, and you're worried *I'm* going to queer your *luck*? All you have to do is wake up in the morning and your luck is in the toilet.

RAY Okay, fine. However you want to run it, Denise. But I'm serious. I need the money. I'm on my knees . . .

DENISE No, you're not. You're waiting to be bailed out. You think I'm going to cave in because I love you and because if our places were reversed you'd help me out?

RAY That's right, there's another reason, I *would* help you . . . !

DENISE Yeah, but you never have two bucks in your kit, so if our situations were reversed you couldn't help me out. I'd have to let Lothar pull the bones from my body.

RAY You know, you love to do this, you love this, you love to get me in a corner and beat the shit out of me, well, okay . . . okay!! Here . . . here I am!

RAY *gets down on his knees.*

RAY Look at me!

DENISE No.

RAY Look at me! I'm on my knees, for the time being, while I still have knees, but Denny, if I screw up with these monsters, I won't have knees, okay? No knees! Please, I'm scared. I want to keep my body intact. I need you to help me.

DENISE (*pause*) Oh, my God.

RAY What?

DENISE It's not enough.

RAY What? What isn't enough, what . . . I'm on my fuckin' knees!

DENISE I don't love you enough.

RAY Excuse me?

DENISE If you'd asked me as a friend it would make more sense. But you asked me as an obligation of marriage, and I realized, just this minute . . . I don't feel that anymore.

RAY Okay, maybe we should talk in the morning.

DENISE No, there's no point.

RAY You're upset, this has been a shock.

DENISE I don't feel married to you anymore.

RAY But we're married . . .

DENISE Yes, but I don't *feel* it.

RAY Denise, marriage is a legal commitment, you fuck feelings because feelings come and go like the tides, but a legal obligation remains valid, that is what is meant by "for better or for worse."

DENISE But it's never gotten better, it's only gotten worse, and I don't know if it's ever been that great between us, it's been more like a friendship, except you don't really like me . . .

RAY That's not true!

DENISE No, not really . . . you don't like to come home.

RAY Of course I do, it's my home, I come here . . .

DENISE No, you don't, you don't like it here, you come in and you sniff the air and you go outside, out to the garden . . . I can tell you're not happy.

RAY Where are you getting this stuff?

DENISE From you. I can tell, you don't like the house, the way I've fixed it up, in fact . . . I know you're going to get mad about this . . . because you do every time I bring it up, but . . . I don't think you ever got over your first wife, I think you're still in love with Sharky.

RAY Oh, *stop it*!! Just, I am so *sick* of your raging insecurity, how can you keep on like this? It's demented, you know, it's psychotic! I have an enormous amount of feeling for you.

DENISE Gratitude maybe, but not love . . . never love.

RAY Denise . . .

DENISE I can't blame you, I forced this marriage. You didn't want to get married. You didn't even want a relationship. You told me that the night I came over in that . . . trashy lingerie with the casserole. God, I've never been so embarrassed in my life.

RAY There's no reason, it was great.

DENISE I scared you to death.

RAY That's not true.

DENISE I couldn't help it. I knew we weren't really connecting, and I wanted you. I wanted to quit working.

RAY You did?

DENISE Yes, I thought maybe we could have a baby . . . ?

RAY Oh, yeah but . . .

DENISE No, I know . . . but I thought marrying a lawyer . . .

RAY Right.

DENISE But that's not the only reason I married you.

RAY Well, if it was . . . ?

DENISE No, it wasn't. I loved you. I loved everything about you. I loved to listen to you talk about your shitty job. I loved how miserable you were. I loved how much you seemed to care about your marriage coming apart, how you felt when your wife left . . . ? I thought if I could make you love me like that . . . I'd really have something . . . great. That's where my un-realistic expectations came into it. I just thought we could make each other happy.

RAY We are happy.

DENISE No, we're not.

RAY I am.

DENISE Ray, it's never been a good fit.

RAY I've been very happy with you.

DENISE Ray? Don't you think I can hear it when you lie?

RAY I'm not lying.

DENISE Do you really think I'm that stupid?

RAY Denise, I don't think you're stupid, I think you're very bright.

DENISE Oh, my God.

RAY What now?

DENISE You really do think I'm stupid.

RAY I don't!!

DENISE You were patronizing me.

RAY No I wasn't. (*Beat*) Maybe just a little, but I do think you're intelligent.

DENISE See, the problem is I tried to love you unconditionally. That's why I've let a lot of your lies go by.

RAY Everybody lies a little.

DENISE You don't. You lie a lot. But think about this, Ray. Think about all that lying. Don't you ever wonder who really knows you? Who really knows your heart? When you die, who will mourn for you? Who will know you well enough to mourn your loss?

RAY I'm close to my brother. Sort of.

DENISE You haven't spoken to your brother since he sold your car to buy crack.

RAY All I'm saying is he knows me.

DENISE He knows all about your gambling?

RAY Yes, absolutely, he's known for months.

DENISE So he knew, and I didn't?

RAY Well, yeah . . . I guess. It's the kind of thing you tell a brother.

DENISE I see.

RAY Look, Denise, this is not the time, I'm just, I can't, I will, but not now, okay, because you've got to help me out here, I mean, this is a very very extra serious problem, you know? It's not like a joke, it's like a big deal, a very big, extra big fat deal. I'm in a lot of trouble, and I need your help. Do you understand, are you getting that?

DENISE Yes, I understand that.

RAY You do?

DENISE Yes.

RAY (*relieved*) Good. Great. So . . . okay. You're going to have to go to the bank tomorrow morning, get the cash, has to be cash, and, okay, new thing, honesty, it's not thirty thousand, I only need twenty, twenty grand, so okay, we'll go get it and you're right, I'm just gonna pay off this guy, forget the investment scheme, we'll do that some other time, when we're back on our feet financially. You know? So you'll go, or . . . hey, we'll both go, we'll go early, we'll have a nice breakfast, you know, out somewhere, maybe by the beach, and we'll go to the bank and then we'll spend the day together, just the two of us, then I'll get the money, take the money, you can come if you want, we'll go find this guy and pay this debt and we'll be free, we'll make a fresh start. I think this has been good, this talking like this, we should do more of this, you know? (*Beat*) So, you feel like spending the day together, just the two of us?

DENISE (*beat*) I'm sorry, Ray.

She crosses to her bedroom, goes in and comes out with her nightgown and toothbrush.

RAY Where are you going?

DENISE I'm going to a hotel. It was your place when I moved in, and I'll move out.

RAY I thought it was all settled.

DENISE Goodbye, Ray.

She exits.
The sound of a car starting and driving away.
Pause. WARREN *comes in from the garden.*

WARREN Wow. That was like watching a big boat sink.

WARREN *makes drinks.*

WARREN (*continued*) You think maybe she has somebody . . . ? Just my observation with women is they walk out very easily when they've got somebody in their head, you know? Like when Sharky left so easily it was because I was in her head. You know? She had a sure thing, somebody she was sure of, so she was able to let you go, just like that . . .

RAY *groans loudly and comes at* WARREN *in a rage,* WARREN *ducks, eludes him,* RAY *is out of control, he screams incoherently.*

RAY Ahhhhhahhahhhhhhhahhahahhghhghgghghhghghahhgah . . .

WARREN *catches him from behind and takes him down expertly; he holds him.*

WARREN Breathe, breathe deeply and relax . . . relax! Come on! Give it up, big boy! Okay! Breathe, now! Come on!

WARREN *is stronger, and* RAY *relaxes and lies limply in his brother's arms.*

RAY How do you fuck if you don't have a penis?

WARREN I don't think you do. You can do other things, but fucking is out.

RAY I've heard of guys thinking they had their legs when their legs had been amputated, swearing they could feel their legs, but what about your dick, what happens?

WARREN (*thoughtfully*) Well, it depends, I suppose, on if they just take the dick.

RAY Right. They could take the balls. I'd have no fluids . . . what do you think would happen . . . would my voice get higher . . . ?

WARREN Stop it.

RAY Seriously.

WARREN It's not productive.

RAY Will I be able to stop shaving?

WARREN What are you doing?

RAY Trying to look on the bright side.

WARREN You know what you need? You need a job.

RAY Maybe if they cut off my dick I could become a woman . . . get married. I wouldn't be able to have kids, the guy would have to love me for myself.

WARREN Are you listening?

RAY Did you ever see *Some Like It Hot?* Jack Lemmon dresses as a woman and by the end of the movie it looks like he's going to make a very good marriage to a millionaire played by Joe E. Brown.

WARREN Look, all you need is one good case and you'd be clear of debt. What about this guy tonight . . . why don't you just take his case . . . this guy that was here with that delicious gumdrop.

RAY I can go back to work for the city.

WARREN You hate that job.

WARREN *finds the check underneath some stuff on the table.*

WARREN Look, here's this guy's check . . . This is a large amount of money.

RAY Gimme that . . .

WARREN Stop grabbing.

RAY Warren?

WARREN *keeps the check away.*

WARREN Rich people and their justice, Ray. It's all for sale.

RAY No, Warren, just stay out of it.

WARREN This girl is going to go to trial for murdering her boyfriend, right?

RAY Yes.

WARREN They have a signed confession, they have the murder weapon. You can get the confession bumped, and I work in the evidence room.

RAY So?

WARREN It doesn't take a genius to figure out why they chose you, Ray, this guy Larry knows about me, knows about you . . . why is that?

RAY I don't know.

WARREN It's a setup.

RAY What are you talking about?

WARREN Losing the knife. I can lose the knife. I lose stuff all the time. 'Cause I'm high, I mean, that's the beauty of working where I work, I can get high whenever I like.

RAY When I suggested that earlier you acted like I was nuts.

WARREN A man without secrets is not a man, so what do you say?

RAY No, Warren! An act like this would change everything. It would change our lives in ways we can't even anticipate.

WARREN Then what difference does it make? We're already off the train, we're already running in the dark . . .

RAY You're talking about cooperating with human evil. That guy is evil, his daughter is damaged.

WARREN Ray?

RAY What?

WARREN Who do we kill when we take a life?

RAY Did you hear what I said?

WARREN This is the argument you made against the death penalty and it worked, you got that guy life.

RAY It doesn't apply here.

WARREN Come on. Who's life do we take when we take a life?

RAY (*sigh*) We take our own life.

WARREN That's right. We take a piece of ourselves we've come to hate, we place it out there, on the face of an innocent person, and we murder that person, right? So, who dies?

RAY Warren, I refuse to become involved in this.

WARREN The girl was operating at her highest level of good, she was trying to the best of her ability to heal the war within herself by committing a murder, can't you understand that?

RAY This is not the first person she's killed.

WARREN (*beat*) That's right.

RAY For God's sake, Warren, she needs to go away. I know you know this.

WARREN (*thinking*) No, I know.

RAY I know the one thing we have in common is our love of justice.

WARREN Okay, so there needs to be some kind of net in place is what you're saying.

RAY Net?

WARREN No, okay, I hear you. How about this? What if when she gets out, instead of just walking away she comes to us.

RAY Us?

WARREN Or me.

RAY If she gets off, she'll be free. It's kind of not our problem at that point.

WARREN But where is the justice in that?

RAY That's what I'm saying . . . !

WARREN But what if when she gets out, we keep her.

RAY Keep her . . . ?

WARREN I could keep her.

RAY You mean, like kidnap her?

WARREN Incarcerate.

RAY That's insane.

WARREN Every day people slip through the holes in the world because they have failed to learn the lessons of life. Failed to refine their sensibilities. They've lost the ability to be sensitive in their dealings with others. Common courtesy is so uncommon as to be a joke. We are neck deep in human excrement wondering where to take our next crap. What is so insane about sequestering a rebellious and murdering girl?

RAY Well, Warren, it's illegal for one thing.

WARREN So is murder.

RAY Warren, what is going on with you?

WARREN I'll tell you, Ray. Sharky has driven me mad. She has tried to fix what is not broken in me and changed the way I look at myself, and now I'm permanently fucked-up. What's the little girl's name?

RAY Vicky.

WARREN I want to heal my relationship with women through my incarceration of Vicky.

RAY How did we get here?

WARREN It's become a twofold plan. I'll lock her up for murder, but I'll rehabilitate her for me.

RAY Will you take pictures of her?

WARREN If I deem it part of the therapeutic process.

RAY And for how long will you sequester this rebellious and murdering girl?

WARREN Seven years, a cycle of time, but maybe, if she's amenable, forever.

RAY Who's going to take care of her again?

WARREN We will. Or I will. That will be my job. You will have to get some kind of job and support us. Because I'll be fired, and I'll just stay home. Like a housewife taking care of the kids. She'll be like a daughter to us, you and me.

RAY Yes, I'm married to my brother, we have one child.

WARREN Think about it. Wouldn't it be great to have a kid?

RAY I am thinking about it. Why am I thinking about this? It's crazy . . .

WARREN Because crazier things happen all the time.

RAY It's because I'm afraid.

WARREN Sure. You're afraid of these evil men that have pulled you into a world of darkness . . .

RAY Stop talking for a minute, okay?

WARREN I am trying to save your life.

RAY Losing evidence can't be that easy. You will be found out, you will be punished. Right?

WARREN Like I said, you have to have an excuse. For instance, you can be on drugs. Drugs are the obvious choice, especially with a cop like me who has a history of abuse.

RAY And it's just a coincidence you lose the evidence on my case.

WARREN You don't take the case.

RAY I don't?

WARREN Anybody could take the case.

RAY But I keep the money.

WARREN You fixed it.

RAY And you'd do this for me?

WARREN Yes.

RAY Why? Why would you do such a thing for me? Give up a job you love, I mean, eventually you would get your old job back.

WARREN I know that.

RAY So why would you give that up?

WARREN You're my brother.

RAY   No. Why really?

WARREN   That's it.

RAY   No, really.

WARREN   I want you to forgive me. For Sharky.

RAY   I have forgiven you, Warren, I couldn't do anything else but forgive you . . . I love you.

WARREN   No, you don't understand.

RAY   Tell me.

WARREN   When Sharky came home and started to scream I struck her not in anger so much as surprise. And she fell into the glass door and, thrashing to keep from falling, ended up cutting herself even worse, in fact, she punctured an artery.

RAY *sits down.*

RAY   Jesus.

WARREN   She was asking me to help, but I couldn't . . . I saw what was happening, but I couldn't seem to consider it an emergency. How could I? It was a triumph. I was finally on level ground. She was so weak and pathetic that all my hatred came out and I remained absolutely motionless and watched her dying. Her screaming turned to begging and the begging turned to crying till finally . . . and this is how I found out she still loved you . . . when she realized she was going to die, she asked me to tell you that she had always loved you, that there was never anyone else in her heart. And then, she apologized to me, she did . . . (*Smiles*) She apologized, which, I must admit, felt good. That broke the spell, the apology. When she did that I tried to help her, but by then it was too late. She was gone.

RAY *looks around, at loose ends.*

WARREN   (*continued*) She told me she wasn't trying to fix me, she was trying to make me more like you. Isn't that sweet? I thought you'd like to hear that.

RAY   Where is she?

WARREN (*moves to the garden*) I put her out there. Out there under the plumeria and the gardenia, where the jasmine is in bloom, where the garden smells the sweetest. I put her out there for you. Deep in the rich fragrant earth. She'll be mother to your garden, nurturing it for years to come, if you leave her alone. Can you do that, Ray? Can you let her rest in peace? If you do, I can lose that knife.

RAY No.

WARREN Think about it.

RAY I have to have a funeral for the same reason I got married. I need the ritual to mark the event. Without ritual, how will this ever be real for me?

WARREN We can have a funeral, we just can't invite anybody.

RAY No, no, I don't . . . I can't, Warren. You know? It's just . . . large.

WARREN I don't think you're thinking about this, you should think about it before you . . .

RAY (*angry*) I thought of her every day, Warren, woke up thinking about her every day. Last thing on my mind at night. First thing in the morning. I still carry her picture in my wallet so when someone I don't know and never expect to see again asks to see a picture of my wife I show them Sharky and pretend we're still married, and that she's at home, waiting for me at home . . . the love of my life waiting for me to come home but I can never go home to her now, can I . . . ?

WARREN Ray, you could have gone home to her anytime.

RAY Anytime, but now.

WARREN You knew she was unhappy.

RAY She was the love of my life.

WARREN Love is easy. Forgiveness is something else entirely.

RAY *She fucked up!!!*

WARREN Well, Ray, we all fucked up.

RAY She could have come back anytime, I would have taken her back anytime, all she would have had to do is come to me, call me, come home . . . that's all she would have had to do!

WARREN I'm sure she thought, as we both did, because you lead us to believe, that you were a happily . . . married . . . man.

RAY (*beat*) I didn't do this, you did it, you did it, I didn't do it . . .

WARREN I know that.

RAY I'm calling the police on you, you fuck! How dare you . . . ! You cock-sucking motherfucking immoral shithead . . . ! How dare you blame me!?

RAY *scrambles through the debris looking for the phone.*

RAY (*continued*) Where's the fuckin' phone!?

WARREN When you call ask for Bigelow and Demetria. They hate my guts. Tell them to come and get me. Tell them to come and get your brother. He's just killed the love of your life, and now you're a free man.

RAY Shut up!

WARREN You won't fantasize about accidentally meeting in a dark bar and running away because it's over, Ray. And you have me to thank.

RAY Thank *you*?

WARREN *hands him the phone.*

WARREN You're welcome.

RAY (*dialing*) I don't think you should have done this, Warren.

WARREN I know, but I did and I'm sorry. And that's all I'm ever going to say about it.

RAY (*waiting*) Hello. I'm looking for Detective . . . ?

WARREN Demetria or Bigelow.

RAY (*covers the mouthpiece*) Are you sure?

WARREN They'll love it, go ahead.

RAY   Demetria or Bigelow. Yeah, I'll wait.

RAY *turns to the garden and stares out. He takes a deep breath. A moment.*

RAY   Mother to my garden for years to come. Where do you get that stuff?

WARREN   I did a little research, because all organic matter is not the same. I didn't want to ruin the garden.

RAY   You bury her good and deep?

WARREN   Six feet down at least. Dusted her with lime. Not too much. But this kind of weather, she'll compost pretty fast.

RAY   Lime adds alkali to the soil.

WARREN   I didn't want to screw anything up by using too much.

RAY   It's already a fairly acidic soil.

WARREN   Can I say one more thing?

RAY   I wish you wouldn't.

WARREN   If you leave her there in the garden, she'll always be there to come home to. No more fights, no more scenes . . .

RAY   Warren . . . ?

WARREN   No, I know, it's not the happiest ending . . . but at least you're together, Ray. It's a way of looking at it, I don't know if you can appreciate the symmetry, but it's there. You have what many people long for with their exes. Closure.

RAY   How can you ask me to do this?

WARREN   Because we're lost men, Ray. And all we have is each other.

The two men watch each other. Lights fade. Blackout.

End of Play.

Teri Reynolds

I Did It for You

One of the few comforting things about the *Mystery of Attraction* is that the worst has already happened when the play begins—you just won't know about it for a while. This is small comfort, but in a world where a loan shark's "collector" waves a human clavicle and says, "The trick is to take the bone while the guy is alive," it is something.

The simplest event—a man waiting in the garden to say hi to his brother—accumulates such sinister meaning by the end that it leaves you thinking it would be safer to pay close attention to your loved ones' small talk from now on. The strategy of the play, rather than to surprise you with a twist, is to seduce you into an edgy state in which you are still no better prepared for what will come. There is simply an accumulating sinking feeling that we cannot trust these characters—their accounts, their decisions, their impulses—and that perhaps they deserve what they get. What is uncomfortable, though, is that we still hope for their redemption, because Marlane Meyer has an eerie talent for combining the squalid and the dignified in a single character. These characters have principles—

The *South Atlantic Quarterly* 99:2/3, Spring/Summer 2000.
Copyright © 2001 by Duke University Press.

misguided though they may be—and therefore it matters that they might betray them. They are souls that will probably be lost soon, but aren't quite yet.

"I believe there is a balance and order in the world that we will all have to reclaim for ourselves one day," Ray says early in the play. "Today is my day." But Ray is a man with a problem, "a shitty little twenty-grand note," and a rich man named Roger has offered to clear his gambling debts in return for a rigged trial that will get Roger's stepdaughter off on a murder charge and allow Roger to marry her now that her mother (his fourth wife) is dead. Incidentally, Roger also claims to know which body part the collector (Bone Daddy) wants to remove from Ray—it's not his clavicle. While we wait to see if Ray is going to make his stand or cash Roger's check, the plot slowly accumulates a structure strong enough to render his decision much more complicated. But the structure is so tight that all of the rules of the universe are laid out in this first interaction.

First, family relationships between men and women are hard to define— and always a little dodgy. "She's like a daughter to me, but she's not my daughter, she's my fourth wife's daughter," Roger says of his stepdaughter/fiancée in the play's first line. Later we find out that Ray's sister-in-law is also his ex-wife.

Second, everyone has another side. We begin with almost no information about the characters: the cast of characters describes Ray as a man "in his late forties," Warren as a man in his "late thirties," and Roger as "a businessman in his fifties." Everything else about them is revealed in conversation. One version of events slowly emerges, and just when your loyalties find a place to stand, the ground shifts. Ray is a gambler in way over his head— and a lawyer. His brother Warren is a drug addict—and a cop—and possibly a child pornographer. Sharky, who "ran that credit card scam that eventually got her popped for grand larceny," has belonged to Mensa for years, although "she never goes to the meetings." And Denise, who seems like the biggest dupe of all, is arguably the only one who manages to stand up for herself. There is a characteristic rhythm to the way Meyer reveals these characters. She never delivers these incongruent elements simultaneously. The effect is one not of paradox, but of initial expectation and disorienting revision. (There is also a great deal of humor in these reversals: when Warren starts to have what looks like a psychotic break, it turns out that he is diabetic and needs a cracker.)

And finally, these characters almost never lie outright, but it takes more than one question to get the truth. As the play goes on, you learn enough about the ground rules—everything has an underbelly—so that the most ordinary of statements makes your ears prick up. So "what were you doing when she got mad?" Ray asks his brother.

WARREN Well, you know, whatnot.
RAY What's whatnot?
WARREN This and that, this and that.
RAY Warren?
WARREN Well, art projects. Okay?
. . .
RAY What do you mean by art projects?
WARREN Why do you say it like that, I went to college.
RAY Just tell me what that means.
WARREN I take photographs.

Many questions later, what Warren first describes as a photographic "still life" turns out to be Polaroids of his neighbor's daughter, a fourteen-year-old aspiring model.

RAY Shit!
WARREN I was trying to help her out, help her get started. Where do you think Marilyn Monroe would be if that calendar guy hadn't taken her picture?
RAY What was she wearing?
WARREN Have you ever seen the painting of Venus on the half shell?

When you want to pretend that the world isn't what it is, and yet leave each statement, in the technical sense, true, language gets in the way of talking. In a play made up almost entirely of two-person conversations, Meyer has invented an extraordinary dialect of oblique reference and hesitation (she uses *beat* as a stage direction more than once). She creates the impression that the characters are hiding something no matter how much truth they tell, and that they never quite connect, as if they don't really inhabit the same conversation. When Roger first describes his problems with his stepdaughter:

ROGER . . . I'm on the verge of taking her as my bride when suddenly she is always in trouble. Escalating calamity as she matures. Disappearing every other weekend, lowlifes shaking me down, shoplifting, drug abuse, and a string of accidental homicides.

RAY *looks at* ROGER.

ROGER She says accidental and I believe her.

RAY Who did she kill?

ROGER Let's talk about who she killed this time.

RAY Okay.

When Denise rebukes Ray for quitting his job at a law firm, he says, "Oh great, another version of 'I told you so.'"

DENISE Well, it was stupid to go out on your own. . . . you're not a leader, you're a sheep.

RAY *Oh, God! Denise???* (*A moment*) This is . . . damnit, this is, you know . . . I just . . . this is what's wrong with the whole bloody system of marriage.

DENISE What? All I said is you're not an ambulance chaser.

RAY That's not what you said!!!

DENISE What did I say?

RAY You said I was a goddamn sheep!

DENISE That was just my way of saying you're not an alpha wolf.

These are not misunderstandings made of circumstance where something else interferes with communication. Those are plays of avoidable tragedy— the ones like *Romeo and Juliet* that twist your gut because the world could have been otherwise—but there's nothing standing between these characters except too much history and a lot of dysfunction. They fail to communicate all by themselves. Given time enough and world, these characters would dig themselves in even deeper.

The mystery of attraction is not really that at all—all of the characters are actually extremely insightful when it comes to articulating the nature of their connection to one another. Warren says he wanted Sharky because of how she loved Ray; Sharky tells Warren she was trying to make him into Ray; and Ray explains that he's never really loved Denise, but ended up with her because "I felt like there was this hole in my life I had to constantly maneuver around to keep from falling into." The real mystery here is why they can't ever deploy this insight to the end of self-preservation.

In a world where most narrative shocks have lost their bite, this play retains its power because each charge surfaces slowly and from underneath a sort of banal dysfunction. These local subversions of expectation are writ large in the play as a whole. The plot you glean is never just the events laid out for you, but also the way you fill in the blanks—the work your mind will do even against your will to extrapolate a narrative. There are (at least) two plays here: the one you get the first time through, that builds slowly and tangles the characters together, and the one that flickers rapidly through your mind as you hit the end and retrospectively revise the significance of all of the events that have come before.

The play ends as it begins, with Ray trying to make a stand. What he is asked to do in the last scene is precisely what he is asked to do in the first, and in a very neat bit of plotting, the decisions are actually piggy-backed onto each other. (Even the argument he makes in the first scene about why Roger's stepdaughter, Vicky, should go to jail could be dropped intact here.) The play leaves him on hold to the police station, suspended as he was at the beginning, deciding how to save himself from Warren's attempt to save him, and whether Warren can be forgiven for the act that has "freed" Ray. "I did it for you," Warren says to Ray to explain why he has stayed married. "I did it for you," Ray says to Denise to explain his gambling. As Warren sums it up in the play's last line, "All we have is each other." If only they didn't.

Jody McAuliffe

Interview with Marlane Meyer

Jody McAuliffe *What got you interested in the-ater?*

MARLANE MEYER I remember sneaking into the living room to watch TV when I was about six or seven years old, and a movie made during the thirties called *Hellzapoppin'* was on. I knew it wasn't an ordinary movie, but a play about show business with a demonic theme. It was very funny, and it had naked people roasting in hell on big spits. I couldn't stop thinking about that movie. At about the same time *Peter Pan* with Mary Martin was on television, and that was really important to me because she was the first woman I'd seen doing the fun things that boys get to do. And once again, it was a play. It was so much different than TV because it had content. Something I can see now, but then it just seemed "better," a more entertaining experience.

What kind of theater attracted you?

When I was in college I had my first collision with a kind of theater that changed the way I thought about theater. Before that, I was inter-ested in theater I could do in my garage or whatever made it to the movie screen. I never

The *South Atlantic Quarterly* 99:2/3, Spring/Summer 2000.
Copyright © 2001 by Duke University Press.

saw much theater as a kid. But in college I saw The Open Theatre, and that was a big deal. I was so excited I couldn't really sleep for a long time. I knew that something really drastic had happened in my head. Because for one thing I always wrote poetry, and I saw how poetry could find its way to theatrical expression. Susan Yankowitz did this great job of writing for that company.

What was your first play?

I had plays I did in the garage, and plays I did in college that were never produced, but I guess my first play was one I wrote about this kid who performed this ritual to bring back his dead father on Halloween.

Can you cite any influences on you as a writer?

Sick and *Mad* magazine, monster movies and screwball comedies, Edgar Allan Poe, old sitcoms, and cartoons. Later, when I started to get interested in language, I liked T. S. Eliot and W. B. Yeats, William Carlos Williams and Dorothy Parker. I didn't get interested in playwrights till a long time after I started writing plays. I was too insecure to really appreciate other people's work before that. I liked Beckett, Pinter, Mamet, but then I got hooked up with the Padua Playwright's Festival and Murray Mednick, Irene Fornes, and John Steppling became really important to me.

How do you begin a play?

From a kind of divine discontent. An argument that won't go away. A kind of misery that needs to be addressed that swims up and stays up until you answer it back.

Have you ever directed your own work?

I did in the beginning because it was easier. In retrospect, after having a lot of directors go at it, I think it might still be easier.

How much writing do you do in production?

I write a lot, usually it's when I finish the play. You can't really finish a play until it's produced.

Can you comment on your use of language?

I think it's evolved out of poetry and seeing what you can get away with not saying. I know when I write commercially the complaint is often that I underwrite. I do that because I rely on subtext to get the meaning across, and you can't do that when you write for the mass media.

How does the American theater look from your perspective?

It's very broad, and yet hard to find something that really grabs me. I still like all the experimental groups that manage to hang on, like the Wooster Group or Richard Foreman. It's so important that the form be explored in new ways. Most of what's out there has been done a lot, but people go because it's friendly and familiar and they can understand the story and be entertained. But it's not fun if you're serious about theater as an art form.

What has the difference been between your experience in regional theater and in New York?

There isn't really much difference; the acting pool is larger, but I don't get produced regionally all that much. Although *The Chemistry of Change* seems to be getting a lot of regional productions. It's actually my most accessible play, plus it has a happy ending.

Can you comment on your evolution as a writer?

It took me a really long time to take writing seriously. I was very defensive and afraid to be engaged by it; I still suffer from that. I apply myself to it; it's not always easy; it's been very hard lately so I've let myself do more commercial work while the other more serious work takes a rest.

Are you a political writer?

I think maybe everyone who writes is political at this point. It's so hard not to be because of the amount of media saturation we experience.

The Mystery of Attraction *has a seamless propulsion in real time. Is that something you had in mind when you started working on it?*

I've always wanted to write a play in real time, like *Cat on a Hot Tin Roof*. I was writing this play that had these very long scenes I kept trying to cut, but they wouldn't cut. It was then I started to appreciate the part of my writing animal that knows more than I do, that knew that this was the time to write my real-time play. It was doing it for me. I think I would trust a play more now to know its way into the world without my having to worry it along.

Can you comment on the difference between writing for TV and for theater?

TV writing is more lucrative and less satisfying in that it's writing to put legs on another man's vision. At least that's been my experience so far. Playwriting is very personal and much scarier and is a totally unique experience. At least it has been. Recently I decided to try and write my own TV pilots and see where that leads. I know it's wrong to like television, but I'm very comfortable with TV, and it's the way I was brought into contact with theater. I spent a lot of time alone when I was young, and TV was always there to keep me company. Theater gets very abstract when you're not in production on a play.

Interviewer's Note

Other works by Marlane Meyer include *Etta Jenks*, *Kingfish*, *The Geography of Luck*, *Why Things Burn*, *Moe's Lucky Seven*, and *The Chemistry of Change*.

Don DeLillo. Photo: Joyce Ravid.

Don DeLillo

The Mystery at the Middle of Ordinary Life:
A One-Minute Play

EDITOR'S NOTE: In a letter to Frank Lentricchia,
Don DeLillo wrote:

> This is really 2 acts in 2 minutes.
> It's all in the playing of course but I think the
> 2nd part—the one-line exchanges—ought to
> be done without reference to the first part,
> as if the characters had completely forgotten
> the woman's exfoliation of the state we call
> marriage.

The *South Atlantic Quarterly* 99:2/3, Spring/Summer 2000.

A man and a woman in a room.

WOMAN I was thinking how strange it is.

MAN What?

WOMAN That people are able to live together. Days and nights and years. Five years go by. How do they do it? Ten, eleven, twelve years. Two people making one life. Sharing ten thousand meals. Talking to each other face to face, open face, like hot sandwiches. All the words that fill the house. What do people say over a lifetime? Trapped in each other's syntax. The same voice. The droning tonal repetition. I'll tell you something.

MAN You'll tell me something.

WOMAN There's a mystery here. The people behind the walls of the brown house next door. What do they say and how do they survive it? All that idle dialogue. The nasality. The banality. I was thinking how strange it is. How do they do it, night after night, all those nights, those words, those few who do it and survive?

MAN They make love. They make salads.

WOMAN But sooner or later they have to speak. This is what shatters the world. I mean isn't it gradually shattering to sit and listen to the same person all the time, without reason or rhyme. Words that trail away. The pauses. The clauses. How many thousands of times can you look at the same drained face and watch the mouth begin to open? Everything's been fine up to now. It is when they open their mouths. It is when they speak.

Pause.

MAN I'm still not over this cold of mine.

WOMAN Take those things you take.

MAN The tablets.

WOMAN The caplets.

Pause.

MAN Long day.

WOMAN Long day.

MAN A good night's sleep.

WOMAN Long slow day.

Lights slowly down.

Frank Lentricchia

Aristotle and/or DeLillo

The *Mystery at the Middle of Ordinary Life* is not an episode, or scene, that might have been part of a larger—I will not say "full-length"—dramatic work, because Don DeLillo's work *is* a full-length play, though not, obviously, of the standard full-length sort that Aristotle had in mind when, twenty-three hundred years ago, he wrote his benchmark meditation on the nature of dramatic action.

Aristotle thought "plot" (a *rigorous* "arrangement of the incidents") the central structural agency, the means of representing an overarching "action," by which he meant not a physical act, or even a series of physical acts, but (in the words of Francis Fergusson) "a movement of the spirit," the entire organic process of change that takes place from beginning to end. A "beautiful" action would be "serious," "complete," and of a "magnitude" apparently far in excess of what DeLillo could permit himself to try for, in the one-minute format demanded by the festival for which his play was commissioned and performed.

DeLillo's small mystery play (let the medieval allusion stand) has an action in the Aristotelian

The *South Atlantic Quarterly* 99:2/3, Spring/Summer 2000.
Copyright © 2001 by Duke University Press.

sense, though two people "do" little but sit and talk about the puzzlement presented by their long-term being together. (The incidents of plot, in DeLillo's plays, tend to be verbal ones, of poetic intensity.) How is it possible, a man and a woman living together, day in and day out? The action is furthermore "complete," satisfyingly worked through from the first line of dialogue to the last, without the aid of exposition to tell us what came before they began to speak, and without teasing us into thinking about what might go on after the lights go down. The concentrated action of this one-minute play is, in fact, all about what goes on now, what went on before, and what will go on afterward in "ordinary life," till death do they part; precisely the sort of life that Aristotle, with his focus on the tragic action of an aristocratic hero of high renown, could not have been interested in, and believed to lie outside the proper domain of tragedy. Of course, the action in this (very American) play could not be tragic in the Aristotelian sense; it is not tragic in any sense. It is, rather, genially comic, featuring a wedding of spirits at the close.

As usual, DeLillo's tone is mixed. The line that sits at the play's virtual center—"They make love. They make salads."—encapsulates both the play's mystery and the writer's seamless blend of tone. I would guess that the temptation for an actor to play this line for laughs would be great. But to ironically debunk the love-making, by ruthless reduction to the banal, is wrong for this play, which is a leap beyond modernist irony; wrong because it would drain precisely from the play its allure of mystery. Salad-making and love-making are better thought of as analogical equivalents, not in the classical vertical form of analogy (low to high, material to spiritual), but horizontally, as would befit ordinary people living in a postaristocratic society. Love-making and salad-making: *at once* banal and mysterious, mundanely physical and transcendent. Much is asked of the actor.

As for Aristotle's prescription of "magnitude": in DeLillo's social context, it would appear irrelevant. The overarching action of the ordinary life of cohabitation lies in the small, repetitive banalities of its domain. They have to talk! How do they get through all the talking without being "gradually shattered"? This is how:

> "I'm still not over this cold of mine."
> "Take those things you take."
> "The tablets."
> "The caplets."

Do I imply that this play, in one minute, lacks magnitude of action? We begin in puzzlement, with talk about the mystery. Then a pause. Talk about the mystery has ended. Then the talk about the common cold: the chatter of intimates that is the center of ordinariness, the familiar chatter, which *enacts* the mystery that is their daily bread. This is the "serious" action that they make "in spirit," together. And the viewer, or reader, is also moved: from ignorance to knowledge, a movement that lies close to the heart of our experience of important drama.

A man and a woman in a room. Any man, any woman. In looks and in dress, undistinguished, one hopes. An uncluttered, nonrepresentational set of elegantly understated evocation, one hopes. Any room. And this is DeLillo's poignant allegory of the quotidian.

I see him in heaven, Aristotle, reading *The Mystery at the Middle of Ordinary Life*. He's making a small revision in his *Poetics*. It takes him one minute to do it: in an ancient text, a fresh, sympathetic insight is entered, bearing on the middle-class life that lies so far in the future.

Jody McAuliffe

Interview with Don DeLillo

DON DELILLO Do you need to know anything about the provenance of this little playlet?

JODY MCAULIFFE *Oh, yes.*

I wrote it because I was asked to by Robert Brustein for the American Repertory Theatre. It was a benefit event called a One-Minute Play Festival, and I think this was in 1992.

I know you published The Engineer of Moonlight *in 1979, and that was between publication of* Running Dog *and before you went away for three years and worked on* The Names.

Yes.

Was this your first foray into playwriting?

Yes, it was, and I'm not quite sure how to explain what brought it about. I think I saw people on a stage, actually, and began to follow them and to listen to them. I would also say that I was aware at the time that I was writing something that probably was not stageworthy, in a way.

In what way, do you think?

Well, I think that play needs a greater thrust than it has, a kind of forward motion. And it's awfully

The *South Atlantic Quarterly* 99:2/3, Spring/Summer 2000.
Copyright © 2001 by Duke University Press.

conversational. But I had a surer sense of a piece of theater that seemed a little more stageworthy when I was doing *The Day Room*.

What got you interested in theater in the first place?

Being a New Yorker, I always, even as a kid, was aware of theater, but I never really became fervent about theater the way I did about movies. And that, in fact, is still true.

Do you have a sense of what kind of theater attracts you?

I'm looking at two photographs of Samuel Beckett at the moment. In fact, they're passport photos that somebody sent me. Probably the theater represented by Beckett.

Pinter as well?

I think so.

Do you have any thoughts about your process as a playwright as opposed to the way you work as a novelist?

Yes, it's quite different. When I sit down to work on a stage play, I do so with a much deeper sense of openness. That is, I know that I'm just involved in the first stage of something that isn't going to be realized until it begins to operate three-dimensionally on a stage with living actors. And I don't necessarily explore psychological states the way I do when I'm writing a piece of fiction. I write dialogue. And I don't always feel a sense of predetermination concerning the meaning of this dialogue or the possible interpretations of this dialogue. I feel fairly open about this. And through the rehearsal process, I find it's possible to be enlightened by the ways in which actors render dialogue.

Since The Day Room *was your first production, was it a strange experience coming from novel-writing, and even playwriting up until that point, to the communal atmosphere of the theater?*

It was very strange. I welcomed the communal spirit of the theater. But after the rehearsal period and the previews and the opening, I think I was probably ready to go back into a room all alone and work on a piece of fiction. For me, each form, play and novel, is an antidote to the other.

So you like the balance?

I like the balance. Which doesn't mean I'm going to write one play for every novel, but I do like the balance. For me, another enormous difference is that when you write a novel you have the published book, and that's your novel, for better or worse. When you write a play, the feeling is much more elusive. The script isn't quite the play; the published text isn't quite the play; usually there's no single evening, no single performance, that represents the play in your own mind. So it's ever transient and ever elusive.

How much, if any, rewriting do you do in production?

In production, I would say fairly little. I did make changes in both plays, but not even remotely extensive changes. I do rewrite the dialogue as I'm composing, over and over. Much more than I do when I write fiction.

It's wonderful that you're open to what actors might bring to it even though you do rewrite it so much. Because a lot of times you hear it in a certain way and then it's difficult when actors speak it.

Right.

It can be clashing.

And then there are different productions, which is another aspect of elusiveness. Which production is the one? And I don't know that I've found a definitive answer for that in the case of *The Day Room*, where I saw three productions. An actress in one production was, it seemed, much more skilled than in the other two, but there were other aspects of this production that perhaps were not so expert.

There are so many variables in theater over which we have varying levels of control.

Yes.

Do you have a sense when you have finished the play what kind of an effect you want it to have on any audience?

Not really, no. It's a little mysterious to sit in the audience, particularly when it's the first or second time that the play's being exposed publicly. It might be a preview or one of the early nights of the run. And it's interesting to get a sense of the audience reaction. I don't have an idea of this in advance, and so it can be quite surprising. And what I sensed most recently with *Valparaiso* was a thoughtfulness—

On the part of the audience?

Yes, a sense in which they were very receptive, line by line, to what was being said and what was being conveyed to them. And also, and this was perhaps even more curious, a sense that I'd written quite a strange play, which hadn't occurred to me. It hadn't occurred to me through all the days of rehearsal. It did occur to me in the presence of an audience, because that's what they seemed to be feeling. A sense of the play's strangeness.

What do you begin with? You mentioned with Engineer *the image of people on a stage. I wondered if with* Valparaiso *that central image of him in the bathroom with the bag over his head was a starting point, or was that something that emerged?*

No, that was something that emerged. The starting point was a man getting on a plane and going to the wrong city, a city that had the same name as his destination but turns out to be a totally different place. That was the idea, and it was an idea that I've had for many years. And I'm not sure what compelled me to begin working on it. I started working on *Valparaiso* before I wrote *Underworld* and felt the work was not proceeding satisfactorily. I did, in effect, write the first act, but I wasn't particularly energized by what I'd done, so I just forgot about it. Then when I finished *Underworld* I went back to it. I'm not quite sure why, but I did. And it began to seem a lot more clear to me the second time.

Well, Valparaiso *is a very compelling variation on that notion that you have in* The Names *where the names of the towns and the initials of the murder victims match up. This is a haunting, mysterious thing.*

Right. And in the play everybody pronounces *Valparaiso* the same way even though the three actual cities are pronounced differently. They collapse into each other. Everything in the play sort of melts into everything else. So there's an unreality about the cities themselves. Only the name is real.

You've written a couple of short, but very complete plays, The Mystery at the Middle of Ordinary Life *and* The Rapture of the Athlete Assumed into Heaven. *I wonder what your thought is about the difference, in terms of your process, between a very short but complete work and a full length?*

In a curious way it's harder to write a three-page play than it is to write a one-hundred-and-three-page play.

I would imagine, because it's as if you have to complete a total action except in a very brief amount of time.

The first one, *The Rapture of the Athlete*, came more easily, I think because it's a monologue. But what came first was the image of a victorious tennis player on his knees with his racket raised, I believe, and he's kneeling in blinding light. That's what got me going on that. And in the second case it was a much less describable process—*The Mystery at the Middle of Ordinary Life*. I don't know quite what got me into it, and what I would say about this little play is that it's a curious fusion of stage play and novel. Of course, it's written in play form, but I think it articulates a question that novelists have asked themselves for a couple of hundred years. Simply, who are the people next door? What do they say to each other? What are they really like? How do they live minute to minute, year to year? And it's that commonplace mystery that attracts a novelist's imagination, and it strikes quite deep.

What's interesting to me about this play is how these people become the people next door of someone else. And they begin their own little cycle at the end. He reflects on this mystery, and they begin to engage in it.

They become the people next door—

Yes, to the other people in the brown house across the way in whom they're so interested. Just as there's a beautiful sense of repetition internally in the text, there's that repetition. It's as if you were in a helicopter and you pulled up and looked down and saw a bunch of houses that all looked the same.

First they're talking about something, and then they become something—

Yes, and then they're doing it. Talking about the tablets and the caplets.

I also realized, curiously, when I looked at the play again, that I lifted a couple of lines from this little play and used them in *Underworld*.

So somehow Underworld *was already germinating.*

There is this kind of a conversation in *Underworld* without the self-referring aspect. The kind of conversation that a novelist might imagine people next door have. And it goes on for four or five pages. This, obviously, was the genesis.

It has a marvelous phrase in it—the notion of something "gradually shattering." Somehow it embodies a weird tension that I think is in the whole little world and little big world that these people live in.

It's a curious thing to write dialogue that you know is going to be enunciated, going to be spoken aloud. And you find yourself fitting together words that have a kind of poetic kinship, more than a kinship based on meaning, and preferring it that way. Not just because it's going to be spoken out loud, but because it's more interesting. There's something to "gradually shattering." The words are related acoustically.

Yes. And there's a beautiful surprise in it somehow, too.

The dialogue I write for theater sometimes resembles the narrative prose in my fiction. It has a conscious meter and beat.

How does the American theater look from your perspective?

It's harder to get a sense of new writers in theater because the work is being done in many cases two or three thousand miles away. But in film, in many cases, the work becomes available. The New York Film Festival is running right now, and there seem to be half a dozen really good movies by young people. I don't know if you see that in theater so much.

In any case, you don't find that you do yourself?

No.

I don't know. Some people may find that they do, but I don't see a lot that I really like. One of my former students who runs a company in New York says that most of the theater he sees he doesn't like. It's always known as an invalid. Theater is forever dying.

I have a nostalgic feeling for theater even while it's alive and well. It's as though it's an anachronism in a way.

Well, there's something about it, as if it's almost occurring in one of those snow globes.

Theater seems to become more important even as there's less and less of a serious audience.

Do you have a favorite among your plays?

No. I think *Valparaiso* is more adept than *The Day Room*. It has less problems of structure. I don't necessarily prefer it. I think, potentially, if I were to go back to work on the first play, *The Engineer of Moonlight*, it might turn out to be more rewarding than the other two. But I don't know if I'd ever do that.

Why do you think it would be more rewarding?

I think it's because at least potentially it's more deeply rooted in real people and real things. At least that's the way I would have to gear it if I were to work on it again. But the curious thing about my plays is they are not nearly as established in the world around me as my novels are. And that, in my own limited sort of outlook on theater, is an aspect of theater itself. It's not about the force of reality so much as the mysteries of identity and existence.

Interviewer's Note

Other works by Don DeLillo include *Americana*, *End Zone*, *Great Jones Street*, *Ratner's Star*, *Players*, *Running Dog*, *The Engineer of Moonlight*, *The Names*, *White Noise*, *The Day Room*, *Libra*, *The Rapture of the Athlete Assumed into Heaven*, *Mao II*, *Underworld*, *Valparaiso*, *The Body Artist*, and *Pafko at the Wall*.

Notes on Contributors

NEAL BELL's plays, including *Two Small Bodies, Cold Sweat, Ragged Dick Somewhere in the Pacific,* and *On the Bum,* have been produced off-Broadway at theaters including Playwrights Horizons, and regionally at theaters including South Coast Repertory Theatre, the Cricket Theatre in Minneapolis, Denver Center Theatre, and Manbites Dog in Durham, North Carolina. Bell has also written adaptations of Zola's *Therese Raquin* and Frank Norris's *McTeague.* The recipient of grants from the NEA, the Rockefeller Foundation, and the John Simon Guggenheim Foundation, Bell has also recieved an Obie Award for sustained achievement in playwriting.

NILO CRUZ's work has been developed and performed in theaters across the country. His play *Two Sisters and a Piano* received the Kennedy Center Fund for New American Plays Award and premiered to critical and popular acclaim at the McCarter Theatre Center for the Performing Arts. He is an artist-in-residence at the McCarter Theatre through a TCG grant from the National Endowment. He has taught playwriting at Brown and the University of Iowa.

DON DELILLO is the author of twelve novels and two full-length stage plays. The playlet in this issue was originally written for a benefit evening at the American Repertory Theater.

FREDRIC R. JAMESON is William A. Lane Jr. Professor of Comparative Literature, professor of Romance studies (French), and chair of the Literature Program. He received his Ph.D. from Yale in 1959 and taught at Harvard, Yale, and the University of California before coming to Duke University in 1985. His most recent books include *Postmodernism, or, The Cultural Logic of Late Capitalism* (1991, which won the MLA Lowell Award), *Seeds of Time* (1994), *Brecht and Method* (1998), and *The Cultural Turn* (1998). He serves on the editorial advisory board for Duke University Press and the *South Atlantic Quarterly.*

WILLIAM DAVIES KING is professor of dramatic art at the University of California, Santa Barbara, and chair of the department. He is the author of *Henry Irving's "Waterloo": Theatrical Engagements with Late-Victorian Culture and History, Writing Wrongs: The Work of Wallace Shawn,* and *A Wind Is Rising: The Correspondence of Eugene O'Neill and Agnes Boulton.* He is currently writing about the portrayal of darkness and sixth sense on the nineteenth-century English stage.

FRANK LENTRICCHIA is the Katherine Everett Gilbert Professor of Literature. His most recent novel, *Lucchesi and The Whale*, was published by Duke University Press in 2001. His critical books include *After the New Criticism*, *Ariel and the Police*, and *Modernist Quartet*. He is currently writing a book with Jody McAuliffe, entitled *Loose Cannons: Studies in the Criminality of Art*, for the University of Chicago Press.

JODY MCAULIFFE is associate professor of the practice of theater studies and Slavic languages and literatures at Duke University, and a member of the Society of Stage Directors and Choreographers. Her fiction has appeared in *Southwest Review* and *Literary Imagination*, and her criticism includes *Plays, Movies, and Critics* (Duke University Press).

MARLANE MEYER's plays have received numerous awards and prizes and have been produced to wide acclaim. They include *Etta Jenks*, *Kingfish*, *Why Things Burn*, *Moe's Lucky Seven*, *The Geography of Luck*, and *The Chemistry of Change*.

JOSÉ ESTEBAN MUÑOZ is an associate professor of performance studies at the Tisch School of the Arts, New York University. He is the author and editor of various books, most recently *Disidentifications: Queers of Color and the Performance of Politics*. He is currently working on two book projects, tentatively titled *Feeling Brown: Ethnicity, Affect, and Performance* and *Crusing Utopia: Figuring Queer Futurity*.

TERI REYNOLDS received her Ph.D. in the Department of English and Comparative Literature at Columbia University. She has published in *American Book Review*, *Germanic Review*, *Lingua Franca*, and *Brief*. She has taught Literature and Medicine for the New York Academy of Medicine and is currently in medical school at the University of California, San Francisco.

ERIN CRESSIDA WILSON is an internationally produced and award-winning playwright, screenwriter, and professor at Duke University. Her feature film, *Secretary*, starring James Spader and directed by Steven Shainberg, is due next year. She has won awards from the National Endowment for the Arts, the Rockefeller Foundation, and the North Carolina Arts Council. Her book, *The Erotica Project*, cowritten with Lillian Ann Slugocki, was originally produced theatrically at Joe's Pub at the Public Theater, and is now published by Cleis Press.